THE CAUSES OF WAR

Geoffrey Blainey

Third Edition

THE FREE PRESS

NEW YORK

THE FREE PRESS
A Division of Simon & Schuster Inc.
1230 Avenue of the Americas
New York, N.Y. 10020

Copyright © 1973, 1977, 1988 by Geoffrey Blainey
All rights reserved, including the right of reproduction
in whole or in part in any form.

THE FREE PRESS and colophon are trademarks
of Simon & Schuster Inc.

Manufactured in the United States of America

10 9 8

Library of Congress Cataloging-in-Publication Data
Blainey, Geoffrey.
The causes of war/Geoffrey Blainey.—3rd ed., 1st American ed.
p.   m.
Bibliography: p.
Includes index.
ISBN 978-0-02-903591-7
1. War.   2. Military history, Modern—20th century.   I. Title
U21.2.B53   1988   88–6893
355'.027—dc19   CIP

Contents

Preface to the Third Edition

In the decade and a half since this book was published it seems
to have become one of the more widely quoted books on the
causes of war and peace. I have learnt much from the
discussion. I especially accept the criticism that the book, while
offering few direct comments on nuclear war, assumed that the
causes of war remained basically the same since the era of
cavalry. It is still my belief that the causes of war and even the
nature of war have not yet been drastically altered by the
advent of nuclear weapons. In a new chapter at the end of the
book I argue rather than, as before, beg my conclusion that in
international relations there is more continuity than chasm in
the years since 1945. On the other hand I have retreated from
my earlier opinion about the likely duration of a nuclear war of
the future. In the first edition I maintained too emphatically
that 'in the era of nuclear weapons a general war – if it occurs –
will probably be a long war'. While I still see a long nuclear war
as possible I do not think that, on existing evidence, it is more
likely to be long than short: both a long and short nuclear war
are possible.

Some critics of the first edition of this book had argued that
Japan's conduct and expectations on the eve of Pearl Harbor
in 1941, might well defy one of the main conclusions and
therefore the whole scaffolding of my argument. Similarly
Australia's and Britain's expectations on the eve of the fall of
Singapore in 1942 were said by some to contradict my
argument about the causes of war. Accordingly I looked closely
at these events, and, to meet the criticism, wrote a detailed
story leading up to the outbreak of the Pacific war, as seen from
the eyes of Japan and one of her ultimate opponents, Australia.
That story appeared in an Australian paperback edition of the
book published in 1977: a slightly shortened version appears in
this edition as chapter 16.

The argument of this book depends on its dovetailed
conclusions. Like the scaffolding of a building it needs only one

major piece of timber to break loose or topple, and the whole edifice falls. I believe the edifice remains intact; and that chapter 16 on the outbreak of the Pacific War and chapter 17 on the nuclear era both fit into the scaffolding of the original edition.

Geoffrey Blainey
University of Melbourne
June 1987

Preface to the First Edition

This book is based on a survey of all the international wars fought since 1700. It argues that in war and peace there are revealing patterns and clues that have been overlooked. As the book is more like an intellectual detective story than a narrative history, the preface may – if so desired – be ignored now and read as an epilogue.

To analyse war is to enter an arena which is already crowded with entrenched assumptions about why nations fight. In that arena contradictory ideas seem to live together peacefully. Hundreds of books and articles put forward their own interpretation and ignore the others. Among historians – and they have written more about war than political scientists, anthropologists or the members of any other discipline – most controversies hinge on the detailed causes of particular wars rather than on wider assumptions. Some popular generalisations about war have never been debated. They are instinctively rejected or accepted because they conflict with or fit our ingrained notions of human behaviour. To tolerate inadequate explanations of war however is to retard the search for superior explanations. One aim of this book is to compel contradictory theories of war to confront one another and fight or at least to confront the evidence. Among those which appear to be wounded or slain are explanations which originally convinced me.

The first part of the book points to weaknesses in well-known explanations of peace. The second part of the book examines ingredients which are usually prominent in determining a nation's decision to fight or not to fight; and the overall influence of those ingredients is summarised in the chapter called 'The Abacus of Power'. The third part of the book discusses the way in which praise, blame and partisanship produce misleading theories of war. For it is almost a dogma that one nation or group within a nation must be solely or mainly to blame for each war; and the dogma is re-

flected in the sterile international debate on the causes of the
war in Vietnam. On the contrary war and peace are alternating phases of a relationship in which rival nations must be
seen as pairs. To realise that relationship is to undermine
some of the most influential theories of war and some of the
most popular images of past wars: it seems to undermine for
instance the American interpretation of Pearl Harbor, the
Russian emphasis on capitalism as a warmaker, and the
theories of accidental war which have become popular since
the advent of nuclear weapons.

The fourth and final part of the book attempts to answer
questions on 'The Varieties of War'. What makes for the persistence of feud wars between two nations over a long span of
time? What factors create general or world wars as distinct
from two-nation wars? And what factors tend to make wars
long or short? Very little has been published anywhere about
those questions, and yet each question is linked intimately to
the wider question of what causes war and peace. The neglected riddle of why some wars are long and other wars are
short is central to the riddle of war and peace. To enquire for
instance why certain wars lasted only one month is simply to
focus attention on the kind of influences which terminate
wars; to survey what terminates wars is of course to examine
the influences that bring peace; and to examine the causes of
peace is essentially to turn the causes of war upside down.
The last part of the book offers the radical conclusion that the
beginning of wars, the prolonging of wars, the ending of wars
and the prolonging or shortening of periods of peace all share
the same causal framework. The same explanatory framework
and the same factors are vital in understanding each stage in
the sequel of war and peace.

Probably the most revealing of those stages is the outbreak
of peace; it even offers insights into the causes of war. At first
sight the suggestion may seem absurd but this is simply
another way of saying that the transition from war to peace is
essentially the reverse of the transition from peace to war.
What causes nations to cease fighting one another must be
relevant in explaining what causes nations to begin fighting
one another. The outbreak of peace is mostly neglected by
those who study the causes of war; but it is easier to analyse,

being infected less with distorting propaganda and emotion.
One conclusion of this book is that the study of history
offers essential clues towards an understanding of war. Nuclear weapons have not drastically altered international relations. In each generation during the last two and a half centuries many men thought their own era was unique and
therefore could learn little from the past; but their belief was
disproved. While each war and each generation of warfare has
unusual or unique characteristics, the familiar factors seem to
predominate. One unexpected result of examining a long
line of wars and many eras of peace is to observe the old
ancestry of most of the viewpoints and arguments which are
held widely in the nuclear age. The main merit, however, of
looking at scores of wars between 1700 and 1971 is the ease
with which generalisations and hypotheses can be tested.
Such a test is rarely applied.* Even a research foundation
which spends a million dollars in studying the causes of war
often prefers to use a bent pin to fish out historical examples
as 'illustrations' of its theories.

Finally a word about definitions. Throughout the narrative
the words 'war' and 'peace' mean international war and
peace. Civil wars are discussed only when they appear to have
influenced international wars. Occasionally, however, the
border between civil and international war is misty. While
the war fought in north America from 1861 to 1865 is known
as the American Civil War it would not have been so named
if the breakaway Confederacy had won. As it began as a war
between two sovereign states, each of which had all the para-
phernalia of government from president to judiciary and
army, I prefer to classify it as an international war. Just as it
is not always easy to distinguish between international and
civil wars, so it is not always easy to define when peace ends
and war begins. The Malayan–Indonesian clashes from 1963 to
1966 may be called either a tiny war or a disturbed phase of
peace; but the death of 740 men suggests that perhaps it
should be called a minor war. Preference for one definition

* Many extensive tests were to be applied in the 1970s by such scholars as
Melvin Small and J. David Singer. That sentence was fair comment in 1973
but not in 1987.

rather than another does not seem to affect my line of argument.

Nor is the territory covered by the book clearly defined. It would have been neater if confined, as was first intended, to European wars but it became impossible to analyse war and peace in Europe without drawing in North America, China, Japan and many European colonies. The first war discussed in the book was the Swedish crossing of the narrow seas into Denmark in 1700. The last war touched upon was the Indian invasion at the head of the Bay of Bengal in 1971. In between are almost one hundred wars which, scattered in time and place, have much in common.

While working on this theme I was helped by many people. For the opportunity to discuss points raised in the book – and, perhaps more important, some of the points not raised – I am grateful to K. S. Inglis, F. B. Smith and to Lieutenant-Colonel Warren Lennon of Canberra, and to Max Charlesworth, J. P. Fogarty, R. D. Freeman, A. Hodgart, P. Jonson, D. F. Mackay, D. E. Kennedy, J. R. Poynter, J. Remenyi and A. G. Thompson at the University of Melbourne. Arthur Burns of the Australian National University read most of the chapters and offered a blend of incisive criticism and generous encouragement which is rare and invaluable.

I am also indebted to the staff at the Baillieu Library, University of Melbourne, for help that ranged from an instant translation of a Russian page to the buying of out-of-print books not available in Australia; to Mrs J. Edgar, who typed the manuscript; and to the editorial board of *Historical Studies* for permission to republish Chapter 5, most of which appeared in that journal in October 1971.

Geoffrey Blainey
University of Melbourne
February 1972

Book One

The Mystery of Peace

1 : The Peace that Passeth Understanding

I

For every thousand pages published on the causes of wars there is less than one page directly on the causes of peace. And yet the causes of war and peace, logically, should dovetail into one another. A weak explanation of why Europe was at peace will lead to a weak explanation of why Europe was at war. A valid diagnosis of war will be reflected in a valid diagnoses of peace.

One obstacle to studying international peace is perhaps the widespread assumption that it is the normal state of affairs. The assumption however is inaccurate. The talented American sociologist, Pitirim Sorokin, once busied himself by counting the number of years which some of the main European countries spent at war. He found that Russia, the land of his birth, had experienced only one peaceful quarter of a century in the previous thousand years; in every other period of twenty-five years she engaged in at least one foreign war. Since the year A.D. 901, he estimated, Russia had been at war in 46 of every hundred years. To those who comment, 'I always thought the Russians were exceptionally belligerent', Sorokin's survey is not consoling. He found that England, since the time of William the Conqueror, had been engaged in war somewhere in Europe or the tropics for 56 of each hundred years. Spain experienced even more years of war.*

There is another reason for the lack of detailed analysis of

---

* It is dangerous to use these figures to measure the warlikeness or the martial qualities of different countries. One reason for caution, as Sorokin himself noted, was that the figures did not distinguish between major and minor wars, or between a war that covered only several months of a year and a war that was fought for many years. Moreover a nation which had frontiers to many other nations, or possessed many colonies, was more likely to engage in war than a country facing one neighbour. His statistics however clearly reveal that wars have been more frequent than is commonly believed.

the causes of peace. For historians it is a powerful reason. They are usually shackled to the available evidence; in studying events they depend heavily on diplomatic documents, memoirs, newspapers, pamphlets and other written or printed records which have been handed down. These records were created only because a politician, soldier or spectator possessed some opinion or news which he wished to communicate. Each record was as oriented to its author's sense of news as a daily newspaper is oriented in the twentieth century. Since war was more newsworthy than peace, the records ostensibly said far more about the causes of war than peace. And yet the records of peace are as extensive as those of war. They are simply less obvious. Any faded document which illuminates the causes of war must by implication also illuminate the causes of peace. Any document which discusses an international crisis that ended peacefully is a mirror of both peace and war. Nevertheless it is easy to see why peace often appears to be a newsless vacuum, a limbo for which scant explanation is necessary.

Historians' explanations of peace in modern times are centred on the nineteenth century. Two long periods in that century were remarkably peaceful. One ran from the Battle of Waterloo to the short wars of 1848 or to the Crimean War of 1853. The other period of peace ran from the end of the Franco-Prussian War in 1871 to the close of the century, though the most common opinion is to assign the end of the long peace to 1914. Each era of peace therefore ran for about one generation. It is perhaps significant that while each war in history is given a name, no matter how short its duration or how slight its consequences, these long periods of peace have no accepted name.

These peaceful periods were not devoid of war. Their wars – in contrast to those of other periods – were simply fewer and shorter and were rarely between major powers. In the eyes of most contemporary observers however these periods were unusually peaceful, and they inspired confident predictions that a millennium of international peace would ultimately prevail. What made these two eras so peaceful? A few talented scholars have offered answers. Their explanations are important, for they are often bold generalisations about the conditions which, they believed, promoted peace during many eras of recent centuries.

II

Lewis F. Richardson was one of the thousands of Quakers who have been crusaders for peace; his own crusade was a search for the causes of peace. Born at Newcastle upon Tyne in 1881 he studied science at Cambridge, carried out research for companies that mined peat and made lamps, became a teacher of physics at universities and colleges and early in the First World War he was absorbed as a meteorologist in the riddle of predicting the weather. Curious to see the battle-front but appalled at the prospect of seeing men killed, he joined a Quaker ambulance convoy and cared for wounded French infantrymen on the western front. There he wrote his first work on war, which he published in 1919 at his own expense. Even if he had dramatised the work and engaged his nephew Sir Ralph Richardson to act it on stage, he would have won only a small audience. His book was called *The Mathematical Psychology of War*.

Richardson was optimistic that if scholars made a systematic study of war they might discover valuable clues to its causes; and much of his spare time between the two world wars and most of his later years was given to studying war. As a mathematician he believed that exact measurement should be applied whenever possible to the social sciences. Diligently – until his death in Scotland at the age of seventy-one – he sorted, counted and measured wars and their likely causes. Many of his computations were published after his death in a book called *Statistics of Deadly Quarrels*.

Lewis Richardson culled useful negative conclusions about war during the period 1820–1949. Perhaps his most fascinating observations were those which challenged popular ideas. Contrary to the enthusiasts who had long preached that a universal language would reduce misunderstandings between nations, Richardson could not find statistical evidence to suggest that nations speaking a common language were more likely to live in peace; English-speaking nations had fought one another, German-speaking nations had fought one another. Contrary to another popular assumption extremes of wealth and poverty 'seem to have had very little influence during this period'. Any plan for international peace which relied simply on levelling the wealth of nations was therefore a gamble. Nor did he think relations between nations had necessarily been improved when they shared a religion, unless the religion they shared was Confucianism.

One of Richardson's positive conclusions was that war in one sense resembled a deep disease of the mind. A common cure for the disease was unfortunately war itself. He suggested that 'a long and severe bout of fighting confers immunity on most of those who have experienced it'. After a decade or two however the immunity faded, and the next generation was likely to enter war with enthusiasm. He recalled a time in London in the 1920s when books about war were out of favour, and he thought that one sad sign that war-immunity was declining was the bounding sales in 1929 of Erich Remarque's best-seller *All Quiet on the Western Front*. He recalled too that for about five years after the end of the First World War the practice of hiking with a knapsack was out of fashion, perhaps because it reminded people of infantry exercises. It was a sad omen when the knapsacks returned to favour.

Richardson's evidence of war-weariness seems to have come from a knapsack of personal impressions, rather than from the mathematical investigations which he so often pursued; and yet versions of his view were shared by many alert observers. The British general, Sir Ian Hamilton, had warned in 1926 that people seemed to oscillate slowly between enthusiasm for war and weariness of war: 'Because good Europeans hate war in 1926 it does not follow that they hated war in 1914 or that they will hate it in 1964.' Many historians who had lived through the First World War and its aftermath were understandably disposed to think that the mood after the long Napoleonic Wars could well have been similar. Certainly one of the most popular explanations for the long European peace after Waterloo was exhaustion or weariness.

The theory of war weariness was stretched far – stretched even to the point of snapping – by Professor Arnold J. Toynbee in 1945 in the ninth volume of his courageous *Study of*

History. Like Lewis Richardson he belonged to that generation which came of age just before the First World War; and
as a young member of Britain's delegation to the Paris Peace
Conference in 1919 he saw the jaded attitude to a war which,
only five years previously, had been entered exuberantly by
so many Europeans.

Toynbee believed that he could see, curling back century
upon century, a cycle of war and peace which, on average,
completed its full rotation in little more than one hundred
years. In each rotation a general war was followed in neat
sequence by a breathing space of peace, a cluster of supple-
mentary wars, a pause of peace, and finally another general
war. One full rotation appeared in Europe between 1815 and
1914, but whether it appeared in previous centuries is very
doubtful. Nevertheless to Toynbee's eyes the pattern existed
and could perhaps be explained by a stronger version of the
war-weariness theory. According to his 'tentative psychological explanation', a general war such as the Napoleonic war
cut such a deep impression on the mind and spirit that men
were reluctant to inflict this experience on their children.
And so, for a generation, strong restraints impeded the coming of war. The next generation, bred in peace, then leaped
lightheartedly into a series of wars, for example the cluster of
wars from the Crimean to the Franco-Prussian, but were still
restrained by the lingering aversion to war which their par-
ents had handed down. These wars therefore did not last
long, and soon were followed by a spell of peace. Slowly however the memory of the devastation of war was completely
effaced, leaving a peace-bred generation who ultimately began a world war which was fierce and unrestrained. In turn
the fighting reared a generation which possessed such resistance to war that a long era of peace ensued.

The grand sweep of Professor Toynbee's theory invites
admiration, but perhaps he demands too much of his rhythm
of war-weariness. His theory, by implication, warns us to be
aware of lands which have long enjoyed peace: beware of
Sweden and the Canary Isles! It could also be said that his
theory lacks supporting evidence. How did he know that
people were weary of war? Because there was a long peace.

It is also difficult to detect any semblance of a cycle of war and peace before 1800 and easy to see that the cycle performed erratically after the First World War. Toynbee himself was puzzled that the Second World War should have come at a time when, according to his theory, mental immunity against war should still have been high. At least he tried to face the dilemma; he confessed that either his theory was jeopardised or else human nature must have changed. Like most of us in a similar quandary he plumped for his theory. The Second World War, he suggested, was 'manifestly something contrary to Human Nature'.

To reject Toynbee's theory is not necessarily to reject the humbler idea that war-weariness was one of the forces promoting peace at certain periods of history. Even then the idea has to be examined carefully. It is often seen as an essential ingredient of the long peace after Waterloo, and yet Europe had an equally long time of peace from the 1870s without similar signs that statesmen and street sweepers were tired of war. Some historians place so much emphasis on war-weariness as the promoter of the long peace after Waterloo, that when they come to the second long period of peace they skip it without offering an explanation. Their master key having failed to unlock the mystery, they discard the mystery and keep the key.

Moving forward to the brittle peace of 1918–1939, the symptoms of war-weariness are abundant. But whether weariness ultimately furthered peace is open to debate. If war-weariness was one of the spokes in Mr Neville Chamberlain's umbrella of appeasement, and if it was one of the Anglo-French attitudes which fed Hitler's confidence, it cannot be called a peaceful influence.

The theory of war-weariness usually sees the nation as the personification of the individual: Germany was weary or France was exhausted. But the way in which men and women reacted to a long war varied widely from individual to individual and from war to war. Adam Smith, the Scottish economist, who had lived through some of the longest wars which Britain fought in the eighteenth century, complained in 1776: 'In great empires, the people who live in the capital, and in the provinces remote from the scene of action, feel, many of them, scarce any inconveniency from the war, but

enjoy at their ease the amusement of reading in the newspapers the exploits of their own fleets and armies.' He added
sadly: 'They are commonly dissatisfied with the return of
peace, which puts an end to this amusement, and to a thousand visionary hopes of conquest and national glory.' Even at
the end of the Napoleonic wars – wars which ran with brief
pauses for 23 years – one cannot be sure who was weary. In
the British Isles those farmers and manufacturers who had
earned high profits during the war might have been weary
less of the war than of the subsequent peace. In France, when
that long war seemed to have ended, Napoleon Bonaparte's
unexpected return from his brief captivity in the island of
Elba in 1815 was not received with weary indifference
throughout the country; he quickly gathered enough soldiers
to take the war to Waterloo. Similarly in China in the
twentieth century the long civil war was followed by the war
against the Japanese invasion; and when in 1945 the Japanese
withdrew, the war-weary theory clearly pointed to a long
peace in China. If ever a country was exhausted by two
decades of war it was China. And yet the civil war was renewed and did not cease until in 1949 the communists won
mainland China.

Enthusiasm for war, or weariness of war, did not have
simple and predictable effects. War-weariness for instance
could increase the chances of war and at other times increase
the chances of peace. Nevertheless those changing attitudes
and moods merit a niche in any theory of war and peace. The
memory of recent wars affects the attitudes not only of leaders
but of the hundreds of thousands without whose support no
war can be fought. Any nation's decision to fight, or to cease
fighting, is based on a picture of what that war or that peace
will be like; and one of the many influences on that picture is
the fluctuating and intensely-coloured memory of past wars
or past periods of peace.

III

Perhaps a long era of peace reflected the existence of strong
outlets for militant energies and ambitions. European
nations, it was sometimes implied, were like steam engines.

In some decades nations had surplus steam which exploded into fighting and in other decades all available steam was required for peaceful pursuits. 'Men were too busy growing rich to have time for war,' wrote one historian. 'Nations turned their energies to domestic growth and industrial expansion,' wrote a second historian. Industrialisation, wrote a third historian, 'absorbed energies which might otherwise have been devoted to international strife'. To a fourth historian the fast expansion of European population after the end of the Napoleonic Wars was one dangerous boiler of surplus energy:

> Inside the rigid and artificial structure of the power states, crowded together on the cramped Continent, the vast awakening energies of modern civilisation (of which the huge population increase was but one indicator) could not find a broad and appropriate field of activity such as the Anglo-Saxon spaces provided. So these energies, pent up in one form or another, sought outlets in revolutions or wars.

That the vast Anglo-Saxon spaces of the United States provided not only an outlet for millions of Europeans but also the burial grounds for perhaps 600,000 soldiers between 1861 and 1865 is a slight blow to the argument.

'The tremendous energy of a rapidly growing population', wrote a fifth historian, 'was finding plenty of outlets in the economic conquest of the globe.' He saw a world abuzz with peaceful energy in the middle of the nineteenth century. 'Gold rushes, railroad building, the struggle to eliminate individual bad men, the outfitting of fleets of steamships, the use of power-driven machinery to triumph over swamp and desert, kept people so busy that they had little time to think of organising to fight one another.' Later the dizzy energy seemed to subside. 'With the increasing ease provided by material success at the juncture of the nineteenth and twentieth centuries, people were left with more empty time on their hands. They were not able to resist the temptation to fill it with dreams and expressions of fear and hatred.'

These are examples of a delinquent theory of war. Nations are lads who scuffle and fight in the streets because they are bored or idle; if the nations are busy, they can be kept out of mischief. Some versions of this theory almost hint that the abolition of the fourteen-hour shift in mines and factories was a catastrophe. Most versions of the theory assume that a nation, like an individual, has one pair of hands, and so only with difficulty can she carry on two activities at the same time. And yet the United States in the late 1960s could simultaneously land men on the Sea of Tranquillity and the coast of Vietnam and have energy to spare for racial riots, industrial expansion and the ubiquitous sit-in and love-in. Even in the nineteenth century men could busy themselves in growing rich while their nation was at war, and some grew rich because their nation was at war. Americans dug gold and built railroads and eliminated bad men and still had time 'to think of organising to fight one another' in what became the deadliest war of the century – the American Civil War. This delinquent theory, in some of its variations, is an economic interpretation of war: it suggests that there is a tendency for energetic prosperity to foster peace while economic adversity fosters war. The evidence seems to reject this hypothesis, but there does seem to be a vital link between economic conditions and war; it will be discussed in the chapter, 'War Chests and Pulse Beats'.

IV

The delinquent explanation assumes that nations have a fixed stock of energy which is alternatively channelled into peaceful and warlike pursuits. A more pessimistic explanation hints that nations have a continuing tendency to be warlike. The long periods of international peace therefore tended to come when governments were engaged in or nervous of civil strife. Dr David Thomson, writing in Cambridge his thousand-page book on *Europe Since Napoleon*, observed that the four decades after Waterloo experienced far more revolutions than wars. He suggested that perhaps 'revolutions had served as a kind of substitute for war'. For good measure he added a dash of the delinquent theory: 'enemies at home seemed more immediate and more menacing than enemies abroad, and civil war absorbed belligerent spirits later to be diverted into the cause of militant nationalism'.

The explanation raises one immediate difficulty. The most tempestuous year of that long peace was 1848. Monarchs and humble citizens from St Petersburg to Scotland agreed that it was a tumultuous year. As a Scottish gentleman wrote to a friend in distant Tasmania: 'Since the smoke of Waterloo rolled away, no such important events have taken place as those of 1848. The present is a chaos, the future a mystery.' Even in Scotland, far from the street fighting of so many continental cities, many of the devout were predicting that 'some mighty change, if not the end of time, is at hand' and that in a few years 'Christ as a King shall appear upon this earth'. The Scottish letter-writer was not one of the fanatics; he was simply a sharp observer of the mood of a year marked in his mind by 'the crash of empires, the fall of governments, and the anarchy of kingdoms'. Now if it is true that civil commotion lessens the chance of international war, 1848 and 1849 should have been free of international wars. On the contrary there were four wars, each of which sprang from civil strife. Indeed one can suggest that the long period of European peace ended in 1848 rather than at the outbreak of the Crimean War five years later.

Dr Thomson, in suggesting that revolution might have been a substitute for war, had observed that one long period of international peace was studded with civil strife; he offered no other evidence. As the second long era of European peace, beginning in the 1870s, was astonishingly free of revolutions, his suggestion has to be treated with caution.

Another interpretation of peace in the nineteenth century points mainly to the influence of powerful statesmen. In the first period Palmerston of England was said to have been the peacemaker, and in the second period Bismarck of Germany. Palmerston and Bismarck might well have been peacemakers during some stages of their long careers, but the extent of their influence can only be measured against the environment in which they worked. Their ability as statesmen to hammer peaceful links between nations depended at least as much on the malleability of their environment as on their skill with the hammer. Moreover their skill depended on the kind of hammer provided by their own nation; Palmerston was backed by the world's most powerful navy and Bismarck was backed by the most powerful army. Accordingly it is vital to enquire how much of their influence came from their personalities and policies, how much from the contemporary international situation, and how much from their superior military backing.

Knowledge of leaders, their perceptions and aims, is vital in explaining the outbreak of peace and war. Generalisations about war and peace are valid only if the selected factor influenced the minds of those leaders who had to decide for war or peace. At the same time it is usually guesswork, in the present state of knowledge, to single out certain leaders as great peacemakers or villainous warmakers. To assess the influence of abnormal men – whether Palmerston or Hitler – requires knowledge of how leaders normally behaved in similar situations. Evidence on leaders' behaviour is set out indirectly in many of the following chapters.

v

While some historians argued that in the nineteenth century great statesmen did much to keep the peace, others argued that great ideas kept the peace. One weaver of that argument was John Ulric Nef. 'For a brief period of weeks', he recalled, 'I had been in training as an infantry soldier for service in the First World War.' The armistice however saved him from leaving the United States to take part in 'those mass slaughters', and instead he became an economic historian, studying the rise of British coal mining and then the turbulent economic life of the century 1540–1640. The turbulence of that distant century of the Spanish Armada and the wars of religion made him wonder about the wider causes of war and peace. What reasons, he asked, could help explain 'the unprecedented conditions of peace and gentle manners that had prevailed, as it seemed, among the Europeans and Americans at the time I was born?' He asked that question a few months before the Japanese bombing of Pearl Harbor, and completed his answer just when the United States entered the Korean War.

Professor Nef threaded intellectual and material influences

into such a subtle carpet that to quote sentences from his
argument is to run the danger of tearing threads from the
carpet. He argued that high ideals kept the peace: 'What
made the peace that followed 1815 more than a mere halt
was largely the culture, the customs, laws and manners, which
had evolved in Europe and had found strong and influential
expression in the great philosophical, literary, and artistic
works of the eighteenth century.' Peace was aided, in his
opinion, by many influences ranging from the new police
force in England to such books as *Tom Brown's Schooldays.*
So the bully Flashman was expelled from the college of
nations primarily by the widespread movement 'to attain
universal peace and culture'. A century increasingly able to
afford devastating wars was surprisingly peaceful. Alas, once
those peaceful cultural influences began to give way to militant influences there was nothing left to spike the powerful
artillery and massive cruisers provided by increasing technical ingenuity. Hence came the devasting and bitter wars of
the twentieth century. Such, in essence, is Nef's theory of
peace.

To chart the changing scale of values of a civilisation calls
for unusual gifts. Nef has those gifts; perhaps no writer has
been so skilful in tracing attitudes to war and peace in the
years since the Renaissance. And yet if Nef insists that a peace-
loving culture curbed warfare between 1815 and 1914, how
then can he explain the midway cluster of wars? Why did the
intellectual and moral restraints fail to prevent the wars of
1848, the Crimean, Mexican, and Italian wars, the American
Civil War, and the three Prussian wars? Nef's theory cannot
adequately explain why one period of the same century was
relatively peaceful and why another was studded with serious wars.

Nef's courageous theory also has to pass another test. If the
moral and intellectual reins against violence and hatred were
really strong enough to curb international war, they must
also have been strong enough to curb civil war. Nef believed
that they were strong enough. He suggested that the 46 years
between the battle of Waterloo and the all-American battle
of Sumter were unparalleled in their relative freedom both
from wars between nations and from 'violence, piracy, and

almost every kind of crime' within western nations. It is difficult however to recognise his white age of virtue. It was in
fact so sprinkled with civil wars and revolutions that Dr
David Thomson, as seen earlier, was prompted to suggest that
civil turmoil had reduced the likelihood of war between
nations in that period.

VI

Perhaps a war which ended with a moderate treaty was more
likely to create a lasting peace. Thus several historians
praised the men who shaped the treaties at Paris and Vienna
in 1814 and 1815 as the creators of a long period of peace.
Nevertheless as a perceptive American historian observed, the
praise cannot be carried too far, for many of the important
decisions of 1814–15 were quickly altered by the eddy of
events. In contrast the century's second era of peace followed
a treaty which was often regarded as harsh and punitive.
While the territory and gold which Germany took from
France in 1871 were later to be singled out as a major cause of
the First World War, it is salutary to recall that the harsh
treaty of 1871 also marked the opening of a remarkably long
era of peace.

In the last three centuries the peace settlement to which
has been attributed the most disastrous effects was the Treaty
of Versailles at the end of the First World War. The emphasis
on Versailles' influence is intriguing. The fact that it was
followed twenty years later by another world war partly explains the blame placed on the treaty. That blame was two-
fold: while some blamed the harshness of the treaty, others
blamed the treaty's economic effects. The rocket-like inflation
in central Europe in the early 1920s, and the world depression of the early 1930s, were often blamed on the economic
decisions made by the victors at Versailles. How far Versailles
created economic havoc in the world is a thorny question.
One may suggest that the huge war debts which were demanded of Germany merely aggravated an international
situation which was already dangerous. The economic ill-
nesses of the 1920s and 1930s mainly reflected events or trends
which had happened before the victors met in France: the

fragile kind of capitalism which had existed before 1914; the
dearth of economic and political knowledge to cope with the
monetary system; the effects of the war on economic conditions and attitudes; and the quickening transfer during the
war of financial dominance from London to New York.

Some of these arguments were hammered or implied in
The Economic Consequences of the Peace, the powerful
book of 1919 which encouraged the belief that Versailles was
a crucial influence on international relations in the following
two decades. When John Maynard Keynes wrote that book in
a two-month spasm of energy after returning wearily from
the peace conference in Paris, he used his astonishing literary
and mental gifts to stress the likely effects of the economic
penalties imposed on Germany. But he also stressed that a
sane treaty was essential because the economic omens were
already so gloomy. He explained that the cobweb of buying
and selling, borrowing and lending, which for long had
linked every port and factory in the world was delicate. A
peace treaty which tautened any strand of that cobweb was
therefore perilous. Ironically Keynes' best-selling book came
to be associated years later with a different message. Like
many bold predictions it was tinged in popular memory by
the later run of events. As Keynes had warned of economic
perils, and as perils had appeared, the peace treaty was increasingly blamed for the perils. What was remembered after
his book was no longer read was simply the title, *The
Economic Consequences of the Peace*. In fact Keynes had
pointed out that most of the 'consequences' were present before 1919. And indeed one of the quiet implications of his
more celebrated book, *The General Theory*, which in 1936
rewrote a vast area of economics, was that even a magnani-
mous Treaty of Versailles might not have averted a world depression nor some of the political events which followed that
depression.

The harshness of the treaty which ended the First World
War was also said to have been a major cause of the Second
World War. If that argument is valid, then one would expect
to hear more vigorous denunciations of the terms imposed on
Germany in 1945. For Germany after 1945 was possibly
treated more harshly than after 1918. For more than a

quarter of a century Germany has been occupied by foreign troops. The old heart of imperial Germany – the Prussian provinces – has been severed from the main German territory. And the old capital – Berlin – has been partitioned and walled and occasionally besieged. Admittedly after the Second World War the reparations imposed on Germany were milder, but then the reparations extracted from Germany in the 1920s had been exceeded by the American loans which flowed into Germany.

The eighteenth century experienced a series of mild peace treaties. Nearly all historians would agree that wars of the eighteenth century rarely ended with the imposition of punitive terms on the vanquished. Unfortunately a lenient peace treaty was usually followed with surprising speed by another war. Perhaps the most moderate peace treaty was in 1748, at the end of nine years of war, but by 1756 almost half of Europe was enmeshed in the Seven Years' War. Nor do the colonial wars fought by European nations endorse the idea that harsh peace-terms quickly provoked wars of retaliation.

One would like to believe that generous terms of peace yielded a dividend of international goodwill. It may be that they rarely yielded a dividend simply because they were rarely applied. When a war ended with lenient terms it was usually because the victor was not strong enough to impose severe terms. Nevertheless the weight of evidence suggests that a severe treaty of peace was more likely to prolong the peace; and there is a powerful reason why that should appear to be so. A harsh treaty was mostly the outcome of a war which ended in a decisive victory. And, it will be suggested later, a decisive victory tends to promote a more enduring peace.

2 : Paradise is a Bazaar

I

The mystery of why the nineteenth century enjoyed unusually long eras of peace did not puzzle some powerful minds. They believed that intellectual and commercial progress were soothing those human misunderstandings and grievances which had caused many earlier wars. The followers of this theory were usually democrats with an optimistic view of human nature. Though they had emerged earlier in France than in England they became most influential in the English-speaking world and their spiritual home was perhaps the industrial city of Manchester, which exported cotton goods and the philosophy of free trade to every corner of the globe.

Manchester's disciples believed that paradise was an international bazaar. They favoured the international flow of goods and ideas and the creation of institutions that channelled that flow and the abolition of institutions that blocked it. Nations, they argued, now grew richer through commerce than through conquest. Their welfare was now enhanced by rational discussion rather than by threats. The fortresses of peace were those institutions and inventions which promoted the exchange of ideas and commodities: parliaments, international conferences, the popular press, compulsory education, the public reading room, the penny postage stamp, railways, submarine telegraphs, three-funnelled ocean liners, and the Manchester cotton exchange.

The long peace that followed the Battle of Waterloo was increasingly explained as the result of the international flow of commodities and ideas. 'It is something more than an accident which has turned the attention of mankind to international questions of every description in the same age that established freedom of commerce in the most enlightened nations.' So wrote one of the early biographers of Richard

Cobden, merchant of Manchester and citizen of the world. Variations of the same idea were shared by Sir Robert Peel, William Gladstone, John Stuart Mill, scores of economists and poets and men of letters, and by England's Prince Consort, Albert the Good. His sponsorship of the Great Exhibition in the new Crystal Palace in London in 1851 popularised the idea that a festival of peace and a trade fair were synonymous. The Crystal Palace was perhaps the world's first peace festival.

In that palace of glass and iron the locomotives and telegraphic equipment were admired not only as mechanical wonders; they were also messengers of peace and instruments of unity. The telegraph cable laid across the English Channel in 1850 had been welcomed as an underwater cord of friendship. The splicing of the cable that snaked beneath the Atlantic in 1858 was another celebration of brotherhood, and the first message tapped across the seabed was a proclamation of peace: 'Europe and America are united by telegraphic communication. Glory to God in the Highest, On Earth Peace, Goodwill towards Men.' That cable of peace was soon snapped, and so was unable to convey the news in the following year that France and Austria were at war, or the news in 1861 that the United States was split by war.

Henry Thomas Buckle was one of many influential prophets of the idea that telegraphs and railways and steamships were powerfully promoting peace. Buckle was a wealthy young London bachelor who in the 1850s studied beneath the skylight of his great London library, writing in powerful prose a vast survey of the influences which, to his mind, were civilising Europe. A brilliant chess player who had competed with Europe's champions at the palace of peace, Buckle thought human affairs obeyed rules that were almost as clear-cut as the rules of chess; and those rules permeated his writings. The first volume of the *History of Civilisation in England* appeared in 1857, the second volume in 1861, and they were devoured by thousands of English readers, published in French, Spanish, German, Hungarian and Hebrew editions, and translated four times into Russian.

One of Buckle's themes was the decline of the warlike spirit in western Europe. As a freethinker he attributed that

decline not to moral influences but to the progress of knowledge and intellectual activity. The invention of gunpowder
had made soldiering the specialist activity of the few rather
than the occasional activity of the many, thereby releasing
talent for peaceful pursuits. Similarly Adam Smith's *The
Wealth of Nations,* 'probably the most important book that
has ever been written', had perceived and popularised the
idea that a nation gained most when its commercial policy
enriched rather than impoverished its neighbours: free trade
had replaced war and aggressive mercantilism as the road to
commercial prosperity. Buckle argued that the new commercial spirit was making nations depend on one another
whereas the old spirit had made them fight one another.

Just as commerce now linked nations, so the steamship and
railway linked peoples: 'the greater the contact', argued
Buckle, 'the greater the respect'. Frenchmen and Englishmen
had curbed their national prejudices because they had come
to know one another, and he believed that nothing had done
more than railways and steamships to increase their friendship. As he affirmed in his clear rolling prose: 'every new
railroad which is laid down, and every fresh steamer which
crosses the Channel, are additional guarantees for the preservation of that long and unbroken peace which, during forty
years, has knit together the fortunes and the interests of the
two most civilised nations of the earth'. Buckle thought
foreign travel was the greatest of all educations as well as a
spur to peace; and it was while he was travelling near Damas-
cus in 1862 that he caught the typhoid fever which ended his
life.

Many readers must have thought that the outbreak of the
Crimean War rather dinted Buckle's argument that the warlike spirit was declining in Europe. Buckle was composing
that chapter of his book when war was raging in the Crimea,
and he forsaw the criticism and met it head on:

> For the peculiarity of the great contest in which we are
> engaged is, that it was produced, not by the conflicting in-
> terests of civilised countries, but by a rupture between
> Russia and Turkey, the two most barbarous monarchies
> now remaining in Europe. This is a very significant fact. It

is highly characteristic of the actual condition of society, that a peace of unexampled length should have been broken, not, as former peaces were broken, by a quarrel between two civilised nations, but by the encroachments of the uncivilised Russians on the still more uncivilised Turks.

Buckle still had to explain why France and England, his heroes of civilisation, had exultantly joined in the barbarians' war. He explained that simply; the departure of their armies to the distant Crimea was a sign of their civilisation. France and England, he wrote, 'have drawn the sword, not for selfish purposes, but to protect the civilised world against the incursions of a barbarous foe'.

The shattering civil war which began in the United States in the last year of Buckle's life should have been a blow to his theory. On the contrary it seems to have heartened his supporters. They interpreted that war as another crusade against barbarism and the barbaric practice of slavery. At the end of that four-years' war Professor J. E. Cairnes, an Irish economist, wrote a powerful article reaffirming the idea that 'all the leading currents of modern civilisation' were running steadily in the direction of peace. He thought that the way in which the North craved the sympathy of foreign nations during the war was a sign of the increasing force of public opinion in international affairs. He believed that the enlightened public opinion was coming mainly from the expansion of free commerce, the railways and steamships, and the study of modern languages. Henry Thomas Buckle would have sympathised with the emphasis on modern languages; he spoke nineteen.

The idea that ignorance and misunderstanding were the seeds of war inspired the hope that an international language would nourish peace – so long as the chosen language was purged of nationalism. In 1880 a south German priest, J. M. Schleyer, published a neutral language of his own manufacture and called it Volapük. It spread with the speed of rumour to almost every civilised land, claiming one million students within a decade. To Paris in 1889 came the delegates of 283 Volapük societies, and even the waiters at the dining tables of the congress could translate the following manifesto into Volapük:

> I love all my fellow-creatures of the whole world, especially those cultivated ones who believe in Volapük as one of the greatest means of nation-binding.

The rival nation-binding language of Esperanto was then two years old. Its inventor, a Russian physician named Zamenhof, had come from a feuding region where Polish, German, Yiddish, and Russian were all spoken; and he trusted that his Esperanto would ameliorate dissensions between races. Before long, however, many supporters of Esperanto and Volapük were feuding. Even the disciples of Volapük tongue discovered that their universal language did not necessarily lead to harmony. They split after a quarrel about grammar.

In the generation before the First World War there were abundant warnings that the Manchester gospel was not infallible. The very instruments of peace – railways and international canals and steamships and bills of lading – were conspicuous in the background to some wars. The Suez Canal was a marvellous artery of international exchange, but for that reason England and France were intensely interested in controlling it; without the canal it is doubtful if there would have been an Egyptian War in 1882. The Trans-Siberian railway was a great feat of construction and a powerful link between Europe and Asia, but without that railway it is doubtful whether there could have been a Russo-Japanese war in 1904–5. This is not to argue that these new arteries of commerce *caused* those two wars; but certainly they illustrated the hazards of assuming that whatever drew nations together was an instrument of peace. The Manchester creed, to many of its adherents, was a dogma; and so contrary evidence was dismissed.

II

As ignorance and misunderstanding were seen as the enemies of peace, more avenues of understanding were obviously needed. They multiplied in the half century before the

First World War. In the 1870s came international bureaux to organise posts, telegraphs, copyrights and weights and measures, along with two competing institutes of international law. In the 1880s was born the Inter-Parliamentary Union, where members of many parliaments hoped to promote the idea that arbitration should rule the relations of nations. At the Paris International Exhibition of 1889, scene of that congress where the delegates ordered their coffee and bread rolls in the Volapük tongue, the peace societies that had sprung up in many nations were now strong enough to organise their first international congress. In the following two decades they ran seventeen such congresses. Even governments set up international conferences on peace: Nicholas II of Russia sponsored the gathering at The Hague in 1899 which failed to agree on a pause in the armaments race but agreed on many other issues, including a decision to ban the firing of explosives and projectiles from balloons. Whereas the first meeting drew twenty-four nations to The Hague, the meeting of 1907 drew forty-four. Those meetings of national leaders were successful enough to nurture a widespread hope that the third, planned for the year 1917, might make arbitration an effective substitute for war in most parts of the world.

Monetary incentives helped to popularise the idea that peace was becoming the norm. The £50 prize or the gold medallion for the best essay on ways of preserving peace among nations promoted popular contests in scores of cities of the western world. The idea was carried further by Alfred Nobel, the Swede who invented dynamite and made those smokeless powders which were to increase death and diminish pollution on the battlefields. When Nobel died on the Riviera in 1896 and bequeathed much of his fortune to create five permanent prizes for international achievements – three for the sciences, one for literature and one for services to international brotherhood – his prizes reflected the belief that the frontiers of knowledge and of peace advanced together.

That great crusade, which spanned Manchester and Washington and The Hague and Hyde Park, had faith in progress and in the goodness of man. Its idealism – and its epitaph –

may be read in the 1911 edition of the *Encyclopaedia Britannica* where the article on Peace was written by an authority on international law, Sir Thomas Barclay. In the House of Commons he represented the Lancashire textiles town of Blackburn, a citadel of the creed that the free flow of communications and cotton dresses were the clarions of peace. Three years before the beginning of the most calamitous war the world had known, Barclay confidently predicted the reign of brotherhood. He rejoiced that in the continent of America 'progress is being rapidly made towards the realisation of the idea that war can be superannuated by elimination of its causes and the development of positive methods for the preservation of peace'. He praised the United States for pioneering the idea that 'peace is the normal condition of mankind'. Even the continent of Europe, where millions of civilians had been conscripted to serve part-time in the huge armies, provided promising omens, because the conscript soldiers had been trained in civic responsibilities as well as in soldiering. Germany, said Barclay, had taught her conscripts to think as well as to obey. Similarly he believed that drill halls and weekend bivouacs had helped to make France, once so militant, the most pacific nation in Europe. 'Militarism on the Continent has thus become allied with the very factors which make for the reign of reason,' he decided. Heartened by the growth of international conferences and agreements and by a surge of opinion calling for peace and working for peace, he prophesied that the causes of war would ultimately be eliminated: 'war is coming, among progressive peoples, to be regarded merely as an accidental disturbance of that harmony and concord among mankind which nations require for the fostering of their domestic welfare.'

Three years later, when the world crisis called for these progressive peoples to stand and be counted, thousands stood and enlisted. The influences favouring peace seemed to have been so shattered that in the twelfth edition of the *Encyclopaedia Britannica* the article on 'peace' was a long essay on how the victors punished the vanquished at the Peace Conference of 1919.

III

If foreign travel, a web of world commerce, democratic discussion, bi-lingualism, Olympic Games, Esperanto, and many other influences had really fostered peace, then the First World War was a tragic accident. In the summer of the outbreak of war, more Europeans were travelling, conferring, holidaying, or working in foreign lands than ever before. If Buckle and Cairnes and Albert the Good had lived to glimpse the crowded channel steamers and international sleeping cars in June 1914, or if they had heard the babble of languages in the hotels at the German spas or the Riviera hotels, if they had read a list of the international conferences organised for that summer, or if they had seen the warehouses of German goods by the canals of Manchester and St Petersburg, they would probably have prophesied a peaceful autumn for Europe.

A war lasting four years and involving nearly all the 'civilised' nations of the world contradicted all the assumptions of the crusaders. Admittedly most had envisaged that the movement towards international peace could meet occasional setbacks. Wars against barbarians and autocrats might have to be fought before the millennium arrived. Indeed, if the First World War had been fought by Britain, France and Germany on the one hand and Russia and Serbia on the other, the belief in the millennium might have been less shaken. Such a war could have seemed a replay of the Crimean or American Civil War and thus been interpreted as a war against the barbarians. It was however, more difficult for learned Frenchmen, Englishmen and Russians to interpret the war against Germany as simply a war against the ignorant and uncivilised: for Germany in 1914 was the homeland of Albert Einstein, Max Planck, Max Weber and a galaxy of great contemporary intellects. On the other hand German liberals at least had the intellectual satisfaction that the Tsar of Russia was one enemy they were fighting; but another of their enemies was France which in some eyes, was the lamp of civilisation.

There was a peculiar irony in the war which divided

Europe. If the length and bitterness of the war had been foreseen, the efforts to preserve the peace in 1914 would have been far more vigorous and might have even succeeded. But one of the reasons why so many national leaders and followers in 1914 could not imagine a long war was their faith in the steady flow of that civilising stream that had seemed to widen during the peaceful nineteenth century. The Great War of 1914 would be short, it was widely believed, partly because civilised opinion would rebel against the war if it began to create chaos. The willingness of hundreds of millions of Europeans to tolerate chaos, slaughter and an atmosphere of hatred was an additional surprise to those who had faith in civilisation.

Despite the shock of a world war, versions of the Manchester creed survived. Indeed that creed may have been partly responsible for the outbreak of another world war only two decades later. The military revival of Germany had complicated causes, but in many of those causes one can detect the mark of Manchester.

Germany could not have revived, militarily, without the willing or reluctant sanction of some of the victors of the First World War. In particular the United States and Britain allowed Germany to revive. As they were themselves protected by ocean they tended to be careless of threats within Europe; as they were democracies they tended to have trouble in spending adequately on defence in years of peace, for other calls on revenue were more persuasive. A secure island democracy is of course the haven of the Manchester creed; its optimism about human nature and distrust of excessive force reflect the security of its home environment.

One sign of optimism in England and the United States was the widespread belief that another world war was virtually impossible. The idea of a war to end war had been one of the popular slogans in those democracies from 1914 to 1918, and the idea lived long after the slogan dissolved in the mouths of orators and faded on recruiting billboards. The prediction that the world would not again experience a war of such magnitude aided the neglect of armaments among some of the main victors of the previous war. It was probably in England too that there was the deepest faith that the

League of Nations would become an efficient substitute for
the use of force in international affairs; this was not surprising, for the League in a sense was a descendant of the House
of Commons, the Manchester Cotton Exchange, and the old
crusade for free trade. In England public opinion, more than
official opinion, tended to expect more of the League of
Nations than it was capable of giving. That misplaced faith
indirectly helped the Germans to recover their bargaining
position in Europe, for in crises the League of Nations proved
to be powerless. Likewise in England the widespread mistrust
of armaments in the 1920s was more than the normal reaction
after a major war; it mirrored the belief that the armaments
race had been a major cause of the previous war. The Great
War, it was argued, had come through misunderstanding; it
had been an unwanted war. This interpretation of 1914, to
my mind quite invalid, matched the optimistic tenets of the
Manchester creed. And since it was widely believed in England it affected future events. It also was a restraint on the
English government's ability to match German re-arming for
part of the 1930s: to enter again into an armaments race was
to endanger peace, it was believed, even more than to neglect
armaments. The ways in which the Manchester creed affected
Europe between the two world wars represents only one
strand in the rope which raised Germany from her enforced
meekness of 1919 to her might of 1939, but it was still an
important strand.

In the nineteenth century the Manchester creed in all its
hues was favoured more by public opinion than by the reign-
ing ministry in England. On the eve of the Second World
War however it was powerful in Whitehall. Manchester
had taken office, even if it was disguised as a former mayor
of Birmingham. Neville Chamberlain, England's prime
Minister from 1937 to 1940, is now often seen as a naïve indi-
vidualist, an eccentric out of step with British traditions, but
he represented one of the most influential traditions of
British thought. Though he was rearming Britain he did not
trust primarily in arms. He saw, not an evil world which reacted only to force or threats, but a world of rational men
who reacted to goodwill and responded to discussion. He believed that most modern wars were the result of misunder-

standings or of grievances. Accordingly there were rational remedies for the causes of war. As he believed that Germany suffered unfairly from the Versailles Peace of 1919, he was prepared to make concessions in the belief that they would preserve the peace. He was eager to hurry to Germany – not summon Germany to England – in the belief that the conference table was the only sane field of battle. He believed Hitler would respond to rational discussion and to appeasement; so did many Englishmen in 1938.

If those gifted early prophets of the Manchester creed could have seen Chamberlain – during the Czech crisis of September 1938 – board the aircraft that was to fly him to Bavaria to meet Hitler at short notice they would have hailed aviation as the latest messenger of peace. If they had known that he met Hitler without even his own German interpreter they would perhaps have wondered whether the conversation was in Esperanto or Volapük. It seemed that every postage stamp, bilingual dictionary, railway timetable and trade fair, every peace congress, Olympic race, tourist brochure and international telegram that had ever existed, was gloriously justified when Mr Chamberlain said from the window of number 10 Downing Street on 30 September 1938: 'I believe it is peace for our time.' In retrospect the outbreak of war a year later seems to mark the failure and the end of the policy of appeasement, but the policy survived. The first British air raids over Germany dropped leaflets.

IV

The city of Manchester has many epitaphs of that theory of peace of which it was the symbol. When you enter the Victoria railway station you see a memorial to the 'Men of the Lancashire and Yorkshire Railway' who died in the Great War. One of many European railways which, in the words of Henry Thomas Buckle, were 'additional guarantees for the preservation of that long and unbroken peace', its war memorial is inscribed with almost 1500 names. At the other end of the city, inside the Free Trade Hall which was built when free trade and peace seemed synonymous, a plaque reveals that the original hall 'had been destroyed by enemy air attack on the night of the 22nd December 1940'. Only a stone's throw away, in the autumn of 1970, a street placard proclaimed:

DON'T SELL ARMS. ABOLISH THEM.

For the optimistic theory of peace is still widespread. Within the United States it pervades much of the criticism of the war in Vietnam. Within the western world it is visible in the school of thought which expects quick results from the fostering of friendly contacts with Russia and China. It pervades many of the plans by which richer countries aid poorer countries. It permeates a host of movements and ventures ranging from the Olympic Games, Rotary and Telstar to international tourism and peace organisations. Irrespective of whether the creed rests on sound or false premises of human behaviour, it still influences international relations. In the short term it is a civilising influence. Whether it actually promotes peace or war, however, is open to debate. If it is based on false generalisations about the causes of war and the causes of peace its influence in promoting peace is likely to be limited and indeed haphazard. Moreover, if it is inspired by a strong desire for peace, but gnaws at the skin rather than the core of international relations, the results will be meagre.

Something is missing in that theory of peace which was shaped and popularised by so many gifted men in the nineteenth century. One may suggest that, like many other explanations of war and peace, it relied much on coincidence. Those living in the three generations after Waterloo had wondered at the long peace and sought explanations in events that were happening simultaneously.* They noticed that international peace coincided with industrialism, steam engines, foreign travel, freer and stronger commerce and advancing knowledge. As they saw specific ways in which these changes could further peace, they concluded that the coincidence was causal. Their explanation, however, was based on one example or one period of peace. They ignored the earlier

* Likewise one explanation of the relative peace in Europe since 1945 – the influence of nuclear weapons – seems to rely often on coincidence.

if shorter periods of peace experienced by a Europe which had no steam trains, few factories, widespread ignorance and restricted commerce. Their explanation of the cluster of European wars in the period 1848–71 was also shaky. These wars were relatively short, and to their mind the shortness of most wars in the century after Waterloo was evidence that Europe's warlike spirit was ebbing. On the contrary one can argue that most of these wars were shortened not by civilising restraints but by unusual political conditions and by new technological factors which the philosophers of peace did not closely investigate. If neglect of war led them into error their attitude was nonetheless a vital reaction to those studies of war which neglected peace.

Most of the changes which were hailed as causes of peace in the nineteenth century were probably more the effects of peace. The ease with which ideas, people and commodities flowed across international borders was very much an effect of peace though in turn the flow may have aided peace. Similarly the optimistic assessment of man's nature and the belief that civilisation was triumphing was aided by the relative peacefulness of the nineteenth century. That optimism would not have been so flourishing if wars had been longer and more devastating. In one sense the Manchester theory of peace was like the mountebank's diagnosis that shepherds were healthy simply because they had ruddy cheeks: therefore the cure for a sick shepherd was to inflame his cheeks.

It is difficult to find evidence that closer contacts between nations promoted peace. Swift communications which drew nations together did not necessarily promote peace: it is indisputable that during the last three centuries most wars have been fought by neighbouring countries – not countries which are far apart. The frequency of civil wars shatters the simple idea that people who have much in common will remain at peace. Even the strain of idealism which characterised most versions of the Manchester creed cannot easily be identified as an influence favouring peace, perhaps because in practice the creed is not idealistic. Thus Neville Chamberlain's concessions to Germany in 1938 were no doubt influenced partly by Germany's increasing strength: moreover his concessions were not so idealistic because they were mainly at the expense of Czechoslovakia's independence.

The conclusion seems unmistakable: the Manchester creed cannot be a vital part of a theory of war and peace. One cannot even be sure whether those influences which it emphasises actually have promoted peace more than war.

Kenneth Boulding, an Anglo-American economist who brilliantly builds bridges across the chasms that divide regions of knowledge, made one observation which indirectly illuminates the dilemma of the Manchester brotherhood. 'Threat systems', wrote Boulding, 'are the basis of politics as exchange systems are the basis of economics.' The Manchester idealists emphasised exchange and minimised the importance of threats. Believing that mankind contained much more good than evil, they thought that threats were becoming unnecessary in a world which seemed increasingly civilised. Indeed they thought that threats were the tyrannical hallmark of an old order which was crumbling. They despised the open or veiled threat as the weapon of their enemies. Thus they opposed czars and dictators who relied visibly on force and threats. For the same reason they opposed slavery, serfdom, militarism and harsh penal codes. And they mostly opposed the idea of hell, for hell was a threat.

They did not realise, nor perhaps do we, that a democratic country depends on threats and force, even if they are more veiled and more intermittent than in an autocracy. They did not realise that intellectual and commercial liberty were most assured in those two nations – Britain and the United States – which were economically strong and protected by ocean from the threat of foreign invasion. The preference of Anglo-Saxon nations for democratic forms of government had owed much to the military security which the ocean provided. On the rare occasions in the last two centuries when Britain was threatened by a powerful enemy it abandoned temporarily many of its democratic procedures; thus in the Second World War Churchill and the war cabinet probably held as much power as an autocracy of the eighteenth century. Mistakenly the Manchester creed believed that international affairs would soon repeat effortlessly the achievements visible in the internal affairs of a few favoured lands.

Saluting that long procession which seemed to be marching steadily towards a shrine of international peace, the men of Manchester saw the lights of the torch-bearers but failed to see that behind marched a phalanx of sword-bearers.

V

The famous periods of peace in the nineteenth century are still a mystery. The factors so far discussed seem invalid even as fragments of an explanation of peace. The peaceful influence of powerful statesmen, humane cultural ideas or mild treaties of peace, or of the spread of commerce and knowledge, seems to have been much exaggerated. Nor can international peace be partly explained as the indirect effect of civil strife, prosperity or some other safety valve. So far only one fragment – the idea of war-weariness – has merit, and even that fragment must be chiselled before it fits the evidence. Since an explanation of peace is indirectly an explanation of war, the prevailing knowledge of the causes of war must be deeply tinged with myth and superstition.

Book Two

The Web of War

3: Dreams and Delusions of a Coming War

Perhaps persistent patterns in war and peace have not been found for the simple reason that they do not exist. Many historians, reacting against shoddy generalisations, argue that the causes of each war and each period of peace are different. In their mind a search for strong patterns is a search for a mirage. And yet the outbreak of war during the last three centuries reveals recurrent clues which illuminate the causes of war and so of peace. One concealed clue – crucial to an understanding of war – is the optimism with which most wars were commenced by nations' leaders.

On Saturday, 1 August 1914 the tremors were felt throughout Europe. In London restaurants German and Austrian waiters collected their pay and hurried to channel ports. In Berlin and Leipzig scores of English families cut short their holiday and boarded trains leaving Germany. At sea, passenger liners received wireless warnings to change course for friendly ports. Outside newspaper offices from Paris to St Petersburg crowds waited for bulletins to be posted or special editions to be bundled into the street.

On the eve of a war that was to kill more soldiers and involve more nations than any previous war one consolation was believed. The coming war, it was predicted, would be short. The fighting might last three months or perhaps six months. Few of Europe's leaders therefore could foresee the magnitude of the tragedy that was about to begin. When the first nations formally declared war on one another, they were not consciously declaring the beginning of what came to be called the war of 1914–18. They were rather declaring the

beginning of what they hopefully believed would be the war
of 1914 or, if the worst happened, the war of 1914–15. There
was an even greater consolation to leaders who realised that
the war, though short, would be terrifying. That consolation
was victory. Both alliances expected victory.

On the morning of 1 August, at a meeting of the federal
council of Germany, the imperial chancellor, Bethmann
Hollweg, gravely revealed that Germany had sent an ultimatum to Russia and to France. He expected no reply: he
envisaged the most sacrificing war that Germany had ever
fought. 'If the iron dice are now to be rolled,' he said, 'may
God help us.'

While warfare was a game of dice it was also a game of
chess, and in that game the German leaders believed they
were masters. Less than three months before the beginning of
the war Colonel-General von Moltke privately sketched to
the Austrian chief-of-staff the war's likely course: 'We hope
to be finished with France in six weeks after the commencement of operations, or at least to have got so far that we can
transfer our main forces to the east,' there to wrestle with the
massive Russian armies. One day before the war was declared,
the Bavarian minister at Berlin, Count von Lerchenfeld,
privately wrote that the omens for a Germany victory were
unusually favourable – even if England should enter the war
against Germany. At eight that evening, just before he went
as usual to dine at 'The Bristol', he spoke on the telephone
with his government in Munich and confided that the general staff 'counts on being able to conquer France in four
weeks'. Two days later he reported that military circles in
Berlin were utterly confident, even though Germany and
Austria 'will be facing the whole world'. Bethmann Hollweg
had the same confidence, believing that the war should be
over, at the most in four months. On the other hand Germany's ally, the Austrian empire, appears to have been less
enthusiastic. Her leaders did not expect an Austro-German
defeat, but so far as one can judge they were not confident of
a quick victory. They knew that they were second-fiddles in
the central European band.

The speed of Germany's advance through Belgium and the
north of France in the first month of war fostered high hopes

that the German troops would be home for Christmas. Germany's foreign minister now decided that there was no point in wooing Italy to join in the war: her aid was unnecessary. In the sixth week of the war Bethmann Hollweg thought the enemy would soon be seeking terms of peace. The halting of the German advance and the locking of the war in hundreds of miles of trenches soon upset the timetable of victory, but confidence bubbled from time to time. On 4 February 1915, when the war was entering its seventh month, Germany announced that she was placing a blockade around the British Isles and using submarines as a shock weapon against naval and merchant ships. Germany then had only twenty-one submarines in the North Sea but the chief of her naval staff, Admiral Bachmann, was so sure of the ability of submarines to sink the merchant vessels on which Britain relied that he predicted panic in Britain and surrender within six weeks. Germany, ironically, was already short of some raw materials and was preparing to ration bread and to use potato flour in the bakehouses. She had not prepared adequately for a war that had now lasted half a year, let alone a war eight times that long.

In London most ministers also expected a short war. Winston Churchill, first lord of the admiralty and an astute student of military affairs, thought the weight of evidence pointed to a short though terrible war. Britain's navy, he predicted as early as 1911, would deprive German factories and warehouses of raw materials and 'would react on German credit and finances already burdened with the prodigious daily cost of the war'. With this opinion Britain's chancellor of the exchequer, Lloyd George, agreed. In June 1914 Churchill asserted that Britain's stocks of oil, essential for battleships that were ceasing to burn coal, were adequate for the critical period of a modern war and perhaps for the whole war. As the tanks of oil on the shores of British harbours were neither large nor numerous the assumption was a short war. Most cabinet ministers, and those close to their ear or mouth, seem to have shared this view in the first month of the war. Viscount Esher, who sat on the Committee of Imperial Defence, jotted optimism in his journal. While he did not share the cheerfulness of English high society – 'these people mostly

look upon the war as a sort of picnic' – he thought the war
would end quickly. On the third day that Britain was at war
he thought that victory might come soon after the Russians
advanced their way into Germany 'a month hence'. On the
tenth day of the war he heard from General Sir Archibald
Murray that the war, with luck, would last only three
months; it was unlikely to last more than eight months because of unbearable financial strain and a scarcity of food for
armies and cities. On the day that Viscount Esher heard one
soldier's optimism, he heard the pessimism of another. He
spent two hours with Lord Kitchener, the hero of many
Indian and African campaigns and now secretary of war.
What Kitchener said was unpalatable. He spoke of a war
raging for at least three years. Kitchener did not expect static
warfare in the trenches; instead he predicted that the French
armies would be defeated early in the war, and that the Allies
would take several years to recover lost territory and push
back the Germans.

Whether French ministers were as hopeful as the British is
not clear. Certainly the higher soldiers of France seemed
confident in facing the same enemy which had humiliated
them in 1870. In February 1914 they secretly issued plan 17,
which envisaged strong French thrusts into Germany should
war arise. While German generals predicted that within six
weeks of the outbreak of war their vanguard would be near
Paris, many French generals predicted that their soldiers
would be at or across the Rhine. One of Frances' finest
generals Victor Cordonnier, recalled that in the first excite-
ment of war 'no heed was paid to the needs of the country,
since it was hoped the war would very soon end'. Did any
Frenchman holding high office envisage that four years after
the start of the war the front line would still be on French
soil?

Even in the elegant Russian capital of St Petersburg the
gilded domes reflected a halo of optimism that one would
hardly expect in a nation which less than a decade ago had
been humiliated by Japan in war. The war minister, General
Soukhomlinov, in March 1914 dictated an article to the
Petersburg Bourse Gazette affirming that Russia alone was
powerful enough to carry out an offensive war against the

massive weight of Germany and Austria. Admittedly that was a public statement: it could have indicated what the war minister intended the public to believe rather than what he himself believed. But in private conferences he was confident. He believed that victory would be achieved in a few months, and most of the Russian ministers agreed. Baron Rosen, a Russian diplomat who was in St Petersburg when the tsar reluctantly agreed to mobilise his forces, was one of many who observed in senior military circles the faith in a glorious victory.

A complicated trellis of hope – a criss-cross of military and financial fact and fantasy – tempered the horror of the coming war. A war involving many nations, it was commonly argued, could not conceivably last long. The war would be ended either by decisive events on battlefields or decisive events in the economic field; if the former did not happen, the latter was certain to happen.

III

In 1962 an American author, Barbara W. Tuchman, completed a fascinating history of the eve and opening of the First World War. President Kennedy is said to have read her new book when he faced the Cuban missile crisis, and if so the book could have been a rein on any tendency to indulge in wishful thinking; for *The Guns of August* captured the false optimism and the aggressive day-dreaming in Europe in the summer of 1914. The faith in the short war surprised Barbara Tuchman; and to her credit she was one of a small band of historians who saw it as part of the atmosphere which caused the war rather than an ironic but irrelevant example of folly. She attributed the faith that the war in 1914 would be short to prevailing opinions on strategy and finance. She summed up her view in a capsule, so compressed that it was slightly over-dosed:

> Clausewitz, a dead Prussian, and Norman Angell, a living if misunderstood professor, had combined to fasten the short-war concept upon the European mind. Quick, decisive victory was the German orthodoxy; the economic impossibility of a long war was everybody's orthodoxy.

Others, before and after her, came to a similar conclusion. The essence of their conclusions was that the war-eve faith was a recent phenomenon, and could only be explained by recent causes. The explanation for the optimism was mainly said to lie in the recent series of short wars in Europe and the growing mesh of financial and commercial dependence in the western world.

The case however has crucial gaps. It seems to explain why so many Europeans – both leaders and followers – expected the war to be swift, but can it explain why they expected it to be victorious as well as swift? In a mind's picture of a forthcoming war the likely duration of the fighting and its likely outcome are almost inseparable. And if we try to explain why an optimistic picture of a coming war took shape in the mind of a Russian minister or a German general, we are likely to conclude that the reasons for their faith in victory also explained why victory would come slowly or rapidly. It is perhaps significant that in England the prediction that the war of 1914 would be short was based heavily on the economic arguments. England was the leading financial power: accordingly, if economic collapse was to come early in the war, it would hit England's enemies first and so lead to their surrender. In contrast German leaders predicted that the war would be short because of the decisiveness of modern military technology: in that field Germany was the recognised master, and so could expect victory. Expectations of the outcome of the war had a strong subjective, inarticulate streak. The lesson of the last half century was that most wars were of brief duration; and Europe in 1914 was happy to accept that lesson. An equally relevant lesson was that those wars, whether long or short, had conferred victory on only one side. In 1914 however both sides were confident of victory. Even Russia, France and Austria, each of which had lost its last major war, expected victory. Underlying the optimism of European leaders in 1914 was something more powerful than their knowledge of recent military and financial history.

The war-eve optimism of 1914 has usually been seen as an exceptional mood. It was not exceptional, but simply more conspicuous. It could be detected more readily in the crisis of 1914 because of the publication, after the war, of piles of secret documents and hundreds of memoirs and autobiographies, which together made the outbreak of war in 1914 the most documented in history. An analysis of the hopes and fears held on the eve of earlier wars reveals a similar optimism.

It is not easy to discover how an approaching war was pictured by those who had to decide whether to make war or avoid war. Public predictions of what a war will be like have to be fingered gingerly; they may be propaganda rather than predictions. A sounder guide is what leaders predicted privately. Even private statements however were often exaggerated in order to persuade reluctant colleagues that the war would be glorious. Moreover if war-eve expectations oscillated from day to day, they cannot easily be pinned down. To muster evidence of war-eve expectations is a slow task. They are not mentioned in hundreds of books and articles on the causes of particular wars, usually because these anticipations are considered irrelevant. Sometimes they are not mentioned by historians because the documents which they consulted did not clearly reveal them. When a ruler and the chief of his armed forces both believed that they would win a war, and win it quickly, their belief was not necessarily expressed in letters that passed between them: it was pointless to discuss something upon which they agreed. Nevertheless sufficient evidence survives to suggest that optimism was a persistent prelude to war.

From the expectations which preceded more than a score of wars since 1700, a curious parallel emerges. Nations confident of victory in a forthcoming war were usually confident that victory would come quickly. Nations which entered a war reluctantly, hoping to avoid defeat rather than snatch victory, were more inclined to believe that they were embarking on a long struggle. The kinds of arguments and intuitions which encouraged leaders to expect a victorious war strongly influenced their belief that the war would also be swift. The belief in a short war was mainly the overflow from the reservoir of conscious superiority.

IV

Many long wars in the eighteenth century were opened with optimistic trumpetings. The attack against Sweden by the strong alliance of northern powers in 1700 seemed likely to yield quick victory: instead it led to twenty-one years of war. When in London in May 1702 the Council met to frame a British declaration of war against France it expected a quick battle and a 'good peace obtained in little time'. The war in fact was to last more than a decade. Russia's rulers seemed to hope that their invasion of Poland in 1733 would arouse no resistance. England's declaration of war against Spain in 1739 was accompanied in English palaces and alleyways by such glib hopes of easy conquest that Sir Robert Walpole quipped: 'They now ring the bells; they will soon wring their hands.' When Frederick the Great sent troops into Silesia in 1740 he believed that the new Habsburg empress, Maria Theresa, would be too busy cementing her fragile empire to offer resistance; Frederick even offered to help her fight other enemies if she would peacefully surrender Silesia to his own troops. The Swedish forces which invaded Russia in 1741 expected a swift march to the walls of the Russian capital. And the leaders of those nations which went to war in 1756 did not seem to envisage that their war would be remembered as the Seven Years War.

When England decided to crush the rebellion of the American colonies, both sides envisaged victory. At Philadelphia in July 1775 the congress of the United Colonies gave thanks to God that he had not allowed them to enter such a war 'until we were grown up to our present strength'. Major John Pitcairn, who commanded the English marines in the first engagement of that war, was astounded at the Yankees' confidence: 'The deluded people are made to believe that they are invincible.' One journal even argued that the American armies on their own soil could defeat all the armies of Europe. Major Pitcairn disagreed; he thought the cheap rum which his battalion was drinking was a greater danger than American firearms. 'I am satisfied', he wrote in March 1775, 'that one active campaign, a smart action, and burning

two or three of their towns, will set everything to rights.'
Three months later his letter was shown to King George III
whose endorsement was emphatic. By then the major was
dead, one of the tens of thousands of casualties of what proved
to be another seven years' war.

While that war went on, Joseph of Austria quietly sent
troops into Bavaria in January 1778 in the faith that he could
occupy territory without firing a shot. He predicted that old
Frederick of Prussia, now grounded with gout, would not
fight the Austrians; but his prediction erred and the War of
the Bavarian Succession ensued.

The longest war fought in Europe during the last three
centuries began in 1792 as a Franco-Austrian war in which
both sides were supremely confident of a quick and overwhelming victory. Britain at first was a spectator of the war
across the channel, and her ministers awaited news of a
French collapse. In the sixth month of the war Henry Dundas
– Britain's home secretary and navy treasurer – was mainly
worried about the effects of the expected French defeat; he
feared that when the Duke of Brunswick's invading army
reached the fringe of Paris, fleeing French revolutionaries
would enter England and stir up trouble. When in the tenth
month of the war France and Britain were also on the verge
of fighting there was more complacency than fear among
British ministers. Edmund Burke, the orator, realised this
when he discussed the crisis in the presence of Henry Dundas
and William Pitt, the prime minister:

Dundas: 'Well, Mr. Burke, we must go to war, for it will
be a very short war.'
Burke: 'You must indeed go to war, but you greatly mistake in thinking it will soon be over ...'

Mr Pitt too was greatly mistaken. He thought the financial
exhaustion of France in 1793 would make for a short war; but
when thirteen years later he was dying, the French war chest
was far from empty and her armies were victorious in much of
Europe. Entering his house on the outskirts of London in
January 1806, the month of his death, Pitt's eyes fell on a wall
map of Europe. 'Roll up that map,' he said despondently, 'it
will not be wanted these ten years.' The extreme optimism at

the start of many wars was often matched by extreme pessimism later.

Europe in 1815 could recall less than three years of peace in the preceding quarter century. The idea that wars were fleeting adventures had been stunned, but the stunning was temporary. French forces invaded Algeria in 1830 and their hope of quick conquest seemed rational, but it was seventeen years and many reverses later that the conquest was complete. Meanwhile in 1828 Russia and Turkey went to war again, the Turks with the sense of invincibility which a holy war aroused, the Russians with bold plans for a quick march all the way to Constantinople. The war lasted two years; even to Russia the cost of the war and the prize of the victory were disappointing.

On the eve of the Crimean War the Russian emperor thought that Turkish resistance would be feeble. As the British ambassador in Russia confided in February 1853: 'The Emperor came up to me last night, at a party of the Grand Duchess Hereditary's, and in the most gracious manner took me apart, saying that he desired to speak to me.' The emperor confided that Turkey was about to collapse. 'I repeat to you that the Bear is dying' said the Russian emperor; 'you may give him musk, but even musk will not long keep him alive.' A short and glorious war was envisaged in St Petersburg; but when Britain and France provided the staggering Turkish bear with musk, the war became long and inglorious for the Russians. Any prediction of the duration and course of a war involves a prediction of whether third or fourth nations will intervene; and this prediction was often too optimistic.

In 1859 Franz Josef, the Austrian emperor, thought his war with France and Italy would be fortunately short: it was short but not fortunate. In 1866, on the eve of the Austro-Prussian war, the Austrians again seem to have expected victory. One splinter of evidence, according to Bismarck's memoirs, was in 'the proclamations that lay in the knapsacks of the Austrian soldiers, together with the new uniforms ordered for the entry into Berlin'. The proclamations were never read, and neither the uniforms nor their owners reached Berlin. In the summer of 1870, on the eve of the

Franco-Prussian war, the French emperor said privately on several occasions, 'We are entering upon a long and arduous war.' He expected a painful victory but the Empress Eugénie and most French ministers seem to have expected a swift victory. One ironic mirror of expectations within the French army was that the officers had been issued with maps of Germany but not of France. Alas, maps of the roads leading to Paris would have been more useful, so fast was the enemy's advance.

When the United States and the breakaway Confederacy began to fight in 1861, few if any of the rival leaders believed that they were beginning a four years' war which would kill more than half-a-million men. On 15 April 1861, three days after the first engagement at Fort Sumter near Charleston, President Lincoln ordered his militia and ships to seize quickly all the forts and property of the Confederacy, and in a confident proclamation he ordered the Confederacy's leaders, officials, and soldiers to 'retire peacefully to their respective abodes within 20 days'. The United States at first voted little money to the war and her volunteers were enlisted for a term of only ninety days; true, there were legal obstacles to a longer enlistment, but the tolerance of the obstacles was itself a sign of how much the government minimised the task ahead. In the third month of the war President Lincoln asked Congress to 'give the legal means for making this contest a short and decisive one' – 400,000 men and 400 million dollars. He received them and more, but the contest remained indecisive. On the other hand the Confederacy in the south, outnumbered in men and materials, expected ultimate rather than easy victory. One cushion of Confederate confidence was the hope that the economic life of Britain – so reliant on the manufacture of textiles – would shiver when the precious shiploads of Confederate cotton ceased to reach Liverpool; Britain would then intervene and end the war. Since the Confederacy was a kind of Rhodesia of the Americas, it is ironic to observe that indirect 'economic sanctions' were as frail in the 1860s as they were in the Rhodesian dispute of the 1960s.

In launching a war against Turkey in the spring of 1877 the Russian leaders expected a swift march to Constantinople. Russia's confidence was easily seen in her plan of campaign. A more vivid testimony was buried in a reminiscence written by one of the most observant scholars of war, Ivan Bloch. A Polish financier, he was president of the company which owned a railway linking Kiev and Brest in western Russia, and in the spring of 1877 his railway conveyed a large part of Russia's forces on one stage of their journey to the Turkish front. It was apparently the custom for the railway president to accompany royalty when they travelled on his line, and on the eve of the war he travelled in the imperial train conveying Tsar Alexander II to the frontier. Out on the green-grassed plains the train was stopped to allow the tsar to have his morning shave, and Bloch and several of the high generals took the opportunity to climb down and stroll along the track. Bloch chanced to tell them that in a day or two he would travel to the holiday resort of Karlsbad in Germany to take the waters, and to his astonishment he was rebuked. 'You surely don't mean it!' said one general. 'Why we shall be coming back to St Petersburg too soon to permit of your going so far away. We shall return in two or three weeks from now ... You see our expedition will resolve itself into a mere military promenade.' The war did not last the expected three weeks; it lasted for 303 days. Undoubtedly it was Russia's greatest success against the Turks for more than a century, but the course of the war did not follow Russia's predictions or, still less, Turkey's.

Most British ministers in 1899 expected the Boer War to be short and swift. Their soldiers had won so many wars in India and Africa that the two republics in the interior of southern Africa – Transvaal and the Orange Free State – did not seem capable of long defying them. A common British attitude to the farmer-armies of these republics was expressed by Alfred Milner, Britain's governor in Cape Colony and one of the men whose views strongly influenced Britain's attitude to the Boers. At a private luncheon in Cape Town, eight days before the war began, he said in a quizzical manner to the new commander of the British forces: 'Surely these mere farmers cannot stand for a moment against regular troops?' The ministry in London was also optimistic. The chancellor of the exchequer, Sir Michael Hicks Beach, informed the

House of Commons that the short war would cost no more than £11 million. The war in fact was not to end for two and a half years, the cost to Britain was more than twenty times the original estimate, and that balance sheet made no allowance for the death of 22,000 British soldiers. At least the British had the compensation of military victory. The Boer republics had also initially believed that they would win, and their ultimate defeat – with 6000 soldiers killed, thousands of farm-houses and flocks and herds destroyed, leaders banished, and 20,000 of their children and women dead in British 'concentration camps' – was not what they had envisaged. As the Boer politician, Schalk Burger, confessed when the fighting was virtually over: it was a 'war of miscalculation'. Similarly the Russo-Japanese War of 1904–5, the Italo-Turkish war of 1911–12, and the two Balkan Wars of 1912–13 were, at least for one side, wars of miscalculation.

So the optimism on the eve of the First World War belonged to a long but unnoticed tradition. In one sense only was it unusual. That was probably the first war since 1803 to involve, from its very commencement, more than two major powers, and so the fighting was expected to be serious and destructive. As expectations of that war therefore carried a pessimistic thread, the optimistic threads must have been far thicker in order to weave the prevailing mood.

v

Even after the great blood-drench, the start of many wars was marked by optimism. The victorious allies intervened in Russia in 1918 in the belief that they could quickly aid the White Russian forces to defeat the Bolsheviks.* At the same time Greece fought Turkey, and Poland fought Russia, in the belief that they would win and win easily. When Japan fought in Manchuria in 1931 and began in 1937 the long war against China, and when in the mid 1930s Italy invaded Ethiopia, the familiar expectations of quick victory seem to have been held.

* One of the rosary beads of U.S. nationalism during the Vietnam war was the belief that U.S.A. had never lost a war. The war of intervention in Russia had been forgotten.

The Second World War was not launched in the presence of cheering crowds. The war of 1914–18 was remembered vividly, and most people in Europe probably expected that the new war would be the same slow-moving and gargantuan event. The mood in 1939 seemed to be a strong exception to the optimistic expectations held on the eve of most wars; and for some time it seemed futile to bother to search for evidence of optimism among those who made the decisions that led to war in 1939. When belatedly I decided to make a quick search I turned first to books which I had read at a time when high war-eve expectations seemed more an example of human folly than a vital clue to war. On that first reading I had seen the folly and missed the clue.

The fighting began on 1 September 1939 between Germany and Poland, and the man who chose the day had high hopes that it would simply be a two-power war. Adolf Hitler, lecturing to the leaders of his armed forces on 14 August, had predicted that Britain and France were not likely to help Poland. He believed that the Anglo-French leaders were timid and their military advisers were not confident of the outcome of a general European war. Hitler also insisted that Britain expected the next world war if it should come, to be long and costly; and Britain would not rush into such a war. Even if Britain and France decided to aid Poland against a German invasion they would surely be unable to defeat Germany or even effectively aid Poland. Hitler certainly did not envisage a deadlocked war in Europe. He believed that even a general war would not be long because no nation wanted a long war. So one pillar of the optimism of 1914 reappeared in the hopes of a man who had fought in that war and had seen that pillar crumble.

The signing, on 23 August 1939, of a pact of friendship between Germany and Russia increased Hitler's confidence. Poland was now cut off from aid. On the Wednesday evening when Stalin in the Kremlin was drinking toasts to Hitler, the toasted leader was in Germany secretly ordering that the invasion of Poland begin on the following Saturday. On the evening of the planned invasion however Hitler was forced to halt his troops, for England had signed a firm promise to aid Poland. Hitler's hesitation was temporary. He believed that he could win a general war against France and Britain, but he still had hopes that they would not fight. This is clear in the 'most secret' directive, issued in Berlin on 31 August and setting down the invasion of Poland for 4.45 on the following morning. Furthermore, while German troops were moving towards or across the Polish frontier on that first dawn of autumn, Hitler made no move against Britain or France. 'If Britain and France open hostilities against Germany,' said his secret directive, then Germany must retaliate. He had pinned much on that 'if'. Even after he had crushed Poland he still hoped briefly that the torn peace of Europe could be patched. He was not willing however to surrender the Polish territory that would provide the essential patch, for he remained confident that he could master that Anglo-French alliance which had failed to help Poland.

In 1939 confidence was far from as exuberant in London as in Berlin. The British attitude was more defensive – an island outlook. There was no pervasive belief that victory would come quickly, but there was no expectation of a British defeat. Our memory of British attitudes in 1939 is inevitably coloured by the military disasters which came a year later; but there was no premonition of those disasters in high places. On the eve of war the government was rather inclined to overestimate its military strength. Lord Halifax, the foreign secretary, thought Poland was of more military worth than Russia as an ally in the event of war. When General Sir Edmund Ironside visited Poland in July 1939 he was also impressed with an army which was as large as the French and nearly as large as the German army of peace time: the fact that Polish officers placed such emphasis on galloping horses did not unduly shake Ironside. As British chief-of-staff he prized experience and tradition in military affairs, and thought that a hidden weakness of the German army was that none of its present commanders had been higher than captain in the Great War. This in fact was to be one source of Germany's strength and was one reason why they chose to employ armoured vehicles against the Polish cavalry.

When in 1939 the Soviet Union fought Finland – one of those rare wars to begin on the eve of a northern winter – Stalin expected the Finns to wilt quickly in the face of his powerful army. He had even selected the Russian who was to rule Finland. But his army was to suffer hundreds of thousands of casualties before winning a Finnish strip that was too small to require a special ruler.

A generation which had experienced two long world wars was perhaps more likely to be cautious in viewing the prospects of future wars. Were most of the international wars since 1945 launched with clipped hopes? One cannot be sure until many of the secret documents become available, but much evidence points to the familiar optimism. When in June 1950 North Korea invaded South Korea she is said to have expected victory by 15 August, the anniversary of V-J Day. The Anglo-French campaign at Suez in 1956 and Israel's wars with Egypt seem to have been spurred by hope of swift victory. And in Vietnam the United States' decisions to 'escalate' or intensify the war were a concealed confession that the original hopes of quick victory had been unrealistic.

In 1962 the most populous nations on the globe, India and China, fought a border war which illustrated the sheer fantasy that so often preceded and accelerated the outbreak of war. In the west it was widely believed that India was the target of Chinese aggression and that therefore India's leaders were unlikely to have entered with confidence a war in which they so soon had to concede defeat. And yet the confidence in the high places in New Delhi was high, so high that the simplified picture of Chinese aggression fades. In the opinion of Neville Maxwell, who was *The Times'* correspondent in India when the war began and was later the author of one of the most observant books on recent war, the high civilians and soldiers in New Delhi had 'convinced themselves that the Chinese would not stand up to fire'. So irrational was their confidence that they had decided on the eve of the war to evict the Chinese troops from a stretch of border where the Indians were outnumbered by more than five to one, where the Indian guns were inferior, where the Indian supply route was a tortuous pack trail, and where the height of the mountains made breathing difficult and the cold intense for the Indian reinforcements who marched in cotton uniforms.

VI

Although faith in victory and indeed a quick victory seems to characterise the leaders of the clashing nations on the eve of each war, the mood was not usually like that of soldiers setting out on a picnic. As the decision to fight became firmer, the confidence was often tinged with nervousness, second thoughts, and the clutching of talismen. Like mountaineers at the start of a dangerous ascent or boxers at the start of a fight, knowledge of the dangers and risks that must precede victory suddenly fluttered up, even challenging for an instant the hope of victory. Kaiser Wilhelm II, who led Germany into the Great War, became famous for his fluttering moods during international crisis; and it came to be believed that they were signs of his neurotic or disturbed mind. But he was not alone in his second thoughts. Sir Edward Grey, who as foreign secretary did much to steer the British Empire into the same war, is remembered not for his assumption that Britain and her allies would win, than for his apocalyptic saying that lamps were being snuffed across Europe and 'we shall not see them lit again in our lifetime'. Sir Edward Grey and the Kaiser Wilhelm, in their second thoughts about an imminent war, belonged probably to a long tradition of hesitancy.

Among national leaders the fear and doubts often seem to be more conspicuous on the threshold of a war than a fortnight earlier or a fortnight later. The mood on the threshold is so conspicuous that it influences many explanations of how wars begin: it influences the idea that many wars arise through misunderstandings and confusion and a mistaken sense of alarm, rather than because the rival nations really wish to fight. It is significant however that the anxious mood is more widespread on the eve of what seems likely to be a many-sided war than on the eve of what is expected to be a two-sided war. As scholars tend to examine more the outbreak of many-sided or great wars, they therefore observe often the fear in the minds of those who had to decide whether to fight or not to fight. And yet there are valid reasons why fear should briefly vie with confidence on the eve of a many-sided war. Such a war was more dislocating to social and

economic life. It involved higher casualties. More important,
no nation on the eve of a many-sided war could be independent and self-reliant. Since most of the major nations entangled in the crisis belonged to alliances they depended
heavily on what their allies would do. In the last hours of
peace they could not be completely sure how their allies
would act. The alliance or friendship might have existed for
ten or twenty years of peace and survived much strain, but
the ultimate test of an alliance is action rather than promises.
Would an ally honour its pledge to give aid in the event of
war? Would it enter the fighting quickly and strenuously or
would it wait to see whom the first phase of fighting favoured? Would its strategy in the first months of the war be
designed more to protect its own borders or would it wage
war in the interests of the alliance?

On the eve of a war between rival alliances such doubts
were not surprising. Even when the alliance appeared to be
tight, doubts crept in. France and Russia were firm allies on
the eve of the First World War. President Poincaré of France
visited St Petersburg in a great French warship, and on the
evening of 23 July – nine days before the start of the war – he
was farewelled by the tsar. As the French warship sailed away
the tsar boarded his own yacht and, sailing across the moonlit
waters of the Gulf of Finland towards his summer palace, he
chatted with the French ambassador Maurice Paléologue:
'I'm delighted with my talk with the President. We see absolutely eye to eye.' Even that tight alliance, which proved to
be firm when war broke out, nourished fears. One day after the
German armies invaded Belgium the French ambassador
called on the tsar at his summer palace, and in a study which
looked through wide windows to the sea he anxiously explained that far away the French faced 25 German corps: 'I
therefore beg Your Majesty to order your troops to take the
offensive immediately. If they do not do so there is a risk that
the French army will be crushed.'

There is perhaps another reason why doubts seem prominent on the eve of some wars. Leaders might have decided to
fight long before they become conscious that they had made the
decision. When, however, they became conscious of the decision and its implications, they were alert for any circum-

stance or argument which could make that decision seem dubious or premature. So their mood swam erratically from hot to cold, and from cold to hot, in those final days when they could still reverse or postpone the decision to fight.

VII

This chronicle of wars that began with high expectations is far from exhaustive but is still startlingly long. It is doubtful if there was any war, since 1700, in which initial hopes were low on both sides. On the eve of many wars both nations or alliances expected the campaign to be short and victorious; on the eve of many other wars both nations expected victory though only one of the nations expected quick victory; and on the eve of some wars one side expected swift victory while the other side held a humbler definition of victory and fought in the belief that it could avoid defeat rather than with any hope of mastering the enemy. Similarly when latecomers joined in fighting which had already commenced they also carried with them a prediction of what that war would be like. Latecomers however were less likely to have fantasies of a short war if they had already seen the pattern of fighting.

While it is easy to recall wars which fulfilled the initial hopes – or even exceeded the hopes – of one side, it is doubtful if there ever was a war which fulfilled the initial hopes of both sides. It is probable that in the majority of wars the initial hopes of neither side were fulfilled. In the First World War neither alliance fulfilled its initial hopes. Of the major members of each alliance perhaps only the United States carried out her aims, and then only because she belatedly entered the war in 1917 with aims that had been frugally tailored to fit the deadlocked war.

Why did nations turn so often to war in the belief that it was a sharp and quick instrument for shaping international affairs when again and again the instrument had proved to be blunt or unpredictable? This recurring optimism is a vital prelude to war. Anything which increases that optimism is a cause of war. Anything which dampens that optimism is a cause of peace.

This optimism does not arise from a mathematical assess-

ment. It does not simply represent one nation's careful calculation that its military and economic capacities exceed those
of the potential enemy. When Russia and Japan faced war in
1904 or when Europe faced war in 1914, the rival expectations were based not only on relative assessments of military
strength. They were also influenced by relative assessments of
each other's ability to attract allies, their ability to finance a
war, their internal stability and national morale, their qualities of civilian leadership and their performance in recent
wars. The importance of each factor varied so much from one
mind to another, and from one nation to another, that the
same evidence could support different conclusions. Even if
rival nations followed a similar formula, and each gave the
same weight to particular factors, they would probably reach
different conclusions. For predictions of how a nation will
perform in a coming war are flavoured by moods which cannot be grounded in fact. Optimism may come from economic
conditions, the seasons, ideologies and patriotism. It may
come from a failure to imagine what war is like; for time
muffles the pain and sharpens the glories of past wars, and
national mythology explains away defeats and enshrines victories. Whatever their source, these moods permeate what
appear to be rational assessments of the relative military
strength of two contending powers. A prediction of a war
about to be fought is thus a crystallisation of many moods and
arguments, each of which has some influence on the decision
to make war.

The process by which nations evade reality is complicated.
Patriotism, national languages and a sense of a nation's history are all dark glasses. Leadership itself is provided with a
hazy telescope that does not always focus on reality. In the
eighteenth century a king could surround himself with courtiers who purred in his presence. In the twentieth century a
military dictator or an elected president was vulnerable to
those who pandered to his pride and his opinions. Woodrow
Wilson, president of the United States in the First World
War, preferred to live within a protective circle of admirers:
'All of Wilson's close friends – the men, the women, the professors, the politicians, the socialites – shared one characteristic: they were, or at least had to seem to him to be, *uncritical*

admirers of the man and of everything he did.' Dr Lester
Grinspoon, a research psychiatrist in Boston, argued in a restrained article in 1964 that every leader becomes partly the
prisoner of his position:

> We have described how a man, as he moves into posts of
> ever-increasing importance in business or government be-
> comes increasingly isolated and lonely; he is surrounded by
> an aura of his own importance, sagacity and omnipotence
> which is reflected by those about him. Paradoxically
> enough, as his decisions increasingly affect a greater num-
> ber of people, he becomes more isolated from them, and as
> he becomes increasingly well-known, he grows lonelier.

One does not have to blame only the national leaders. The
halo of omnipotence could also be shared by the multitudes:
the London crowds which in 1739 clamoured for war against
the Spanish who had sliced poor Jenkins' ear, the American
colonists who in the 1770s called for the British to be driven
into the Atlantic, the Parisians who gloried in the declaration
of war against the foreign enemies of the revolution, crowds
in Milan who in 1848 believed that volleys of stones would
drive the Austrians across the Alps, the Englishmen who
clamoured in 1854 for war against the Russians, the Germans
who crowded railway stations in 1870 to cheer their departing
troops, the Russians who lit bonfires when war against the
Turks began in 1877, the Americans whose blood pressure
rose as Spain refused to abandon Cuba in 1897, and all the
cheer-leaders in Iran and Iraq in 1981. Defeat to them was
inconceivable. Doubt was the voice of the enemy and therefore incomprehensible.

Expectations – and particularly expectations in the short
term – seem a crucial clue to the causes of war and peace. If
two nations are deep in disagreement on a vital issue, and if
both expect that they will easily win a war, then war is highly
likely. If neither nation is confident of victory, or if they expect victory to come only after long fighting, then war is unlikely. Admittedly it may be argued that if the two contending nations did not go to war, and if the deep disagreement
persisted, diplomacy would be unmanageable and the tension

would ultimately break into open warfare. This argument seems doubtful. Diplomacy would be more manageable simply because neither nation held hope of solving satisfactorily the contentious issue through warfare.

The start of a war is – almost by the definition of warfare – marked by conflicting expectations of what that war will be like. War itself then provides the stinging ice of reality. And at the end of a war those rival expectations, initially so far apart, are so close to one another that terms of peace can be agreed upon.

Whatever causes that contradictory optimism in nations must be classified as a cause of war itself. One obvious cause of the contradiction is differing calculations of the power of the rival forces and rival equipment. But not less influential are the indirect or more subtle factors that will affect the outcome and, above all, the predicted outcome of a war. Among these factors are nationalism and other ideologies, economic conditions, the seasons, the prospect of intervention by outside nations, and the prospect of internal unity or disunity within the warring lands. How each factor influences the coming of war or peace is the theme of the four following chapters; the collective influence of these factors is assessed in the chapter entitled 'The Abacus of Power'.

4: While Waterbirds Fight

I

During the Napoleonic Wars the blockade of French ports was one of Britain's sharpest weapons. The British used this weapon as determinedly as the Germans were to use submarines a century later, and moreover they applied the blockade to the ships of neutrals as well as enemies. As the United States was neutral and continued to trade across the Atlantic, many of her ships were sunk or captured by British squadrons. The British gambled that the United States, despite monthly provocations, would prefer not to wage open war, but by 1812 a majority of leaders in Washington favoured war.

Every decision to wage war is influenced by predictions of how outside nations will affect the course of the war. And one of the factors that emboldened Washington in its preparations to fight Britain was the knowledge that France was indirectly on its side. In the coming war the United States would not be a formal ally of France: American commerce had suffered too heavily from French frigates and commercial edicts. But so long as France was supreme on the continent, and so long as she remained strong at sea, she would tax Britain's strength. Britain therefore seemed unusually vulnerable; her colonies in Canada were open to invasion from the south.

In Washington in April 1812 a secret sitting of Congress decreed that no American vessels or cargoes should leave the ports of the United States during the following ninety days. The precaution, intended partly to catch the enemy by surprise, was a foretaste of the tactics to be used against the United States at Pearl Harbour a century and a quarter later. On 18 June 1812 the United States declared war on Britain. While the news of war sailed slowly to Britain, American squadrons sailed out in search of British frigates and merchantmen, and a small army marched towards Canada.

Those American politicians who were eager for war had exaggerated the might of Napoleon and minimised the might of Britain. The French retreat from Moscow in the following winter, Wellington's invasion of France in 1813, and the capture and banishment of Napoleon in 1814 cut away one of the main props of Washington's confidence. The British, at last able to divert heavy reinforcements across the Atlantic, marched on Washington in August 1814, captured the town, and set fire to the White House. But the American armies fought back, and on the other side of the Atlantic the French were no longer so subdued. In November 1814 the British prime minister Lord Liverpool became as eager as the American president for peace. Lord Liverpool privately pointed to Britain's financial exhaustion, the delicate negotiations now facing the congress in Vienna, and the 'alarming situation' in the interior of occupied France. Four months later Napoleon was to escape from Elba and harness that unrest in France, but Lord Liverpool had no inkling of that escape; he was simply nervous that revolution in France might rise again. Expectations of what France might do had again flavoured Anglo-American decisions for war and peace.

At the end of 1814 British and American delegates were content to sign a document of peace which implied that neither side had been the victor. Nevertheless national memory is selective and a drawn war often slips surreptitiously into the list of victorious wars. Since every nation tends to believe that each of its past wars was fought in self-defence, a drawn war is more likely to be remembered as a victory. It is in the same tradition that a minister who controls the armed forces is entitled the 'minister for defence' rather than the 'minister for attack'.

A nation's decision to go to war always includes an estimate of whether outside nations will jeopardise its prospects of victory. The United States in 1815 might not have sent a naval expedition to the shores of Tripoli to punish the Barbary pirates if she had believed that a European power would side with the pirates. The United States might not have gone to war against Mexico in 1846 if European nations had seemed likely to offer effective aid to the Mexicans. By the 1860s the sword was in the opposite hand. The war between the Confederacy and the United States enabled European nations to send naval and military forces to interfere in other parts of the American continent. In the Caribbean the Spanish would probably not have fought the Negro rebels of San Domingo between 1863 and 1865, if the United States had remained united: nor would a Spanish squadron in 1864 have seized the Chincha Islands and their rich guano beds from Peru.

Armies and fleets from western Europe would not have dared to attack Mexico in 1861 if the neighbouring United States had remained strong. Back in November 1855 Lord Palmerston in London had predicted privately that the ultimate swallowing of Mexico by the United States 'is written in the Book of Fate'. He added that Britain and France would not fight to prevent the United States from annexing Mexico, 'and would scarcely be able to prevent it if they did go to war'. Six years later however, when the United States was skewered on its own internal war, France and Britain and Spain became bolder. They invaded Mexico, mainly to recover unpaid debts which the new Mexican government repudiated. France persisted with the war even after her allies withdrew. Nearly 30,000 French troops reached Mexico in 1862; they captured Mexico City in the following year and then installed as Emperor of Mexico the French nominee, Ferdinand Maximilian I, brother of the Emperor of Austria. Every protest which the United States made against French interference in Mexico was hollow until the American Civil War was over. Then the warnings from Washington could no longer be ignored. The French troops began to embark for home. The young Empress fled, her husband stayed, and his fate can be seen in the National Gallery in London, where Edouard Manet's famous painting depicts a blue-coated firing squad, standing raggedly in the warm Mexican light. That royal execution of 1867, and Russia's sale of Alaska to the United States in the same year, marked the start of a generation during which no outside power intruded in the United States' zone of influence.

Across the Pacific, in 1873, Japanese leaders debated privately whether they should send an invading expedition to Korea. Okubo Toshimichi for his part thought invasion

would be unwise, and one of his warning arguments envisaged Japan exhausting herself in a war in Korea and thereby tempting the Russians to move south and pounce. Japan
and Korea, he warned, would then resemble two waterbirds
fighting over a fish while the Russian fisherman made ready
to snatch the fish away. The same vivid analogy was used at
the beginning of the First World War by Yamagata Aritomo,
a 76-year-old soldier who was adviser to the Emperor of
Japan. He claimed that 'America enjoys, because of the war,
the full advantage of the proverbial fisherman': she was steal-
ing the catch while the waterbirds of the world were quarrelling. Some would say that Japan herself was to become the
perfect fisherman in international affairs, but if this is true
she was emulating the master fisherman of the west.

When the waterbirds fought, the fishermen were often
tempted to spread their nets. But a fisherman did not necessarily have to wait for the waterbirds to begin fighting; he
could snatch the fish while the birds were merely glaring at
one another. The short war between Serbia and Bulgaria –
the only international war fought in Europe in the 1880s –
was one of many variations on the parable of the waterbirds.

II

In September 1885 a bloodless revolution in Eastern Rumelia
threw out the Turks. Bulgarian troops quickly moved in to
defend the territory against the likelihood of a Turkish return. As the winds became cold, the small Bulgarian army
stood guard on the border of Turkey, waiting to see whether
the Turks replied with force. Then came a curious happening. While the Bulgarian regiments were poised on the
eastern frontier, their distant western frontier was endangered by Serbia. The king of Serbia believed that, if Bulgaria's
army remained pinned down on the distant Turkish border,
he could easily snatch territory. It was almost as if the French
were guarding the German border in expectation of an invasion, when suddenly the Spanish crossed the border and
dashed towards Paris. Indeed the capital of Bulgaria, the
small city of Sofia, was more vulnerable than Paris because it
lay only about fifty miles from the Serbian border. On 14

November 1885 Serbian troops crossed the Dragoman Pass, met virtually no opposition, and marched towards the undefended Bulgarian capital.

Throughout Europe the expectation of a quick Serbian victory was so widespread that many influential journals did not even discuss whether Serbia would win the war; they simply assumed that she would win. On the opening day of the war Bulgaria's strategic position seemed desperate. If she moved troops from the Turkish frontier she risked a surprise attack by Turkey. And if she decided to risk a Turkish attack how could she rush troops from the eastern frontier in time to save Sofia? The only railway in Bulgaria was a single line which, beginning at Constantinople and running west through Adrianople, crossed the Bulgarian frontier and ran almost half-way to Sofia. The railway had been built and operated by the Turks, but during the revolution of 1885 the railway bridge at the Turkish border had been blown up in order to prevent Turkish troop trains from entering. That left only five locomotives on the western side of the border; even more unfortunate there was no railway workshop in Bulgaria. Those five locomotives, running on a track which permitted a speed of only 15 miles an hour, had to carry most of the Bulgarian troops towards Sofia in order to meet the advancing Serbian army. And when the first troop trains reached the terminus in central Bulgaria the soldiers had to march 80 miles across the Balkan Ranges, past the city of Sofia, and so towards the advancing Serbs.

Winter was setting in, the poor road to the west became slushy with the passing of bullocks and baggage drays, and the Bulgarian Army's commissariat was unable to feed and supply the marching troops adequately. And yet one Bulgarian regiment, marching from the railhead towards the front, covered 60 miles in a mere 32 hours; only one man in seventy fell out because of sickness or lameness. One battalion, on reaching Sofia, procured cavalry horses, and two men mounted each horse and rode towards the enemy. On the third day of the war, in an icy wind that rippled the new snow on the ground, the vanguard of the two armies fought the Battle of Slivnitza. To the astonishment of most European observers the Bulgarians held their ground and even pushed forward, military bands playing at the head of the storming column. The strange spectacle of fanaticism and pageantry was appropriate, for this was to be the last European war in which both frontline armies were commanded personally by the monarchs.*

A war which had begun with all the dice loaded against Bulgaria became within one week an equal encounter and within a fortnight a Bulgarian triumph. The Serbs were pushed back across the ranges, back across their own frontier. All that saved them from the sweeping invasion which they had hoped to inflict on Bulgaria was Austria's threat of intervention on 28 November. Austria was the ally and financier of Serbia, and Austria's ultimatum ended the war exactly a fortnight after it had begun. Just as Serbia was the fisherman which had intervened while Bulgaria and Turkey were quarrelling, now Austria threatened to fish while Bulgaria and Serbia were fighting.

III

The promised or expected neutrality of a third party could also promote the appeal to war. When Japan and Russia were approaching their war of 1904, Japan was emboldened by Britain's promise to use her seapower to prevent any other European power from interfering in the war. When Italy suddenly attacked Turkey in 1911 and invaded her colony in Libya, she derived some of her confidence from the diplomatic crisis which was absorbing France, Germany, Britain and Austria – the very powers who otherwise might have warned Italy to withdraw her troops and ships from the war. And in 1912, when Turkey was losing the war against Italy, four small Balkan nations prepared to attack the remaining Turkish territory in Europe. On 8 October 1912 the tiny kingdom of Montenegro declared war on Turkey. On 13 October Bulgaria and Serbia, having mobilised their armies, sent an ultimatum to Turkey. On the following day the

* Bulgaria's ruler, Prince Alexander, was a brother of that German-born naval officer who became Britain's First Sea Lord of the Admiralty in 1912, who later changed his name from Battenberg to Mountbatten, and whose son won fame in Burma in the Second World War.

Turks hastily agreed to a preliminary peace treaty with Italy, thus surrendering Libya but freeing all their forces for the crisis in the Balkans. On 17 October Turkey went to war with Bulgaria and Serbia and, a day later, with Greece. The four Balkan fishermen seemed to have strong nets. In invading the Turkish provinces they could rely on the support of the Greek, Bulgar, Croat, Serb and Macedonian inhabitants of those provinces. The four invaders were also, by Balkan standards, financially sound: even the pig and plum economy of Serbia seemed as capable as Turkey of financing an expensive war. The invaders could quickly mobilise about 700,000 soldiers, almost twice as many as Turkey could field at short notice, and an omnipotent warship. In an era when new warships were believed to be making all old ships obsolete, the Greeks held superiority by virtue of their cruiser *Georgios Averof*. That was proven on 17 January 1913 when a Turkish battle squadron emerged from the Dardanelles, found that the Greek monster was waiting, and after a long-range duel was forced to retreat to the safety of the Dardanelles. On land the Turks also seemed vulnerable. Their provinces in Europe formed a spoon-shaped region, and the narrow handle of the spoon was only forty miles wide and was flanked by the Aegean on the south and by the Bulgarian enemy on the north. The Turks had to cling to the handle of the spoon, for the 300-mile railway that twisted along the handle from Constantinople Junction to the Turkish port of Salonika was their vital link with the wide Turkish province extending to the Adriatic. Within three weeks of the outbreak of war, the Bulgarians marching from the north and the Greeks arriving from the south had cut the railway, isolating the Turkish forces in the west.

These advantages would not have spurred the decision to fight if one other advantage had been missing. The Balkan League had gambled that none of the great European powers could thwart their invasion. Although, on the eve of the war, the great powers had affirmed that 'under no circumstances would they agree to any change in the status quo', their warning was rejected by the Balkan League as an empty threat. The tensions between the mighty of Europe were as visible in 1912 as they were in the great war which began two years later. And in those tensions, the Balkan League had placed its trust.

The Turks were no sooner defeated than their conquerors began to quarrel among themselves. The spoils were unexpectedly impressive: measured in square miles they were perhaps larger than those won in any European war for almost a century. Of the spoils Serbia and Greece demanded more than Bulgaria was willing to concede. Bulgaria's obstinacy was easy to understand because in a few months her army had suffered at least 93,000 casualties – more than the total of her allies. The Bulgarians had fought fiercely on the front where the Turks were strongest, and for a time had even seemed capable of reaching the Golden Horn. In victory their leaders lapped up the cabled compliments that they were the 'Prussians of the Balkans' and the 'Japanese of the West'. They not only exaggerated their military prowess but also decided rashly that if the waterbirds should quarrel no fisherman was likely to intervene and snatch the catch. Russia and Austria, they decided, were friendly. There remained neighbouring Rumania, hostile but neutral, and the Turks who had recently conceded defeat in war. All in all the Balkan landscape seemed to smile on Bulgaria in their summer of victory.

On 29 June 1913 Bulgaria suddenly attacked the Greek and Serb armies at many points along a front-line stretching from the Danube down to the sea at Salonika. A foretaste of the long French front in the Great War, it absorbed all the strength of the Bulgarians and so exposed their unguarded eastern and northern borders to attack. Less than a fortnight after the war had begun, the Rumanians swarmed in from the north. With a huge army at their call, and hardly a Bulgarian regiment to check them, they marched unopposed towards the Bulgarian capital of Sofia, thus repeating the Serbian strategy of 1885. Even the Turks, defeated in the spring, declared war on Bulgaria in the summer and reoccupied Adrianople without firing a shot. Soon four armies were converging on Bulgaria: five armies if we count the retreating Bulgarians. The Second Balkan War lasted one month.

The parable of the waterbirds and the fishermen was visible again at the start of the First World War. In every capital city they had to predict whether their own allies would support them, whether the allies of the enemy would join in the war, and whether uncommitted nations would fight, give economic aid, or remain aloof. In the aftermath of that war, Poland's decision to fight Russia and Greece's decision to fight Turkey were partly influenced by their expectations of outside aid. In 1935, on the eve of the war in Abyssinia, Italy gained confidence from the prediction that European nations would not intervene and the Ethiopians gained courage from their contradictory prediction. As Emperor Haile Selassie sadly told a meeting of the Assembly of the League of Nations: 'In October 1935 the fifty-two nations who are listening to me today gave me an assurance that the aggressor would not triumph'. Their glib promises of aid, he had hoped, would more than compensate for 'the inferiority of my weapons, the complete lack of aircraft, artillery, munitions and hospital services'. When Japan went to war in 1937 she assumed that no European nation would intervene on China's side. When Poland went to war with Germany in 1939 she believed she would receive crucial aid from Britain and France: Hitler on the contrary suspected that Poland would receive no useful aid. In the Suez War and Hungarian uprising of 1956 expectations of how outsiders would behave were crucial to the beginning and ending of those wars.

The same expectations influenced many decisions to end wars. The United States in 1814 became eager to end her war with Britain when the defeat of Napoleon released British regiments for service in North America. In the 1860s France became more eager to abandon her war in Mexico when the end of the American Civil War enabled the United States to threaten to send troops south of the border. In the same decade Prussia's decision to end her short war against Austria was apparently influenced by fear that France might intervene.

These are simply dramatic examples of wars whose beginning or ending were influenced by hopes or fears that outsiders would intervene. Examples can be plucked with ease from every half century since 1700. The dilemma of the waterbirds is less visible in other wars but probably is always present. Every war is preceded on both sides by predictions of how outside nations will behave; and these predictions form one of the causes of war and, similarly, of peace.

Leaders of a nation deciding to fight or to avoid fighting survey the political landscape just as a nightwatchman surveys the surroundings of the place he guards. Political leaders and chiefs of the armed forces may not even be conscious that they have surveyed the international landscape, for they have long memorised it or intuitively observed its changes. Their assumptions of how outside nations will behave are not always visible in the diplomatic documents written as a war approaches. The assumptions may be so obvious, so beyond dispute, to those who write the memoranda and despatches that they may not be recorded. They are carefully recorded however when they perturb the waiting fishermen on the edge of their pond.

IV

To suggest that opportunism pervades international affairs is to run counter to national asumptions. Opportunism in international affairs is usually detected in a particular leader, a Napoleon or a Hitler, or in a particular nation. It is common in the English-speaking world to see opportunism in Germany's attack on Belgium in 1914 or Japan's attack on Pearl Harbour in 1941. But opportunism also marked Britain's reluctance to aid inland Luxembourg and her eagerness to aid coastal Belgium in 1914. Opportunism also marked the United States' policy towards Japan in earlier months of 1941, for she refused to export strategic commodities to Japan in the hope that Japanese troops would be forced to withdraw from China or to fight there with inadequate weapons.

The opportunism in international affairs tends to be ignored for a more important reason. It is more conspicuous when nations go to war, but it is still strong in peace. Our obsession with the causes of war and our reluctance to study the causes of peace possibly blind us to the way in which opportunism underwrites each period of peace. The most popular vision of peace is of nations living independently, each respecting the rights and territories of others; and each belonging to a kind of brotherhood. The brotherhood of nations however tends to be hierarchical and opportunist. Peace depends directly or indirectly on military power. While we observe the role of military power when it dramatically breaks the peace, we tend to ignore its role when it ends a war or preserves the peace. We thus conceal from ourselves the close relation between the causes of peace and the causes of war.

5: Death-Watch and Scapegoat Wars

I

A search for causes common to many wars of the eighteenth century reveals one obvious clue. The death of a king was often the herald of war. The link is embodied in the popular names given to four important wars. Thus there was a War of the Spanish Succession and a War of the Polish Succession, and they were followed by wars of the Austrian and then the Bavarian Succession. It would be illuminating to know who named those wars. Their names persuasively imply that the question of who should succeed to a vacant throne was the vital cause of the wars. It is sometimes said that these wars, 'as their textbook titles suggest', sprang from dynastic rivalries; 'it is not by accident' that they are so named. The eagerness to explain the causes of a war partly in the light of its popular name is slightly puzzling. It almost suggests that the War of Jenkins' Ear was a war about ears and the Seven Years' War was a war about years.

Those four wars of succession were not the only wars which were preceded by and influenced by the death of a monarch. In 1700 the rulers of Saxony, Denmark and Russia went to war against Sweden whose boy ruler, Charles XII, had not long been on the throne. In 1741 Swedish troops invaded Russia whose tsar was one year old. In 1786 the death of Frederick the Great of Prussia prepared the way for the Austro-Russian campaign against Turkey in the following year. And in March 1792 the death of the Emperor Leopold II in Vienna was one of the events that heralded the French declaration of war against Austria in the following month.

In all, eight wars of the eighteenth century had been heralded and influenced by the death of a monarch; and those wars constituted most of the major wars of that century.

Nor did those death-watch wars entirely vanish after 1800. Thus two wars between Prussia and Denmark were preceded by the death of Danish kings, the American Civil War followed the departure of a president in 1861, and the First World War was preceded by the assassination of the Austrian heir.

The kind of events or influences which are capable of increasing the chances of war are also capable of decreasing the chances. The death of a monarch could foster peace as well as war. In January 1762 Frederick the Great was at a crucial point of his long war with Russia and half the armies of Europe when he heard news of the death of the tsarina, Elizabeth of Russia. 'Courage, my dear fellow', wrote Frederick exultantly to a friend. 'I have received the news of a great event.' That great event and the accession of a new tsar led to Russia's prompt withdrawal from a war in which she was favourably placed.

What is the most feasible explanation of death-watch wars? In a century marked by a strong monarchy the death of a king obviously affected the distribution of power between nations. When a long-reigning monarch was succeeded by a seemingly weak monarch then the tilting of the scales of international power was dramatic. Of the eight monarchs whose death heralded war, six had each reigned for more than a quarter of a century. Of the eight inheritors six could be called vulnerable; one was a baby, two were teen-aged princes, one was a pregnant woman inheriting a throne to which female rights were frail, and two others came from outside the kingdom. The accession of a seemingly weak monarch made a land vulnerable to attack. It was additionally vulnerable because in a century where many alliances between monarchs were personal, the death of a monarch often dissolved or weakened defensive alliances. A new monarch could not always be certain of the loyalty of foreign allies or even of his own courtiers and generals. Significantly, the new monarchy was nearly always the target, not the arrow, of foreign attack. Significantly, it was usually attacked by a land which previously had not considered itself strong enough to launch an attack. A royal death, it seems, was most dangerous when it blurred what had previously been a neat ladder of power, suddenly making rival monarchs confident of their own bargaining position.

The death-watch wars were begun with the familiar over-optimism. The kingdom with the new ruler was usually judged to be temporarily too weak to resist the plundering of part of its territory. The plunderers usually believed that they could snatch territory without provoking a war or that, if war erupted, the campaign would be swift and victorious. No war was apparently expected by Louis XIV when in 1701 he quietly began to poach territory from Spain, by Frederick the Great when in 1740 he invaded Austrian Silesia, and by Joseph of Austria when in 1778 his white-coated troops marched into the south of Bavaria. Those annexations however were followed by strenuous fighting. And the fighting only ceased when exaggerated hopes were whittled down.

II

Revolution, in the last quarter of the eighteenth century, was a prelude to at least four wars between nations. The revolt of the North American colonies became an international war in 1778, and other revolutions precipitated Prussia's invasion of the Netherlands in 1787, Russia's invasion of Poland in 1792, and Austria's invasion of France in the same year. Civil unrest, like the death of kings, marked the crumbling of established authority and therefore affected perceptions of national power. Increasingly in Europe the royal funeral was replaced by civil strife as a dangerous disturber of the peace.

Many international wars in Europe after 1800 were not preceded by civil strife, and civil strife did not always lead to war. Nonetheless it is astonishing to discover how many wars had been heralded by serious unrest in one of the warring nations. The following list is long but not exhaustive. It would have been longer if it had included wars outside the period 1815 to 1939, if it had included wars in Central and South America, and if it had included wars between European powers and those coloured people who were too loosely organised to be called nations. The resulting table moreover included only those civil disturbances which seemed to have visible links with the subsequent wars.

1815-1939

Year of Outbreak of International War	War	Seat of Civil Disturbance
1823	French Pyrenees Expedition	Spain
1828	Russo-Turk	Greece
1830	Belgian	Belgium, France
1830	Franco-Algerian	Paris
1848	Danish–Prussian	Berlin
1848	Sardinian–Austrian	Vienna, Milan
1849	Hungarian Expedition	Hungary
1853	Crimean	Danubian Principalities
1860	Italian	Sicily
1861	Mexican Expedition	Mexico
1862	The War of Haiti	San Domingo
1864	Danish–Prussian	Holstein
1876	Serbo-Turk	Bosnia
1877	Russo-Turk	Balkans
1882	Egyptian Expedition	Egypt
1885	Serb–Bulgarian	E. Rumelia
1894	Sino-Japanese	Korea
1897	Greco-Turk	Crete
1898	Spanish–U.S.A.	Cuba
1899	Boer	Transvaal
1900	Boxer Expedition	Peking
1911	Italian–Turk	Turkish Empire
1912	First Balkan War	Macedonia
1914	First World War	Bosnia
1918	White Russian War	Russia
1919	Third Afghan War	India, Afghanistan
1919	Greco-Turk War	Turkey
1920	Russo-Polish War	Russia
1931	Sino-Japanese War	Japan, China
1936	Spanish War	Spain
1937	Sino-Japanese	China

In the space of one century and a quarter at least thirty-one wars had been immediately preceded by serious disturbances in one of the fighting nations. These wars constituted just over half of the relevant international wars of that period. The link between civil strife and international war is clearly vital, and indeed the well-known scapegoat theory attempts to explain that link.

In the nineteenth century war was less often the sport of kings but it was still a sport. Its annual fixtures were less certain than those of cricket, and spectators could not always find a grandstand on the verge of the battlefield, but as a sport war had much to offer. Alexander William Kinglake, an English barrister, was a plain-clothes follower of wars. In North Africa in 1845 he accompanied the flying column of the French general St Arnaud in his campaign against the Algerians. Nine years later he was in the Crimea with the British expedition, viewing the fighting from the saddle or a convenient hill. A fall from his pony on the morning of the Battle of Alma chanced to give him an introduction to the English commander, Lord Raglan, and they dined on victory that evening, the beginning of his deep respect for Raglan. At the end of the war Lady Raglan – her husband had died in the Crimea – invited Kinglake to write a history of the campaign. He wrote eight large volumes, the last of which appeared when he was nearly eighty. Kinglake had a powerful and lucid pen, and the early volumes of *The Invasion of the Crimea* were best-sellers. As the authoritative historian of the main war which Britain fought during the long reign of Queen Victoria, his analysis of that war possibly influenced the explanations of many later wars.

The core of Kinglake's explanations was persuasive; he argued that Napoleon III of France had 'a chief share in the kindling of the war', and that the main aim of his aggressive policy towards Russia was to promote 'the welfare and safety of a small knot of men then hanging together in Paris'. In Kinglake's opinion a major cause of the Crimean War was the internal troubles of the French regime. The invasion of Crimea was designed as a scapegoat to divert the eyes of Frenchmen from their own government's weaknesses.

Kinglake was not the first historian to see a particular war as a foreign circus staged for discontented groups at home. Nor was the Crimean War the first to which this interpretation was applied. It was invoked to explain individual wars stretching from the Hundred Years' War, which began in

1328, to the Vietnam war more than six centuries later. It is still one of the most popular generalisations about war. Professor Quincy Wright, who completed in Chicago in 1942 an ambitious study of war, concluded that a major and frequent cause of international war was the aggressive tendency 'to indulge in foreign war as a diversion from domestic ills'. Wright's argument is more forceful in the current edition of the *Encyclopaedia Britannica*, for which he wrote the article on causes of war; he doubted whether a totalitarian dictatorship could exist without taunting or attacking a foreign scapegoat. Leonard Woolf, in the third of his stimulating studies of communal psychology, also believed that a modern dictator depended on stirring up savage patriotism by blaming foreigners for all his nation's ills: 'his use of hatred as an instrument of government makes it highly probable that he will eventually land his country and his government in war, whether he wants it or not.' A similar warning comes from some political theorists who fear that a troubled nation could use nuclear weapons against an enemy in order to create unity among its own people.

The idea of war as a crusade to rally a divided nation is very adaptable and can be remoulded to fit diverse preconceptions of wars. It can serve as a conspiratorial theory of war, as it served Kinglake. It thus satisfies the belief – often a gospel among liberals of the nineteenth century, anti-communists of the twentieth century and Marxists of both centuries – that autocratic rulers want war but that the common man is duped into supporting it and fighting it by the callous manipulating of his emotions. The theory can also satisfy those who believe that war is a popular event, giving as much satisfaction to firemen as statesmen and enabling all to vent their discontent on a common enemy. The theory also gained strength in the twentieth century from the fascination with psychology. War was seen as a psychological outlet: the enemy was the target for inner tensions. As it was increasingly believed that nations lost more than they gained from warfare, the persistence of war could perhaps be explained only by exploring the dark caves of the subconscious. While those caves were being explored, popular psychology suggested an answer. Was a nation going to war like the sup-

porters of a football team who, frustrated by their team's defeat, irrationally declared war on the windows of the excur-
sion train on the way home?

The scapegoat theory also attracts anthropologists. When
the American Anthropological Association met in Washington in 1967 to discuss the causes of war, that theory was perhaps the most widely voiced. At the seminar Margaret Mead
suggested that one of the functions of warfare was to 'provide
targets outside the country when the maintenance of power is
threatened from within.' At least five other anthropologists
since 1930 had suggested that primitive wars arose when a
society was troubled by dissensions, tensions and grief. Field
work – or field workers – provided some supporting 'evidence'. Thus one anthropologist was told by a warrior in the
Sepik district of New Guinea that he had organised a raid
because his wife had taunted him and made his 'belly hot
with anger'. Whether the warrior was hot with anger against
the neighbouring tribe or against his own wife is not quite
clear. Whether primitive war is comparable with civilised
war is also not quite clear, though it seems likely that the two
forms of warfare have many more causal similarities than
differences.

These variations on the scapegoat theory appear to coexist
peacefully alongside contradictory interpretations of war.
The theory escapes criticism partly because it is believed to
have been proven by an alien discipline. Some political scientists perhaps believe that the scapegoat theory has been culled
from the reading of history; some historians perhaps think it
comes from psychology; some anthropologists perhaps believe
that it has been verified by research in political science. They
don't know where the theory comes from: all they know is its
universal glow. The glow seems to serve as a substitute for
evidence.

IV

It is easy to examine the evidence produced by historians to
support scapegoat interpretations of particular wars. Frequently they produce no evidence, and sometimes they produce fragile snippets. Consider for instance, Alexander King-

lake's argument that Louis Napoleon contrived the Crimean War partly to deflect French eyes from discontent at home. Kinglake, it is sometimes pointed out, had carried a grudge against him since the late 1840s when the emperor-to-be was living at number nine Berkeley Street, London, with Miss Howard, a fashionable beauty. Kinglake had been engaged to give history lessons to Miss Howard, fallen in love with her, and had resented his rival suitor. Kinglake's explanation of the Crimean War, it is said, was simply a way of maliciously taking revenge on Louis Napoleon. Now the commentary on Kinglake may well be unfair. If everybody who in the 1850s damned Louis Napoleon as a warmonger were really a rejected lover of the beautiful Miss Howard, she must have been the most courted woman in European history. More relevant, no evidence has come from French documents to endorse – and much to doubt Kinglake's interpretation of Napoleon's part in causing the war.

The Franco-Prussian War of 1870 sometimes received a similar interpretation. The official German history of that war attributed the outbreak partly to the restless ambition of Napoleon III and partly to popular discontent within France. 'A diversion in foreign politics, so often resorted to under these circumstances, seemed at length the only counterpoise to the continual pressure of the parties at home.' So said the official interpretation from Berlin. This idea neatly absolved Prussia from blame, but it was backed by no evidence. In fact Napoleon III, less than two years before the outbreak of the Franco-Prussian War, had commented on the suggestion that he might wish some day to fight Prussia as a solution to his empire's internal problems; he had privately told Lord Clarendon, Britain's foreign minister, in October 1868 that no internal troubles – and he foresaw none – 'would be appeased by an external war'. He thought that war and the accompanying high taxes would endanger rather than strengthen a dynasty; and he was correct, for war was to drive him from his throne.

Sponsors of scapegoat interpretations nearly always apply them to the enemy, to the nation of which they disapprove. The interpretation is therefore usually abusive and partisan. Its supporting evidence also comes from biased sources rather than from the statements of those men who reputedly decided to go to war for the sake of internal unity. There is one notable exception, and it is often quoted. In 1904, when Russia and Japan went to war, the Russian minister of the interior said: 'We need a little victorious war to stem the tide of revolution.' At first sight this is powerful evidence. Russia's minister of the interior, V. K. Plehve, possibly knew more than anybody about internal unrest in Russia; he had previously been director of police, he had been promoted when the previous minister of the interior was assassinated by a terrorist in 1902, and thereafter he spent most of his working hours trying to suppress dissidents on a wide front running from Armenia to Finland. If one of the arguments which persuaded Russia to go to war with Japan was the desire to restore unity at home, Plehve would be the main beneficiary.

Plehve's statement originated in the memoirs of Count Witte, who was Russian minister of finance until 1903. As Witte recalled:

> In the early days of the Russo-Japanese war, General Kuropatkin on one occasion reproached Plehve, I recollect, with having been the only Minister to desire the Russo-Japanese war and make common cause with the clique of political adventurers who had dragged the country into it. 'Alexey Nikolayevich (i.e. Kuropatkin),' retorted Plehve, 'you are not familiar with Russia's internal situation. *We need a little victorious war to stem the tide of revolution.*'

There are at least six obstacles – not all insuperable – to accepting the dramatic statement as a mirror of Russian policy. The statement was not recorded by Witte until, perhaps eight years later, he completed his memoirs; if Witte's memory was defective or biased the statement could have been diluted or intensified with the lapse of time. As Witte was a bitter opponent of Plehve and as he disapproved of the war with Japan he could have unconsciously given the statement a sharp edge; as the war was neither little nor victorious Plehve would thereby be condemned with his own words. Moreover Plehve's statement, if read carefully, does not affirm that the quest for a scapegoat was the main reason why Russia had decided to fight. Count Witte himself primarily blamed a 'clique of political adventurers' – Russians with ambitions in the Far East – for dragging the nation into war. Nor did Count Witte ever suggest that internal unrest was an additional reason why Russia went to war; Witte devoted twenty-two pages to the causes of the war, but nowhere did he suggest that Russia's policy was influenced by the hope that a war would ease internal unrest. Above all Witte argued that the Russian ruling clique, while utterly obstinate in their negotiations over the future of Manchuria, neither wanted nor expected a war. 'We acted', wrote Witte, 'as if we were certain that the Japanese would endure everything without daring to attack us.' The Japanese attack on Port Arthur in February 1904 snapped that daydream.

It is therefore risky – on the strength of Plehve's two sentences – to argue that Russia went to war in the hope of quenching internal unrest. At the same time it is feasible, if one so desires, to argue that soon after the commencement of the war Plehve believed that internal unity would be one of the bonus dividends of victory. His hope was particularly ironical, and that was probably the main reason why it was recorded in Witte's memoirs. Most of those who read Witte's memoirs did not have to be reminded that, as the war dragged on, the unrest and violence within Russia increased rather than decreased. Readers also knew that the celebrated victim of the violence was Plehve himself. In the sixth month of the war he was riding in his carriage to the tsar's summer palace near St Petersburg when he was blown up by a terrorist's bomb.

The idea that the dilemmas of internal politics often lead to war is indefatigable. It is prominent in many explanations of the First World War. Nearly every nation in the summer of 1914 seemed to suffer from heat rash. London was suffering from the kicks of the Irish, Berlin from the oratory of the strong Social Democrats, St Petersburg from the marches of strikers and Vienna the restlessness of the polyglot peoples within its empire. It is not surprising that some historians should suggest that the Russian leaders' desire to quieten internal dissent was one factor which edged them towards war. 'The idea of a foreign war to avert domestic troubles is, of course', wrote S. B. Fay, 'a very familiar one in the history of many countries'; and he suspected that that motive lay behind Russia's decision to mobilise her army in July 1914. His evidence for that motive however is not strong. The first fragment of evidence is a Swiss newspaper article, written in 1917 by an 'apparently well-informed Russian sympathiser'. One may suggest that the author of the Swiss article can be treated with no more respect than hundreds of other anonymous and apparently well-informed writers in the European press. There is no evidence that the writer had the ear of those Russian ministers who in 1914 debated whether Russia should prepare for war. The second and final fragment of evidence is a report written on 25 July 1914 by the German ambassador to Russia; the ambassador had heard from an anonymous but 'trustworthy source' about the discussions which had taken place the previous day in Russia's Imperial Council. According to that source the Imperial Council had discussed whether Russia, already facing workers' discontent and strikes, could 'face external complications without trouble'. Now this is not evidence favouring the idea that Russia hoped to divert her people's attention from internal troubles. On the contrary it suggests that members of the Imperial Council thought internal troubles provided more a deterrent than an incentive to launching a foreign war.

The same interpretation has been applied to Germany. The government in Berlin, it is said, thought a foreign war would quieten the Socialists and check their increasing influence. The evidence for this interpretation soon shrivels. Germany's foremost soldier, von Moltke, had warned his Austrian counterpart in 1913 that any war would demand the full co-operation of the people. To his mind any idea of waging war in order to unite the nation was folly; his aim was rather to ensure that the nation was united before it decided to wage war. On the eve of the war Germany's chancellor, Bethmann-Hollweg, stressed privately that the support of all classes was essential from the outset if Germany were to fight successfully. Hence his anxiety that the tsar of Russia, the great enemy of Social Democrats, the ruler who had trampled on the 1905 revolutionists, should appear to be the aggressor. If the tsar were to endanger Germany, predicted Bethmann-

Hollweg, the powerful Social Democrats would be loyal to Germany and would not even consider the question of 'a general or partial strike, or of sabotage'. His prediction, made on 30 July 1914, was correct. Next day Russia formally mobilised her army. A day later Germany mobilised hers, and the Social democrats cheered.

The expansionist aims of Germany and Italy and Japan in the 1930s have been widely interpeted as conscious or unconscious attempts to quell internal tensions by setting up external enemies. According to one distinguished Harvard scholar, the dictators of the 1930s 'deliberately preferred conflict abroad to the prospect of intolerable change at home'. One flaw in the idea is that Italy and Germany by the mid-1930s had signs of national unity which England, the United States, France and the democracies could not match. Many Englishmen who did not like the fascism which they saw in Berlin or Rome in the mid-1930s at least observed a sense of purpose and unity that was absent in London or Glasgow. Moreover Germany had recovered faster than the western democracies from the world depression, and so economic distress in Germany was milder. In contrast the eagerness of British and French leaders to appease Hitler in the late 1930s may in part be attributed to their fear that their own people were not united. One is forced to suggest that, if the scapegoat theory is correct, England and France should have been the more militant European nations in the late 1930s, and Germany and Italy should have been striving to maintain the status quo. Admittedly it could be argued that Germany gained much of her unity simply because the government had already set up targets of hatred – the Jews and the Communists – years before the war. But to accept that argument is virtually to abandon a scapegoat theory. Why should Germany in 1939 go to war in order to achieve internal unity if that unity was already conspicuous?

Hitler appears to have been convinced that the nation supported him in 1939. That was one source of his confidence in Germany's ability to win a war. A parallel source of confidence was his belief that so many European nations, unlike Germany, were internally divided. When in 1939 he planned the invasion of Poland he hoped that 'increasing internal crises in France and the resulting British cautiousness' might prevent Anglo-French aid to Poland. When a few months later he wondered whether Russia was likely to attack Germany he decided that Russia was 'not dangerous' at present; 'it is weakened by many internal conditions'. Hitler was one of many leaders in many ages who believed that internal unrest was a deterrent, not an incentive, to the resort of war.

The episodes of armed violence between Indonesia and the new Federation of Malaysia in the 1960s were widely seen as President Sukarno's quest for a scapegoat. He was said to have sought a target for the economic distress and political tensions in his own republic by sending armed parties into Malaysian territory. It is not clear however whether the 'confrontation' supports the scapegoat theory. One doubt is whether the episodes can be defined as a war. Between 1963 and 1966 they led to the death of 590 Indonesians and 150 Malaysian and allied soldiers and civilians; by any definition it was a minor and half-hearted war. Presumably the campaign was seen by Sukarno and other leaders as a unifying influence on Indonesia, but did the goal of internal unity call for a bloody or a blustery foreign policy? If president Sukarno hoped to weld his nation by a glorious foreign adventure, why did he send so few Indonesian troops that they had no prospect of achieving glory? One feasible answer is that Sukarno needed most of his soldiers at home. Another answer is that Indonesia lacked the confidence and the financial strength to wage more than a token war. It is even possible that, but for Indonesia's internal troubles, she might have waged a serious war in order to prevent North Borneo and Sarawak from joining the new Malaysia. Above all, the main effect of Indonesia's internal tension seems to have been on civil war rather than international war. During the three years of 'confrontation' the casualties within Indonesia through civil strife were perhaps several hundred times the casualties suffered by Indonesians in their scuffles with Malaysia. The violence against communists within Indonesia was most intense in the first half of 1966, and so one would expect – according to the tenets of scapegoat theory – that the foreign war would be intensified. Instead it came to an end.

Scapegoat explanations appear to be acts of faith rather

than reasoned arguments. Deep faith is often satisfied with shallow evidence. Those who partly explain wars as the search for a scapegoat rarely offer evidence for their interpretation. The scant evidence which they disclose often points the other way.

v

Another test can be applied to the idea that many international wars were attempts to allay internal tensions. The chronology of most of those events reveals an illuminating pattern. A government facing grave internal tensions did not first attack a neighbouring nation in order to restore unity. More sensibly it attacked, or counter-attacked, the rebels within the nation. In the 1890s the Turkish government, faced with Greek uprisings in the Turkish province of Crete, tried to quell those uprisings long before it went to war with the kingdom of Greece. Hitler's Germany, fanatically hostile to communists in the 1930s, harried the German communists long before it went to war with communist Russia. These are not isolated examples of the sequence of events; they are rather illustrations of the normal pattern. Scapegoat theory seems to ignore that pattern.

One curiosity of scapegoat interpretations is that they are applied more to nations which suffered from mild tensions rather than from open civil war. And yet if a nation suffered from mild tensions it would hardly need to embark on a foreign adventure in order to allay those tensions. Alternatively, if a country had serious tensions it would seem to have less hope of waging a successful foreign war, for its own disunity would lessen the chance of victory. The effect of serious disunity on a nation's attitude to war is particularly visible at the end of many wars. Events in Russia in 1905 and 1917, in Germany in 1918 and perhaps in the United States in the early 1970s suggest that serious disunity within a nation inclines leaders to seek peace rather than war.

Scapegoat interpretations of war seem plausible but are probably erroneous. They rely on dubious assumptions. They usually assume that peace is a newsless limbo which requires little explanation. They usually assume that a troubled nation will seize on an enemy, large or small, near or far; but this assumption is not easy to accept. They assume that one nation can be blamed for a war, and yet war is a relationship between at least two nations and cannot be explained by examining one nation in isolation. Even if, on the contrary, wars can be logically blamed on to one nation, scapegoat theory is still misleading: it assumes that the strife-torn nations initiate the fighting, but in fact the fighting in most of the relevant wars between 1815 and 1939 was not initiated by the strife-torn nation. Admittedly there may have been wars in which some members of a government hoped that one of the many advantages of victory would be a heightened unity among their people, but that does not mean that such a hope was a major reason for deciding to fight. The main virtue of scapegoat explanations is that they recognise that civil unrest and international war are frequently linked. For that link however there seems to be a more convincing explanation.

A nation's preference for war or peace is always influenced, in part, by perceptions of its own internal unity and the unity or discord of its potential enemies. These perceptions are relevant to every outbreak of war and every outbreak of peace, though their influence may not always be conspicuous. Nevertheless these perceptions – whether promoting confidence or caution – do not work evenly either for war or peace.

Internal strife, it seems, was most likely to lead to international war when it muffled what had previously been a clear and accepted hierarchy of power between two nations. Civil strife in the stronger nation was more likely to disturb the peace because it muffled the hierarchy of power and lowered the stronger nation's apparent margin of superiority. On the other hand civil strife in the weaker of two nations was more likely to preserve the peace, because it confirmed the accepted assessment of their relative power. The same pattern probably prevails during the last stages of a war. If one nation was clearly establishing its military superiority, the prospects of peace were enhanced when serious civil unrest erupted within the losing nation: moreover unrest was more likely to erupt in the loser than the winner.

VI

Civil strife was only one of the strands which could lead towards international war, but that strand was often strong and was sometimes threaded with cordite. Civil strife was particularly dangerous when a group or interest in the disturbed nation had strong bonds with another nation. Those bonds could be religious and racial; in the nineteenth century Greece had bonds with the Greeks in many parts of the Turkish empire, and Russia had bonds with Slavs and Orthodox Christians in the same empire. Some bonds were nationalist; Germans in the South of Denmark had affinity with Prussia, and Italians in the southern parts of the Austrian Empire had affinity with the kingdom of Sardinia. Some bonds were primarily ideological; in the 1890s the rebels in Spanish Cuba shared with popular opinion in the United States the belief that the new world should be liberated from European rule, and the counter-revolutionaries in Russia in the civil war of 1919 had ideological ties with the governments of foreign nations.

Of the civil disturbances which preceded international war in the period from 1815 to 1939, at least twenty-six of the thirty-one disturbances formed links with the outside nation which ultimately went to war. Occasionally the government of the troubled nation nourished the link. Thus the Austrian monarchy, faced in 1849 with an insurrection in its Hungarian provinces, persuaded the tsar to help in snuffing a rebellion which could otherwise have inspired similar rebellions within Russia. The normal pattern however was for the rebelling segment – not the government – to forge bonds with an outside nation. In the nineteenth century, for example, the rebels within the Turkish empire nourished strong ties with either the governments of Russia, Greece or Serbia; and those governments at times went to war against Turkey. On occasions the government and the rebels of the troubled nation each formed links with outside nations; that was true in the Spanish war of the 1930s and in South Vietnam in the 1960s. Whereas the government in Saigon had allies in Washington, the rebels had allies in Hanoi.

The links between nations are sometimes viewed as the causes of war. That view is reflected in the question debated in historical journals or, during a modern war, in press and television: are the causes of the war economic or ideological, imperialist, religious, or nationalist? One may suggest however that the links were not the causes of war. They constituted the relationship between two nations; they could nourish either peace or war. They provided the vital issues or transactions for which the two nations had to find a mutually acceptable price. When the transactions between two nations were important, a way of regulating those transactions was also important. The ultimate regulator was military power. When two nations had a contradictory assessment of their own military power, and the issue at stake was vital to both nations, war was likely.

The Greco-Turkish war of 1897 reflects the most common background of conflict. The seat of that disturbance was the Turkish island of Crete, where Orthodox Christians outnumbered the Moslems and frequently rebelled against rule from Constantinople. As the nearest part of the Greek mainland was only sixty miles from Crete, the oppressed Greeks on the island had strong bonds with the kingdom of Greece. Nevertheless Greece, in her first sixty years as an independent kingdom, lacked the military strength to overthrow the Turkish garrisons on Crete or even to aid openly the frequent rebellions on the island. Greeks rebelled in the Crete mountains in 1833, 1841, 1858, 1866–8, 1878 and 1889, but not until the rebellion of 1896 did the kingdom of Greece attempt to liberate the island.

Why did the 1896 rebellion on Crete at last attract strong Greek aid? After Russia's victory over Turkey in 1878 the power of Turkey had, in the eyes of most European leaders, waned steadily. Above all Turkey had waned as a naval power, and yet naval strength was necessary if Crete was to be defended from possible invasion. By the early 1890s the Greek navy was stronger than Turkey's. Greek foreign policy was also emboldened by rising nationalism, of which the revival of the Olympiad at Athens in 1896 was a symbol. For more than a generation Greece had engaged in no foreign war; and war usually had the advantage, dubious though it may seem, of curbing leaders' exaggerated optimism of their nations' strength. The confidence of Greece – the belief that if diplomacy failed she could drive the Turks from Crete – placed a strain on negotiations. That strain was increased because the Turks did not accept the common opinion that their empire was crumbling. Nearly two decades had passed since the Russians in 1878 approached the walls of Constantinople, and that memory had faded. The Turkish army, still one of the largest in Europe and now sharpened by German advisers, was to display its strength on Greek soil in 1897.

The confidence on the Greek mainland helped to inspire the Greeks on the island of Crete in 1896. A militant Greek society, Ethnike Hetaerea, aided the rebels with arms. The initial success of the rebellion in Crete increased the sense of purpose and unity in Greece. It also reinforced the belief that Turkey was weak. Even the concessions which Turkey yielded in the internal government of Crete emboldened rather than appeased the government in Athens. And in February 1897 the civil strife became international war with the arrival at Crete of Greek men-of-war and 1500 troops. An international blockade prevented serious war in Crete but could not prevent Greek soldiers from raiding Turks on the northern borders of Greece. On 17 April Turkey declared war on Greece but within five weeks the Greek army was a rabble and an armistice was eagerly signed. Greece was humbled, was forced to pay a large indemnity to Turkey, and her only consolation was that Crete passed from Turkish to international rule.

The war between Greece and Turkey suggests several conclusions. First, civil strife that affects the interests and prestige of two nations is obviously dangerous. If Turkey had not tried to suppress the rebellion in Crete in 1896 she would have thereby encouraged similar rebellions among the minorities which dotted her wide empire; but if Turkey tried to crush the rebellion she would provoke Greece, where national confidence was now high. A second conclusion is the danger of a diplomatic clash between two nations confident of their ability to impose their own will; if the Greeks had believed that militarily they were the less powerful nation, they would not have been willing to turn civil strife into international war. A third conclusion may be offered tentatively; the civil war within Crete, whether initiated by Christian rebels or Turkish troops, was in part a reflection of the blurred barometer of power between Turkey on one side and Greece on the other. The conflict therefore was partly self-generating. International tension encouraged internal strife which in turn encouraged international war. These conclusions seem relevant to most international wars which sprang from civil strife.

Those conditions which tended to make civil strife overflow into international war suggest that scapegoat interpretations are irrelevant. The government suffering from civil unrest – whether Denmark in 1864 or Turkey in 1897 – usually preferred to avoid an international war, if war could be avoided. A troubled nation could more easily defeat its own rebels if it did not also have to fight a foreign enemy. On the other hand the outside nation often had a strong incentive to go to war: the ball was in the enemy's court and would remain there unless the court was invaded. In 1897, for instance the ball lay in the Turkish court and would almost certainly remain there unless Greece jumped the net. If we have to decide which nation was more eager to convert internal strife into international war, then the external nation was usually more eager.

The spread of civil strife within a nation often resembled the death of a king; the royal funeral bells in the eighteenth century often had the same martial echoes as the bells that rang the curfew in troubled lands in later centuries. Both bells invited an enemy to attack. The bells were most dangerous when they sounded the end of epochs in which the hierarchy of power between pairs of nations had been agreed upon. The opportunism which had kept the peace was thus replaced by an opportunism which fostered war.

those are the times and places which are less capable of financing a war. Since international war is armed violence on a large scale rather than an episode of pickpocketing, arms as well as motives are essential. Moreover since national governments are complicated organisations, they are likely to see war as a problem of organisation as well as a way of solving international disputes.

The theories which point to economic needs as the mainspring of wars assume that inadequate finance did not usually deter nations from initiating a war. Nations, they assume, were willing to launch an attack even if their financial backing was low or economic distress in the countryside was high. The available evidence however suggests otherwise. In the eighteenth century, adequate finance was widely regarded as a prerequisite of war. Admittedly one serious war, the War of the Austrian Succession, began when harvests were poor in lands as far apart as Finland and France, but a financially strong monarch initiated the fighting. Frederick of Prussia, balancing in his mind the advantages of trying to snatch Silesia from Austria, could count on a rich war chest inherited from his father. He also believed that the treasury of Maria Theresa in Vienna was almost empty and would therefore restrict her ability to send troops into the field. Soon after he had marched on Silesia he tried to bargain with Maria Theresa. Give me Silesia, he argued, and I will help defend you against other enemies. 'To place the Court of Vienna', he added, 'in a condition in which it can put up a good defence for itself I will furnish it at first with 2,000,000 florins in ready money; I might even go to three million.'

France, the traditional enemy of Austria, was eager to exploit Austria's weakness but was cautioned by famine and financial strain. Whereas in the summer of 1740 Frederick of Prussia was able to supply corn to many who were suffering from the mean harvest, the King of France could not. Passing through Paris he ignored the cries for bread. It was in a Paris street that summer that a group of hungry women seized the bridles of the horses of Cardinal Fleury, opened the door of his ornate carriage, and screamed at him for bread. 'He almost died of fright,' wrote one contemporary. After all he was aged eighty-seven. The cardinal virtually controlled France's foreign policy, and when in November 1740 he pondered whether to go to war against Austria he was checked by financial pressures:

> Your Majesties are aware of the expenses which we have to meet both to keep up our existing squadrons and to prepare the further ones which we shall need in the coming year; especially as provisions and all the munitions necessary for these armaments are so excessively dear.
>
> But what concerns us still more is the frightful distress in the provinces caused by the dearth of corn and all the grains necessary for subsistence. The principal duty of a King is the relief of his subjects, and, apart from the immense relief which we are obliged to grant, Your Majesties will easily understand what a great decrease there has been in the amount of taxes which we are able to collect, as a result of the poverty of the people.

Is it significant that France did not commit herself to war against Austria until the following summer, when a good harvest was in sight for the first season in four years?

The letters of kings, ministers and diplomats in the eighteenth century often assumed that a country with internal weakness – whether financial or political – could not afford to be adventurous. Maria Theresa's adviser, Kaunitz, wondering in 1749 how the empress could recapture Silesia, argued that 'our internal and external situation does not allow us to undertake a dangerous and far-reaching offensive policy'. In 1763 Louis XV of France wrote, almost with clenched fist: 'Everything that may plunge Russia into chaos and make her return to obscurity is favourable to our interests.' One can almost hear his teeth grinding as he sees the connection between internal distress and external timidity. Two decades later his own France was to drift into a chaos, deepened by meagre harvests and heavy royal debts. England's minister to France, writing a secret despatch in 1786, thought that hopes of peace hinged on the weak French treasury 'much more, I believe, than on the pacific professions of the court'. The Duke of Dorset, writing from the same embassy eighteen months later, did not think France would enter the new

Russo-Turkish war; the white flag of neutrality seemed to suit best the 'domestic distresses of France'. These predictions were falsified when France went to war with Austria in 1792. The French treasury at that time was not ample and dissension within France was high. While the events of 1792 suggest that financial troubles were not a sufficient obstacle to dissuade France from declaring war, this does not mean that economic needs and pressures were the causes of the war.

In the century between the Napoleonic Wars and the First World War it was almost an axiom among major European powers that lack of finance was a strong deterrent against war. Germany imposed an indemnity of 5,000 million gold francs on France in 1871, partly to defray some of Germany's war expenses and partly in the belief that a heavy indemnity would prevent France from spending much on arms in the following decade. After Greece had been defeated in 1897 she was forced to borrow in order to pay an indemnity to Turkey; and Britain, France and Russia acted as guarantors of the loan. Significantly, Sir Michael Hicks Beach, Britain's chancellor of the exchequer, believed that if the big powers supervised Greek finances, they would promote European peace by preventing Greece from spending on armaments that money which she owed to other nations. One month after the start of the First World War the chancellor of Germany wrote a private memorandum on the indemnity which he hoped to impose on a defeated France: 'it must be high enough to prevent France from spending any considerable sums on armaments in the next 15–20 years'. When peace came it was Germany which had to pay indemnities and divest herself of armaments.

A nation whose economy was advanced and whose soldiers were paid and liberally supplied in the field could be expected to be more aware of the need for adequate financial strength in order to wage a war. But even backward nations seem to have stressed financial factors. When Japanese leaders debated in 1873 whether to invade Korea the main architect of modernisation, Okubo Toshimichi, opposed the invasion by listing seven arguments. Five of his seven points stressed the financial implications of the proposed war. He pointed out that if Japan went to war she would suffer from inflation, from high taxes which would foster internal strife, and from a scarcity of funds for modernising her schools and industries, army and navy. 'To start a war and to send tens of thousands of troops abroad would raise expenditures by the day to colossal figures' – and yet Japan was already troubled to balance her budget. He warned that if a war against Korea proved to be long or unsuccessful, 'our inability to repay our debts to England will become England's pretext for interfering in our internal affairs'. The supporters of peace won that debate.

The strong emphasis on adequate finance suggests that it must have a niche in any explanation of war. It also suggests a negative conclusion: that the danger of international war was probably not higher in times of, or regions of, economic deprivation. A more positive conclusion can in fact be drawn, and it was offered by a Scot in the course of one of the most perceptive essays on war ever written.

III

Alec Lawrence Macfie fought with the Gordon Highlanders on the Somme in the First World War and then, at the onset of the world depression, became a lecturer in economics at Glasgow University. His experience of the two most shattering events of his generation came together in an odd way, for about 1937 he detected a thread that seemed to connect the outbreak of the war with certain economic conditions. In February 1938 he issued a short article with an ominous warning. Entitled 'The Outbreak of War and the Trade Cycle', it occupied nine pages of a learned journal at the very time when newspapers were mesmerised by the revival of Germany and the danger of another world war.

Macfie argued that international wars were most likely to begin when an economic recovery was well under way or had mounted the slopes and reached a prosperous tableland. A quick study of the outbreak of twelve international wars in the period from 1850 to 1914 suggested this pattern, but what did the pattern signify? Macfie thought that wars tended to break out at those times when the economic mood was bumptious and when 'hope is alight and obstacles are impatiently confronted'. That mood, he suggested, provides the heat to 'germinate the seeds of war no matter when they are sown'. Macfie's knowledge of economic fluctuations persuaded him that in Europe the danger point would appear again in about two years. 'If these considerations are accepted', he argued, 'we may well pray that statesmen may be granted an access of wisdom between now and 1940.' The prayer was not answered.

The tendency for economic activity to move regularly from slackness to boom and from boom to slackness – the depressed years being marked by a scarcity of jobs and falling profits – was first experienced by England and the advanced industrial countries. Variously called the trade cycle or the business cycle, it reflected the spread of an intricate web of inter-dependence between nations and between producers within each nation; economic specialisation was turning much of the world into a 'global village' long before aircraft, radio and television made the web conspicuous. Thus a fall in the de-mand for Manchester-made textiles was felt in the cotton fields of the Carolinas, the terraces of Liverpool, and in many corners of the globe.

In glimpsing a link between the business cycle and war, Macfie pointed to something that could not neatly be applied to wars before 1800. He did not comment on this dilemma; he humbly disowned any intention of setting up his plate as a historian and merely passed on his observations in the hope that they might 'prove grist to some historian's mill'. Al-though the eighteenth century had ups and downs in econ-omic activity, and although the famous Swedish historian Eli Heckschser thought his homeland had a weak semblance of the business cycle as early as 1763, those oscillations presum-ably did not move with the regularity and the capitalist clockwork that merit the name of 'business cycles'. Wind, ice and rain – and their effects on the harvests – were probably the main pendulum of these earlier fluctuations. The ups and downs of economic activity were probably more influential on war decisions after the Napoleonic wars, partly because the prevailing economic mood was more likely to be shared by many nations, and partly because the oscillations between economic pessimism and optimism tended to become sharper.

Macfie's link is, at first sight, open to some doubt even in his chosen period of 1850–1914. He realised that economists could argue that he had mistaken the causes of war with the preparations for war. It could be argued that the rising prosperity which preceded wars was merely the effect of re-arming and preparing for war. This may have been partly true of the prosperity that preceded some wars but seems untrue of the majority. It is therefore difficult to reject Professor Macfie's observation that economic conditions affected the outbreak of wars.

Changes in economic moods and conditions affect not only bankers, shopkeepers, manufacturers and shipowners, farmers and all they employ: they also affect monarchs, first ministers and chiefs of staff of the armed forces. They affect the revenue and expenditure of governments and they affect the problems which they have to face. They affect social unrest or cohesion. And perhaps most important they subtly affect expectations of what the coming months will be like and whether they can be shaped with ease.*

When trade is deteriorating and when unemployment is increasing the mood of governments tends to be cautious or apprehensive. Dwindling revenue and soaring claims for the state's aid aggravate the mood. On the other hand, when prosperity is high – and this is the time most dangerous to peace – there comes a sense of mastery of the environment. Indeed the economic moods closely parallel those mental moods which psychiatrists study. Such words as 'depression' and 'mania' are common to the vocabulary of those who chart fluctuations in the market places as well as mental asylums. When a contemporary psychiatrist, David Stafford-Clark, describes the emotional conditions of elation, which virtually everyone experiences at times, he is describing a mood which all economists have observed:

> when the sense of well-being and confidence not only exceeds all degree of appropriateness to the patient's life, but begins to colour and cloud judgement and responsibility to a point at which the capacity to adjust to reality and manage

* The short-term future is the dominant outlook in international affairs. Arthur Lee Burns makes this vital point in his book, *Of Powers and their Politics*.

affairs becomes impaired, then it constitutes a condition of illness no matter how little the patient may complain.

More than a trace of this illness is visible in business booms and even in the recurring moods of nations. The eve of the Crimean, Franco-Prussian, Boer and many other wars was tinged with this mania.

One cannot say that economic events alone shape these oscillating moods. Admittedly economic events – partly because they are easily measurable – have been studied so intensely that they can for practical purposes be explained mainly in terms of other economic happenings. But economic behaviour cannot be isolated from the totality of behaviour. Economists have built a deep reservoir of knowledge of how man behaves in economic affairs, but the mental conditions which influence that behaviour are not known so well.

IV

Macfie's observations, made in the month when Hitler personally took over the Ministry of War, caused no wider ripple than a leaf falling on flat water. Observations that come from a factual study of many wars have always been rare, but his rare offering was neglected. He could have been writing from Kabul rather than Glasgow, so little notice was taken of his words. Professor Macfie was careful to offer only a tentative explanation. 'Final judgment,' he wrote, 'is the task of historians.' To my knowledge only one member of the many disciplines studying the causes of war has offered any judgement or comment on Macfie's observations. During a public lecture in London in 1948 a prominent historian, Sir George Clark, briefly outlined Macfie's ideas. He assured his listeners that the historians who had contributed most to an understanding of war had not traced economic trends but rather had 'minutely dissected treaties and dispatches'. This was not surprising, for the historians of treaties outnumbered the historians of trends by one thousand to one. Sir George courteously chided Macfie for preaching certain heresies; in fact Macfie had gone out of his way to disown the ideas which were now mistakenly pinned to him. Sir George Clark's lecture was published in hard covers in 1958, amidst renewed applause.

It seems that Sir George Clark thought that Macfie was laying claim to a continent. Instead he was merely placing his flag on one little island and was careful not to wade into the surrounding surf. Macfie's whole argument rested on one brilliant observation, and he viewed it as a useful clue, not as the essential cause of war. He realised that an upswing in the economy or the bumptious mood of boom were not sufficient to cause a war. He knew of those periods when the economic mood from the Danube to the North Sea was confident, but the confidence was not accompanied by a war.

One can applaud the restraint with which Professor Macfie set out his argument. In one area it perhaps should have been even more restrained. His view 'that wars do not break out in times of business stagnation or increasing depression' is suspect. As Macfie's survey began in 1850 and ended in 1914, he did not notice that some earlier and later wars began during adverse economic conditions. Four short international wars were fought in Europe in 1848 and 1849, hungry years. Japan briefly fought the Chinese in Manchuria in 1931 during the deepest trough in the long history of the business cycle. And there might have been other wars – especially colonial wars – which began during economic conditions that did not match Macfie's prescription.

It would be artless to expect all wars to break out during prosperous or improving conditions. Economic moods were only one of the factors influencing decisions for war or peace, and they were not always the most influential. Wars could break out in adverse economic conditions if other factors were pushing strongly towards war. In the background to the four wars of the depressed years of 1848 and 1849 lay familiar portents of war: internal strife, the death of a king or his authority, and the waterbird dilemma. Thus the Danish–Prussian war of 1848 followed the death of the Danish king, the humiliating of the Prussian king by rebellion in Berlin, and internal unrest in the south of Denmark. Likewise revolutions in Vienna and in the Austrian province of north Italy in 1848 emboldened Sardinia to attack the Austrian empire which seemed to be on the verge of ruin. And the war in

Hungary was both a cause and effect of the erosion of authority in the multi-racial Austrian empire.

Even in these short wars one can possibly glimpse the restraining hand of adverse economic conditions. The ultimate victors were markedly cautious in their approach to war. In June 1848 the government in Vienna ordered its 82-year-old field-marshal, Radetzky, to seek an armistice from Sardinia but he defied his orders and fought on. Similarly in 1931, in the trough of the world depression, the Japanese army which attacked the Chinese in Manchuria was not carrying out instructions from the government in Tokyo. And when in 1849 a Russian army had filed across the mountains into Hungary to put down a rebellion which if triumphant could have spread east to Russia and north to Russian Poland, the Russians were not on an expedition of plunder and annexation. When the Hungarian rebels had been crushed the Russian soldiers – unlike their descendants in 1956 – went home. War was not impossible in times of adversity or of waning economic confidence: it was less likely to occur, and if it did occur was likely to be short.

v

Macfie's forgotten observation may help to explain the optimism with which so many wars were begun. It offers an additional reason for rejecting scapegoat theories: if depressed nations were reluctant to initiate foreign wars, we would also expect the strife-torn nations to initiate few wars. Macfie's observation offers an additional reason for suspecting the dogmas, beloved of many economists, that economic pressures and ills were the main stirrers of wars. By his test those theories flounder. Above all, Macfie's observation seems to fit neatly into the jigsaw of war and peace.

7: A Calendar of War

In the summer of 1911 a German gunboat steamed along the Atlantic to the drowsy Moroccan port of Agadir and so precipitated one of those crises which preceded the First World War. In many European capitals the ministers and military advisers, wondering whether the gunboat incident would lead to war, sought an answer in the seasons. If Germany was about to provoke a war with France and Russia, would she choose to begin the war in summer or winter? As the common assumption was that Germany would first throw most of her men against France in the hope of a quick victory and then swing her armies to the Russian front, anything which delayed the westward advance of Russia's armies would be of incalculable value to Germany. Accordingly the French military attaché in London thought a winter war was more likely, for he believed that the ice and snow would delay a Russian advance. In Britain the War Office advisers also thought the crucial region was the plains of Poland, the launching ramp of any Russian advance. They drew however a different conclusion from the same evidence. As Winston Churchill confidentially explained: 'The bad months for Russia are the spring and summer, when there is a great deal of rain and slush in Poland.'

Although advisers might disagree in naming the season which seemed most likely to produce a war, they believed that weather was one of those factors which influenced decisions to go to war. The seasons seem to have always been a factor. The simplest way to identify their influence is to examine a large region which has a sharp contrast in the seasons and a long experience of wars. The countries north of the Tropic of Cancer – an expanse of land through Europe, Siberia, Japan and North America – provided the battlefields of at least forty-four international wars in the century from

1840 to 1938. A list of the months in which those wars commenced yields a simple pattern:

Spring:	16 wars
Summer:	15 wars
Autumn:	10 wars
Winter:	3 wars

The most popular time for starting a war was the four
months between April and July. More than half of the wars –
26 out of 44 – commenced during those four months of
favourable weather. In contrast no war was begun during
December or January.

II

Why was war more likely to begin in the warmer months? It
is clear that spring and summer favoured an invader. In those
months the drier roads and quieter rivers aided the mobility
of large armies and their cumbersome artillery. An army
could more easily forage food for men and horses along the
way. As the days were longer the soldiers could advance more
rapidly: night fighting was virtually unknown until the
Russo-Japanese war of 1904–5. As the weather was milder the
morale and perhaps the health of troops could also be maintained more easily.

If the advantages of beginning a war in the warmer months
were substantial, an attempt should be made to explain why
three of the forty-four wars should have begun in winter.
Both the Prussian–Austrian war against Denmark in 1864
and the Russo-Japanese war of 1904 began in February;
moreover both wars were fought in regions where the February ice seemed to offer severe obstacles to an invader. The
two exceptions however can possibly be explained in the light
of exceptional strategic advantages. Winter offered the
attackers the very assets which summer usually offered. The
Japanese in 1904 gained by attacking Russia in winter. The
new Trans-Siberian railway was the main supply line for
Russian forces in the Far East, but was not quite completed.
Accordingly Japan, by beginning the war in February rather
than April or May, snatched an opportunity to make quick

advances on an enemy that was not yet capable of sending rapid reinforcements to a front that lay thousands of miles across the iced plains and ranges of Siberia. Forty years earlier the Danish army had slipped on the ice which had seemed to be its protection. When in 1864 Denmark's relations with Prussia and Austria had been tense, the main Danish defence against land invasion was a line of earthworks across the narrow neck of Jutland. Built a thousand years earlier by Vikings and carefully strengthened in the 1850s, the defences ran for about ten miles from marshes in the west to a narrow arm of the Baltic sea near Schleswig. The Danes considered them virtually impregnable: against a frontal attack they may well have been impregnable. But in February 1864 marshes and inlets were frozen, and on a snowy night the Prussians suddenly outflanked the Danish defences.

The advantages of snow and ice may not have been the strongest argument favouring a winter attack against Denmark. Prussia and Austria also had to be wary that great powers, particularly Britain and Russia, did not aid Denmark. Winter prevented those naval powers from offering quick aid. Russia's fleet was icebound in the Gulf of Finland until May, and Britain's fleet was almost as ineffective. At least that was the opinion – or belated excuse – offered by Britain's Foreign Secretary, Lord John Russell, in a memorandum written soon after Denmark's quick collapse: 'we can act only by sea, and that only in the summer time. It would not be safe to shut up a British fleet in the ice of Copenhagen harbour during the winter.'

One cannot be sure that these considerations of strategy prompted the Prussians and Austrians in 1864 and the Japanese in 1904 to start their wars in winter. They might have confirmed rather than inspired their decision. Clearly there is scope for a comparative study of the factors which promoted war in the warmer rather than the colder months. Meanwhile the suggestion of why the wars of 1864 and 1904 began in winter does dovetail neatly into the common interpretation of why most wars began in spring and summer.

The period 1840 to 1939 contained one cluster of European wars whose timing cannot simply be explained by the advantages of weather. They began in the latter half of autumn, when the invaders could not hope that weather would for long favour their advance.* When Russia and Turkey began to fight near the Black Sea in 1853, when the Serbs crossed the Dragoman Pass into Bulgaria in 1885, and when the small Balkan allies attacked Turkey in 1912, the promoters of these autumn wars could hardly hope that their own fury would melt the early snows. The fighting in each of these wars had barely begun when snow covered some of the battlefields and slush slowed the supply lines. The orthodox explanation of how the weather affected the timing of the decision to fight cannot be applied to these wars. There may be a clue however in the region in which they were fought. All were fought in south-eastern Europe. It is possible that in that area the backward economic life and the dependence on agriculture made October a favourite month in which to begin a war: with the harvests gathered, and a surplus of food available to feed the armies, the late autumn may have been the only season in which large numbers of men could be assembled from the farmlands without jeopardising the production of food. This hypothesis can only be tentative. Moreover it totters slightly when placed beside the fact that while three wars in south-east Europe began in autumn another three began in the spring or summer.† The riddle of the autumn wars can be approached with another clue. The three wars were preceded by and kindled by internal unrest or insurrection in one of the warring countries. Is it then feasible to suggest that internal unrest tended to be higher or more dangerous in the autumn in eastern and south-eastern Europe? Certainly two

---

*Another autumn war, the Italo-Turk war of 1911 began early in September. As the main field of fighting was to be western Libya, and as its climate favoured a winter rather than a summer invader, the timing of that invasion fits the idea that the beginning of a war was influenced by the presence of weather which expedited military victory. The same argument is relevant to the war between Spain and Morocco, which began in October 1859. It cannot be used, however, to explain the Russo-Finnish war of November 1939.

† One other point may be relevant to the tendency to begin wars in south-east Europe in the late autumn. Though the First World War began in July 1914. Turkey entered it in *November* 1914 and Bulgaria in *October* 1915.

of Russia's revolutions – 1905 and 1917 – occurred in late autumn. Likewise, 'the most radical revolution in the year of revolutions' broke out in Vienna in October 1848, whereas most of the revolutions in western Europe in that year had come in February and March. Whatever is the explanation for the commencement of wars in October in south-eastern Europe – and the explanation may be complex or even coincidence – the timing of these wars cannot be explained by the orthodox picture of dry roads and long days.

We can glimpse why the seasons, through their effect on strategy and tactics, should often influence the decision whether to fight or remain at peace. As a nation wages war to impose its will on another, and as it can more easily impose that will in certain climatic conditions, it will tend to begin a war during the most favourable season. Nevertheless one has to be wary of the idea that kind weather influenced the timing of wars solely through its ability to hasten military operations. Did the warmer months also contain economic or political ingredients that made international crises more likely?

III

William Stanley Jevons, the English economist, was a sharp observer of the fluctuations in human affairs. The ninth child of a Liverpool iron merchant, Jevons himself blended the imaginative and the practical. At the age of eighteen he emigrated to Australia to work at the new mint in Sydney, where he assayed the gold arriving from the new diggings and studied economics and meteorology. In 1859 he returned to London, and soon after his twenty-fourth birthday he became an undergraduate at University College, quickly outstripping most of those who taught him. A skilful skater on ice, he was even more skilled in skating to the heart of problems in chemistry, mathematics, economics, logic and meteorology. He was one of the first economists to study those alternations in economic activity known as the business cycle, and it was typical of his eagle-roaming mind that he believed he saw a link between sunspots in the heavens and the ebb and flow of economic activity. In his approach to difficult questions he used statistics with the precision of an assayer, almost weighing them to the nearest milligram. He applied to economic explanation a statistical verve which was not to be applied to military explanation – and then only tentatively – for at least another three-quarters of a century. Curiously one of his observations on economics possibly has some relevance to war.

In 1862, when he was aged twenty-seven, Jevons detected a monetary pattern. He noted that the last four great financial panics – 1836, 1839, 1847 and 1857 – had occurred in October or November. He probed the English money market, and in London in 1866 he told the Statistical Society that the autumn panics were partly a reflection of the pressures for money which were felt in most autumns by the Bank of England. At first sight the seasonal demand for gold and credit in the autumn could have come from a decline in economic activities following the gathering of the harvest, but Jevons decided otherwise: the autumn pressures on the Bank of England, he concluded, 'do not appear to be due to any very great or all-extensive influence of the seasons upon trade'. Whatever the explanation for the pressure – and Jevons gave tentative reasons – his emphasis on the dangers of autumn was muffled by unexpected events. He had delivered his paper in April 1866, and in the following month England experienced her first financial panic for nine years; the crisis of Black Friday when the house of Overend & Gurney fell. Jevons' emphasis on the dangers of autumn was again muffled in 1873: the financial panic in Vienna came in May, though the United States' panic in the same year, following the failure of Jay Gould the railway financier, did come in autumn. The panics that came in spring drew some of the sting from Jevons' observations, though he had not said dogmatically that financial panic could come only in the autumn. Nevertheless, after Jevons was drowned while bathing near Hastings in 1882, his brief writings on the crisis of autumn tended to find their way to that collection of his papers which critics labelled 'brilliant but erratic'. Among most economists who study business fluctuations, Jevons' observation is now forgotten.

It so happened that soon after reading Jevons for the first time, Michael Stewart's lucid book, *Keynes and After*, came into my hands. Stewart briefly discussed the great Wall Street crash of 1929, noted that it occurred in October, and decided that there was no particular reason why it should have come in that month rather than any other month'. Jevons' observations promptly came to mind: had his pattern reappeared? It seemed useful therefore to list the main financial panics in the international economy in the century from 1830 to 1930. There were twelve on my list, and nine fell in October or November. Why so many panics should occur in the autumn is not clear. The economic pressures may stem from identifiable events such as the end of the harvest and the decline of tourism and may also stem from a mood which becomes less optimistic with the approach of winter.

A seasonal rise and ebb of confidence – whatever its causes – may provide an additional reason why most wars broke out during the spring and summer. In those months the sense of mastery was possibly stronger in business, political and even military circles. This fits the tendency, observed by Professor Macfie, for wars to come during the more confident years. In short, international wars tended to come during the more optimistic months of the more optimistic years. At those times national leaders were possibly more inclined to over-estimate their bargaining position in international affairs, thus making serious crises more likely. And the ease with which armies could advance in the warmer months might have increased the likelihood that crisis would lead to war.

It may be argued that the favourable seasons provided merely the occasion to begin a war which had already been decided upon. This may be true of some wars. But if it were true of the majority of wars one would expect to find evidence that many nations had firmly decided to wage particular wars months in advance of the beginning of warfare. Evidence of such decisions seems to be sparse. The common attitude held by leaders of warring nations three or six months before the actual outbreak of warfare seems to have been a belief that war was possible or probable. The prediction that a war was inevitable seems to have been rare: moreover such a prediction was not always accurate. The seizing of a favourable opportunity to wage war therefore seems to be part of the very decision to go to war rather than the aftermath of the decision.

War marks the conviction of nations that they can impose their will on one another more effectively by fighting than by peaceful methods of persuasion. Anything which increases leaders' beliefs that they can forcibly impose their will on an enemy, and anything which increases the desire to impose their will, should be called a cause of war. In that sense the seasons are probably one of the lesser influences on war and peace.

IV

That bullish confidence could be aided not only by seasonal conditions and the rising tide of prosperity. It could apparently be aided also by national celebrations and the confidence they reflected and kindled. Some national celebrations were festivals of peace, but the nationalism which they kindled was not always friendly to peace.

In London in 1851 the Great Exhibition of the Industry of All Nations, the finest trade fair the world had known, preached peace through international trade and knowledge but it also preached, with its display of steam engines and textiles and pumps, that Britain was the foremost manufacturer in the world. It is often noted that the Crystal Palace set the mood of Britain in the early 1850s. Did that triumphant celebration contribute to the jingoism with which the British in 1854 entered their first major war for four decades? Similarly, did the celebrations of France's national day on 14 July 1870 help to embolden the Council of Ministers which, meeting in Paris on the following morning, decided to declare war on Prussia?

In Athens on 5 April 1896, the Olympic Games were revived in a new marble stadium. While the games were an idealistic attempt to promote peace through sporting rather than military contests, they were also a revival of Greek glory. For Greece the symbol of Olympia was not the doves released on the opening day but the village postal messenger who ran to the lead in the marathon race and entered the stadium to the delirious applause of eighty thousand people and the congratulations, from the royal box, of the King of Greece. Was some of the reckless confidence with which Greece a year later began her first major war for more than sixty years – a war which ended in quick Turkish victory – mortared in the marble stadium of peace? In the year of the Greco-Turkish war the British Empire jubilantly celebrated Queen Victoria's sixty years on the throne, and two years later it entered the Boer War in the belief that the two South African republics would fall at the first puff from the mightiest empire the world had known. Was British confidence fed in part by these nationalist celebrations? And was a fraction of the defiance of the South African republics fostered by their celebration in December 1898 of the sixtieth anniversary of Dingaan's Day, their 'Day of the Covenant', commemorating the victory of the Boer commandos over the Zulus at Blood River?

In 1908, on the eve of the diamond jubilee of the accession of Franz Josef to the Austrian throne, his empire made its most expansionist step for almost forty years with the annexation of Bosnia-Herzegovina. In the summer of 1911 Italy celebrated her fiftieth anniversary as a united kingdom, and the lavish exhibitions in Rome and Florence and Turin had not long been opened when the government appeared to extend the celebrations into its diplomacy. For in September 1911 it handed Turkey a 24-hour ultimatum to surrender western Libya, apparently believing that Turkey would yield. But force was necessary, and Italy engaged in her first war with a European power for more than forty years.

The outbreak of the First World War might well have been influenced, slightly or strongly, by national festivals. In 1913 the German government celebrated the centenary of the 1813–1815 wars of liberation, culminating in the dedication of a massive memorial at Leipzig. The celebrations were intensified by the twenty-fifth anniversary of the accession of Kaiser Wilhelm the Second. Less than a year after the completion of the celebrations, Germany was engaged in her first war for more than forty years. Similarly the assassination which was the prelude to that war was in one sense an outcome of the fervour of celebrations. When the heir to the Austrian throne, Archduke Franz Ferdinand, agreed to visit Sarajevo, the capital of Bosnia, on 28 June 1914, he was party to a dangerous decision. For that was St Vitus's Day, the anniversary of the Battle of Kossovo, a Serbian defeat which inaugurated four centuries of Turkish domination. 'No historic event has made such a deep impression on the mind of the Serbs as the battle of Kossovo', wrote C. Mijatovich, the Serbian minister to Britain in the last years of Victoria's reign. The battle had become the great South Slav folk epic, the patriotic theme of countless tunes played with the horsehair bow of the *gusla*. As Austria had replaced Turkey as the main enemy of the independent kingdom of Serbia, St Vitus's Day was becoming an anti-Austrian celebration. And on that day, in a city with strong Serbian sympathies, the Austrian heir was shot by a Serbian patriot.

The suggestion that nationalist celebrations sometimes increased the willingness to wage war is a delicate point: if hammered too hard it may shatter. The elated atmosphere might have had no effect on the outbreak of some wars, a weak effect on others, and a strong effect on one or two wars. Several celebrations might have been organised because a bellicose mood already existed, though in turn they intensified that mood: in Germany on the eve of the celebrations of 1913 the chief-of-staff emphasised the need to create unity so that the nation could face any military emergency. Moreover national celebrations were more likely to be lavish if a nation were relatively prosperous. Perhaps the fusion of prosperity, confidence and a sense of national destiny occasionally tempted nations to exaggerate their own power.

Nationalism was not the only mood or ideology which could heighten the sense that all obstacles could be overcome. The Israelites facing their Old Testament enemies with the confidence that the Lord was on their side and worth at least 100,000 men; Revolutionary France facing powerful states in 1792 in the belief that foreign peasants and street sweepers would hail them as liberators; the mystical faith in many circles of the United States in the 1840s that it is 'our manifest destiny to overspread the continent allotted by Providence for the free development of our yearly multiplying millions'; the wide assumption in the British Empire in the late-Victorian age that it was great because God had made it great; the Turks' faith that their wars against Christian states were holy wars and therefore certain to succeed; the Marxist

faith that wars against imperialism must end in victory because it was so ordained by the principles which Marx had
discovered: all these beliefs could heighten the chance of war
by heightening the confidence of victory.

In every decision for war or peace the fluctuating influence
of seasons, moods and ideologies are probably at work, weakening or strengthening those more tangible factors which also
underlie the ultimate decision. In a crisis they may sometimes
hasten or postpone the decision to go to war. During a war
they may hasten or postpone the decision to seek peace. The
ability to hasten or postpone such decisions may appear to be
a negligible matter. 'Nevertheless,' as Sir Winston Churchill
wrote in 1931, 'a war postponed may be a war averted.' Even
if a war were postponed for only one year, it might have become a very different war. If a great European war had begun
a year earlier or a year later than 1914, it might not have
embraced the same allies, the same duration and the same
result.

8: The Abacus of Power

The Prussian soldier, Carl von Clausewitz, died of cholera in 1831, while leading an army against Polish rebels. He left behind sealed packets containing manuscripts which his widow published in the following year. The massive dishevelled books, entitled *On War*, could have been called *On War and Peace*, for Clausewitz implied that war and peace had much in common. In his opinion the leisurely siege of the eighteenth century was not much more than a forceful diplomatic note; that kind of war was 'only diplomacy somewhat intensified'. In essence diplomatic despatches breathed deference, but their courtesy was less effective than the silent threats which underwrote them. The threat might not be mentioned, but it was understood. The blunt words of Frederick the Great had similarly summed up the way in which military power influenced diplomacy: 'Diplomacy without armaments is like music without instruments'.

Clausewitz had fought for Prussia in many campaigns against the French but he had more influence on wars in which he did not fight. He is said to have been the talisman of the German generals who planned the invasions of France in 1870 and 1914. His books were translated into French just before the Crimean War and into English just after the Franco-Prussian War, and in military academies in many lands the name of this man who had won no great battles became more famous than most of those names inseparably linked with victorious battles. His writings however had less influence outside military circles. He was seen as a ruthless analyst who believed that war should sometimes be 'waged with the whole might of national power'. His views therefore seemed tainted to most civilians; he appeared to be the sinister propagandist of militarism. Those who studied a war's causes, as distinct from its course, ignored him. And yet one of the most dangerous fallacies in the study of war is the belief that the causes of a war and the events of a war belong to separate compartments and reflect completely different principles. This fallacy, translated into medicine, would require the causes and course of an illness to be diagnosed on quite different principles.

Clausewitz's tumble of words was overwhelmingly on warfare, and the index of the three English volumes of his work points to only one sentence on peace. Nevertheless some of his views on peace can be inferred from lonely sentences. He believed that a clear ladder of international power tended to promote peace. 'A conqueror is always a lover of peace', he wrote. His statement at first sight seems preposterous, but at second sight it commands respect.

II

Power is the crux of many explanations of war and peace, but its effects are not agreed upon. Most observers argue that a nation which is too powerful endangers the peace. A few hint, like Clausewitz, that a dominant nation can preserve the peace simply by its ability to keep inferior nations in order. There must be an answer to the disagreement. The last three centuries are studded with examples of how nations behaved in the face of every extremity of military and economic power.

That a lopsided balance of power will promote war is probably the most popular theory of international relations. It has the merit that it can be turned upside down to serve as an explanation of peace. It is also attractive because it can be applied to wars of many centuries, from the Carthaginian wars to the Second World War. The very phrase, 'balance of power', has the soothing sound of the panacea: it resembles the balance of nature and the balance of trade and other respectable concepts. It therefore suggests that an even balance of power is somehow desirable. The word 'balance', unfortunately, is confusing. Whereas at one time it usually signified a set of weighing scales – in short it formerly signified either equality or inequality – it now usually signifies equality and equilibrium. In modern language the assertion that 'Germany had a favourable balance of power' is not completely clear. It is rather like a teacher who, finding no equality of opportunity in a school, proceeded to denounce the 'unfavourable equality of opportunity'. The verbal confusion may be partly responsible for the million vague and unpersuasive words which have been written around the concept of the balance of power.

The advantages of an even balance of power in Europe have been stressed by scores of historians and specialists in strategy. The grand old theory of international relations, it is still respected though no longer so venerated. According to Hedley Bull, who was a director of a research unit on arms control in the British foreign office before becoming professor of international relations at the Australian National University, 'The alternative to a stable balance of military power is a preponderance of power, which is very much more dangerous'. Likewise, Alastair Buchan, director of London's Institute for Strategic Studies, suggested in his excellent book *War in Modern Society:* 'certainly we know from our experience of the 1930s that the lack of such a balance creates a clear temptation to aggression'. Many writers of history have culled a similar lesson from past wars.

Most believers in the balance of power think that a world of many powerful states tends to be more peaceful. There an aggressive state can be counterbalanced by a combination of other strong states. Quincy Wright, in his massive book, *A Study of War,* suggested with some reservations that 'the probability of war will decrease in proportion as the number of states in the system increases'. Arnold Toynbee, observing that the world contained eight major powers on the eve of the First World War and only two – the United States and the Soviet Union – at the close of the Second World War, thought the decline was ominous. A chair with only two legs, he argued, had less balance. As the years passed, and the two great powers avoided major war, some specialists on international affairs argued that a balance of terror had replaced the balance of power. In the nuclear age, they argued, two great powers were preferable to eight. The danger of a crisis that slipped from control was diminished if two powers domi-

nated the world.* Nevertheless even those who preferred to
see two powers dominant in the nuclear age still believed, for
the most part, that in the pre-nuclear era a world of many
strong powers was safer.

To my knowledge no historian or political scientist produced evidence to confirm that a power system of seven
strong states was more conducive to peace than a system of
two strong states. The idea relies much on analogies. Sometimes it resembles the kind of argument which old men invoked in European cities when the two-wheeled bicycle began to supersede the tricycle. At other times it resembles a
belief in the virtues of free competition within an economic
system. It parallels the idea that in business many strong
competitors will so function that none can win a preponderance of power; if one seems likely to become predominant,
others will temporarily combine to subdue him. It is possibly
significant that this doctrine of flexible competition in economic affairs was brilliantly systematised at the time when a
similar doctrine was refined in international affairs. While
Adam Smith praised the virtues of the free market in economic affairs, the Swiss jurist Emerich de Vattel praised it in
international affairs. In one sense both theories were re-
actions against a Europe in which powerful monarchs hampered economic life with meddlesome regulations and disturbed political life with frequent wars.

It is axiomatic that a world possessing seven nations of
comparable strength, each of which values its independence,
will be a substantial safeguard against the rise of one world-
dominating power. Even two nations of comparable strength
will be a useful safeguard. When all this has been said we
possess not an axiom for peace but an axiom for national
independence. And that in fact was the main virtue of a
balance of power in the eyes of those who originally practised
it. It was not primarily a formula for peace: it was a formula
for national independence. Edward Gulick, a Massachusetts
historian, was adamant that its clearest theorists and practi-

* The preference for a bi-polar system often seems to hinge on the
idea that wars are often the result of situations which go further than
either nation intended. The idea of accidental war will be discussed in
the following chapter.

tioners – the Metternichs and Castlereaghs – 'all thought of
war as an instrument to preserve or restore a balance of
power'. In essence a balance of power was simply a formula
designed to prevent the rise of a nation to world dominance.
It merely masqueraded as a formula for peace.

III

The idea that an even distribution of power promotes peace
has gained strength partly because it has never been accompanied by tangible evidence. Like a ghost it has not been captured and examined for pallor and pulsebeat. And yet there
is a point of time when the ghost can be captured. The actual
distribution of power can be measured at the end of the war.

The military power of rival European alliances was most
imbalanced, was distributed most unevenly, at the end of a
decisive war. And decisive wars tended to lead to longer
periods of international peace. Indecisive wars, in contrast,
tended to produce shorter periods of peace. Thus the eighteenth century was characterised by inconclusive wars and by
short periods of peace. During the long wars one alliance had
great difficulty in defeating the other. Many of the wars ended
in virtual deadlock: military power obviously was evenly
balanced. Such wars tended to lead to short periods of peace.
The War of the Polish Succession – basically an ineffectual
war between France and Austria – was followed within five
years by the War of the Austrian Succession. That war after
eight years was so inconclusive on most fronts that the peace
treaty signed in 1748 mainly affirmed the status quo. That
ineffectual war was followed only eight years later by another
general war, the Seven Years War, which ended with Britain
the clear victor in the war at sea and beyond the seas, though
on European soil the war was a stalemate. But even the Anglo-
French peace which followed the Treaty of Paris in 1763 was
not long; it ended after fifteen years. It ended when the revolt of the American colonies against Britain removed
Britain's preponderance of power over France.

The French Revolutionary Wars which, beginning in
1792, raged across Europe and over the sea for a decade were
more decisive than any major war for more than a century.

They ended with France dominant on the continent and with England dominant at sea and in America and the East. They thus failed to solve the crucial question: was England or France the stronger power? The Peace of Amiens, which England and France signed in 1802, lasted little more than a year. So began the Napoleonic Wars which at last produced undisputed victors.

This is not to suggest that a general war which ended in decisive victory was the sole cause of a long period of peace. A decisive general war did not always lead to a long period of peace. This survey of the major wars of the period 1700 to 1815 does suggest however that the traditional theory which equates an even balance of power with peace should be reversed. Instead a clear preponderance of power tended to promote peace.

Of the general wars fought in Europe in the last three centuries those with the most decisive outcome were the Napoleonic (1815), Franco-Prussian (1871), First World War (1918), and Second World War (1945). The last days of those wars and the early years of the following periods of peace marked the height of the imbalance of power in Europe. At the end of those wars the scales of power were so tilted against the losers that Napoleon Bonaparte was sent as a captive to an island in the South Atlantic, Napoleon III was captured and permitted to live in exile in England, Kaiser Wilhelm II went into exile in Holland and Adolf Hitler committed suicide. Years after the end of those wars, the scales of power were still strongly tilted against the losers. And yet those years of extreme imbalance marked the first stages of perhaps the most pronounced periods of peace known to Europe in the last three or more centuries.

Exponents of the virtues of an even distribution of military power have concentrated entirely on the outbreak of war. They have ignored however the conditions surrounding the outbreak of peace. By ignoring the outbreak of peace they seem to have ignored the very period when the distribution of military power between warring nations can be accurately measured. For warfare is the one convincing way of measuring the distribution of power. The end of a war produces a neat ledger of power which has been duly audited and signed.

According to that ledger an agreed preponderance of power tends to foster peace. In contrast the exponents of the orthodox theory examine closely the prelude to a war, but that is a period when power is muffled and much more difficult to measure. It is a period characterised by conflicting estimates of which nation or alliance is the most powerful. Indeed one can almost suggest that war is usually the outcome of a diplomatic crisis which cannot be solved because both sides have conflicting estimates of their bargaining power.

The link between a diplomatic crisis and the outbreak of war seems central to the understanding of war. That link however seems to be misunderstood. Thus many historians, in explaining the outbreak of war, argue that 'the breakdown in diplomacy led to war'. This explanation is rather like the argument that the end of winter led to spring: it is a description masquerading as an explanation. In fact that main influence which led to the breakdown of diplomacy – a contradictory sense of bargaining power – also prompted the nations to fight. At the end of a war the situation was reversed. Although I have not come across the parallel statement – 'so the breakdown of war led to diplomacy' – it can be explained in a similar way. In essence the very factor which made the enemies reluctant to continue fighting also persuaded them to negotiate. That factor was their agreement about their relative bargaining position.

It is not the actual distribution or balance of power which is vital: it is rather the way in which national leaders *think* that power is distributed. In contrast orthodox theory assumes that the power of nations can be measured with some objectivity. It assumes that, in the pre-nuclear era, a statesman's knowledge of the balance of international power rested mainly on an 'objective comparison of military capabilities'. I find it difficult however to accept the idea that power could ever be measured with such objectivity. The clear exception was at the end of wars – the points of time which theorists ignore. Indeed, it is the problem of accurately measuring the relative power of nations which goes far to explain why wars occur. War is a dispute about the measurement of power. War marks the choice of a new set of weights and measures.

IV

In peace time the relations between two diplomats are like relations between two merchants. While the merchants trade in copper or transistors, the diplomats' transactions involve boundaries, spheres of influence, commercial concessions and a variety of other issues which they have in common. A foreign minister or diplomat is a merchant who bargains on behalf of his country. He is both buyer and seller, though he buys and sells privileges and obligations rather than commodities. The treaties he signs are simply more courteous versions of commercial contracts.

The difficulty in diplomacy, as in commerce, is to find an acceptable price for the transaction. Just as the price of merchandise such as copper roughly represents the point where the supply of copper balances the demand for it, the price of a transaction in diplomacy roughly marks the point at which one nation's willingness to pay matches the price demanded by the other. The diplomatic market however is not as sophisticated as the mercantile market. Political currency is not so easily measured as economic currency. Buying and selling in the diplomatic market is much closer to barter, and so resembles an ancient bazaar in which the traders have no accepted medium of exchange. In diplomacy each nation has the rough equivalent of a selling price – a price which it accepts when it sells a concession – and the equivalent of a buying price. Sometimes these prices are so far apart that a transaction vital to both nations cannot be completed peacefully; they cannot agree on the price of the transaction. The history of diplomacy is full of such crises. The ministers and diplomats of Russia and Japan could not agree in 1904, on the eve of the Russo-Japanese War; the Germans could not find acceptable terms with British and French ministers on the eve of the Second World War.

A diplomatic crisis is like a crisis in international payments; like a crisis in the English pound or the French franc. In a diplomatic crisis the currency of one nation or alliance is out of alignment with that of the others. These currencies are simply the estimates which each nation nourishes about its relative bargaining power. These estimates are not easy for an outsider to assess or to measure; and yet these estimates exist clearly in the minds of the ministers and diplomats who bargain.

For a crisis in international payments there are ultimate solutions which all nations recognise. If the English pound is the object of the crisis, and if its value is endangered because England is importing too much, the English government usually has to admit that it is living beyond its present means. As a remedy it may try to discourage imports and encourage exports. It may even have to declare that the value of the English pound is too high in relation to the French franc, the German mark and all other currencies, and accordingly it may fix the pound at a lower rate. Whichever solution it follows is not pleasant for the national pride and the people's purse. Fortunately there is less shame and humiliation for a nation which has to confess that its monetary currency is overvalued than for a country which has to confess that its diplomatic currency is overvalued. It is almost as if the detailed statistics which record the currency crisis make it seem anonymous and unemotional. In contrast a diplomatic crisis is personal and emotional. The opponent is not a sheet of statistics representing the sum of payments to and from all nations: the opponent is an armed nation to which aggressive intentions can be attributed and towards whom hatred can be felt.

A nation facing a payments crisis can *measure* the extent to which it is living beyond its means. As the months pass by, moreover, it can measure whether its remedies have been effective, for the statistics of its balance of payments are an accurate guide to the approach of a crisis and the passing of crisis. On the other hand a deficit in international power is not so easy to detect. A nation with an increasing deficit in international power may not even recognise its weaknesses. A nation may so mistake its bargaining power that it may make the ultimate appeal to war, and then learn through defeat in warfare to accept a humbler assessment of its bargaining position.

The death-watch wars of the eighteenth century exemplified such crises. A kingdom which was temporarily weakened by the accession of a new ruler or by the outbreak of civil unrest refused to believe that it was weaker. It usually behaved as if its bargaining position were unaltered. But its position, in the eyes of rival nations, was often drastically weaker. Negotiations were therefore frustrated because each nation demanded far more than the other was prepared to yield. Likewise the appeal to war was favoured because each side believed that it would win.

In diplomacy some nations for a long period can live far beyond their means: to live beyond their means is to concede much less than they would have to concede if the issue was resolved by force. A government may be unyielding in negotiations because it predicts that its adversary does not want war. It may be unyielding because it has an inflated idea of its own military power. Or it may be unyielding because to yield to an enemy may weaken its standing and grip within its own land. Whereas an endangered nation facing a currency crisis cannot escape some punishment, in a diplomatic crisis it can completely escape punishment so long as the rival nation or alliance does not insist on war. Thus diplomacy may become more unrealistic, crises may become more frequent, and ultimately the tension and confusion may end in war.

Disputes about bargaining power will not necessarily matter if two nations have only slight contacts with one another. Prussia and Afghanistan in the nineteenth century probably had completely contradictory estimates of their own bargaining power, but this did not matter. But if two adjacent nations, Prussia and France, had contradictory estimates of their own bargaining power, the contradiction could be dangerous. Their estimates of their own strength for instance were contradictory in 1870. Each nation went to war, relatively confident that it would defeat the other. The more contact which nations have with one another, the more important it is that they should agree about their relative bargaining power. It has long been noticed that adjacent nations fight one another more frequently than they fight isolated nations.

A pioneer of sociology, Georg Simmel, while lecturing in philosophy at Berlin in 1904, set out a sad truth about international relations. He argued that the most effective way of preventing a war was to possess exact knowledge of the comparative strength of the two rival nations or alliances. And this exact knowledge, he wrote, 'is very often attainable only by the actual fighting out of the conflict'. Ironically he moved in 1914 from Berlin to Strasbourg, a city which Germany had annexed at the end of the Franco-Prussian War in 1871; and he was there when Germany and France again sought, through warfare, to learn exact knowledge of their comparative strength. That war ended with the defeat of Germany; and diplomatically she was weak throughout the 1920s. France had the bargaining power; differences could be resolved. Their relationship was dramatically altered in the 1930s when Germany rearmed herself. The German leaders' estimate of their nation's military strength now contradicted that which the French and British leaders held of their relative military strength. And if Georg Simmel, the German philosopher, had been alive during the Munich crisis of 1938, he might have predicted that the likely way of resolving the contradiction was through war.

War itself provides the most reliable and most objective test of which nation or alliance is the most powerful. After a war which ended decisively, the warring nations agreed on their respective strength. The losers and the winners might have disagreed about the exact margin of superiority; they did agree however that decisive superiority existed. A decisive war was therefore usually followed by an orderly market in political power, or in other words peace. Indeed one vital difference between the eighteenth and nineteenth centuries was that wars tended to become more decisive. This is part of the explanation for the war-studded history of one century and the relative peacefulness of the following century. Whereas the eighteenth century more often had long and inconclusive wars followed by short periods of peace, the century after 1815 more often had short and decisive wars and long periods of peace.

Nevertheless, during both centuries, the agreement about nations' bargaining power rarely lasted as long as one generation. Even when a war had ended decisively the hierarchy of power could not last indefinitely. It was blurred by the fading of memories of the previous war, by the accession of new leaders who blamed the old leaders for the defeat, and by the legends and folklore which glossed over past defeats. It was blurred by the weakening effects of internal unrest or the strengthening effects of military reorganisation, by economic and technical change, by shifts in alliances, and by a variety of other influences. So the defeated nation regained confidence. When important issues arose, war became a possibility. The rival nations believed they each could gain more by fighting than by negotiating. Those contradictory hopes are characteristic of the outbreak of war.

v

There is one puzzle in this argument. While a general war which ended decisively set up an orderly ladder of power between victors and losers, did it also set up a ladder between victors? Why did not two or three of the victors, soon after peace was established, fight one another in order to clarify further the ladder of power? For many months this question defied any answers I could muster, but slowly some answers have suggested themselves. After several decisive wars the victors remained nervous that the main defeated nation might ultimately rise again. Although France had been crushed and occupied with the last blows of the Napoleonic Wars, Britain remained nervous that France might rise again; only five years after the defeat of Napoleon, Lord Castlereagh confidentially stressed the 'importance of preventing the Low Countries, the military barrier of Europe, from being lost, by being melted down into the general mass of French power'. In the 1920s some English and all French leaders remained wary of a revival of two of the vanquished of the First World War, Germany and Russia. After the Second World War, the Soviet Union appears to have been nervous of the prospect of a German revival. Such fears helped to retain some unity among the victors of the previous war.

The likelihood of the victors' turning on one another soon after a major war was often lessened by other influences: the links which they had formed during the war, their vivid memory that war was an extremely costly and unpredictable way of solving disputes, and the eruption of internal stresses

which had been temporarily masked during the war or had
been created by the war. The danger of post-war conflict between the victors was also reduced by the negotiations which
had settled the terms and conditions of peace. Although those
negotiations primarily imposed penalties on the vanquished
nations, they also apportioned rewards and spheres of influence to the victors. At the end of a decisive war the pact of
peace not only required agreement between the victors and
the vanquished but some measure of agreement between the
main victors. And the victors, in reaching agreement among
themselves, often settled the kind of dispute which, had it
remained unsettled, would have later endangered the newly-
won peace.

Behind all these influences, which vary from war to war,
hides one other factor. Since war is the final court of appeal
and the undisputed test of which nations are stronger, a
general war weighs not only the relative power of the two
opposing sides. It also weighs the relative power of the
nations which fight as allies. It may weigh the power of individual allies with less accuracy, but at least it offers a more
useful guide than a long period of peace affords. Russia and
the United States were temporarily allies in the Second
World War, and their relative performances in the war provided a measurement of their military strengths and weaknesses. Indeed in the last leg of the war in Europe, when they
advanced on Germany from opposite directions, they were
virtually enemies as well as allies. When at the end of the war
they were thrust uneasily together on the highest pedestal of
power, each at least had received realistic warnings of the
other's strength. Those warnings probably help to explain
why in the following decade their hostility was not expressed
through open war.

VI

These conclusions, it may be argued, are not relevant to the
nuclear age. Many international theorists believe that old
patterns and precedents are now irrelevant. They believe
that the dropping of the first atomic bombs on Japanese cities
in 1945 and the launching of long-range missiles in 1957

transformed the way in which military power influences war and peace. They believe that the old concept of the balance of power has been replaced by a balance of terror. They believe that the way in which leaders of nuclear nations try to estimate the losses and gains of a possible war is now largely subjective. Some also argue that in the nuclear age the existence of two rather than seven powerful states is more conducive to peace: in the nuclear age the two-legged chair is steadier. But is the modern world so different? It may be that these theorists have observed, for the first time, truths about war and peace which were perhaps less visible but clearly present before the advent of nuclear weapons.

In each generation of the last two centuries the military technology and the social and political framework of nations has altered. Perhaps our era marks an unusually abrupt transition. And yet a lot of evidence suggests that the year of Hiroshima was not such a deep chasm in the continuity of international affairs, and that the continuity is more relevant than the chasm. Most nations possess only conventional weapons. All the wars since 1945 have been fought only with the conventional armoury of weapons. Admittedly a few powerful nations possess weapons capable of wiping out huge cities. The hazards of a nuclear attack offer severe warning against lightly undertaking a war, and yet severe warnings and hazards existed earlier. The prospect of a major war in 1938 was a more terrifying prospect than ever before; Chamberlain in 1938 warned Hitler that a world war 'may end civilization'. The prospect of a major war in 1914 was more terrifying than ever before; the British foreign secretary, Sir Edward Grey, believed that a great European war might undermine civilisation. The idea of a balance of terror is highly appropriate today, but it was appropriate a century ago. If a nuclear stalemate or balance exists today between Russia and the United States, it is not the first stalemate between major powers. In many decades statesmen contemplating a general European war have concluded that the losses would far exceed the profits.

It seems unwise to regard international relations since 1945 as an old game obeying completely new rules. It is a slightly different game obeying the same rules. Hence the main reason why France and Germany did not fight in the 1880s was that perhaps they agreed on the relative distribution of their military power. Perhaps the main reason why the United States and Russia did not fight in the 1960s was that they agreed on their relative distribution of their military might. Agreement depends not only on an assessment of the might of the enemy but a prediction of the costs and profits of fighting rather than negotiating. Agreement depends not only on the perceived distribution of power but on the perceived prizes and penalties of using military forces to redistribute that power.

One may suggest that the measurement of international power is a crucial clue to causes of war. War itself is a dispute about measurement; peace on the other hand marks a rough agreement about measurement. If this is true it is vital to distinguish those influences which call for an abacus of international power and which muffle the reading of that abacus.

VII

Wars usually end when the fighting nations *agree* on their relative strength, and wars usually begin when fighting nations *disagree* on their relative strength. Agreement or disagreement is shaped by the same set of factors. Thus each factor that is a prominent cause of war can at times be a prominent cause of peace. Each factor can oscillate between war and peace, and the oscillation is most vivid in the history of nations which decided to fight because virtually everything was in their favour and decided to cease fighting because everything was pitted against them.

They were persuaded to fight because the enemy seemed weakened by unrest at home: they were persuaded to seek peace because they themselves were now torn by unrest. They were persuaded to fight because they were prosperous and confident, and they were persuaded to seek peace because their prosperity and confidence had dwindled. They were persuaded to fight because they knew that a powerful rival was at war elsewhere and so could not interfere, and they were persuaded to seek peace because they feared that the powerful rival was now about to turn against them. They were persuaded to fight because they saw that the enemy's army or fleet was for the moment unprepared, and they were persuaded to seek peace because their own army was about to be encircled. They were persuaded to fight because the spring was favourable for a swift invasion, and they were persuaded to seek peace because the coming season would hasten their defeat. They were persuaded to fight because their intense aims seemed attainable through war, but they were persuaded to cease fighting because these original aims, being now unattainable, had faded. They were persuaded to fight because their nationalism or ideology could not conceive of defeat, and persuaded to cease fighting because their ideology could no longer mask the reality of defeat. They were persuaded to fight because most of their leaders were excessively optimistic and impatient men, and persuaded to cease fighting because those leaders, having failed, had been replaced by more cautious men. They were persuaded to fight because they had forgotten the pain and blood of war and they were persuaded to seek peace because they had been washed in blood.

One may suggest that nations, in assessing their relative strength, were influenced by seven main factors: military strength and the ability to apply that strength efficiently in the chosen zone of war; predictions of how outside nations would behave in the event of war; perceptions of internal unity and of the unity or discord of the enemy; memory or forgetfulness of the realities and sufferings of war; perceptions of prosperity and of ability to sustain, economically, the kind of war envisaged; nationalism and ideology; and the personality and mental qualities of the leaders who weighed the evidence and decided for peace or war.

Not one of these influences worked persistently for war; not one of these influences works persistently for peace. Each can promote either peace or war. It is their combination which determines the chances of peace and war. If they so combine as to convince one nation that it is the more powerful, and so combine as to convince the rival nation that it is the more powerful, the danger of war is high. If on the other hand, through these influences, each nation is not confident of its ability to defeat the other, the prospect of peace is high.

A nation could lack confidence in its own strength even though most of these seven main factors inspired confidence: those factors presumably were outweighed by the others. A nation could be confident of its strength even though one or two of the factors were not very favourable; it was the total effect of these factors which formed a nation's sense of its bargaining position. Occasionally one of these factors changed dramatically; a powerful king died, or civil strife erupted in a rival nation, or the waterbird dilemma emerged. And yet a dramatic swing in one of the seven factors probably led to war only if the collective effect of the others already pointed that way.

These seven powerful influences interacted with one another. While we can quarantine them in order to examine them, they were usually infectious. The infection was most contagious during the last phase of a war or, in other words, the eve of peace. Military defeats eroded morale at home, and that in turn lowered output of military supplies and so increased the chance of further defeats. And those defeats perhaps prompted the withdrawal from the war of a cautious ally and stirred dissension on the home front. In turn dissension often hastened the overthrow of leaders by a group which had long been lukewarm towards the war and was now eager to accept peace on unfavourable terms.

The same kind of interaction, promoting optimism instead of pessimism, was often working slowly and undramatically in the years preceding a decision to go to war. Indeed the extreme optimism which so often characterised the start of war was the quintessence of the causes of the war.

Book Three

The Elusive Warmongers

9: War as an Accident

The high hopes on the eve of wars suggest a sad conclusion. Wars occurred only when both rivals believed that they could achieve more through war than peace. The conclusion however conflicts with the belief that many wars were unintentional. Such wars, it is argued, arose when one nation misconstrued the aims of a rival and drifted into a war which neither nation desired. The belief in accidental war is sometimes a latter-day edition of the Manchester creed. Some of its advocates believe hopefully that no statesman could have wanted those twentieth-century wars which created so much devastation and yielded such spurious victories.

Several historians argued that certain wars were unintentional. The encyclopaedic *New Cambridge Modern History* reveals that the War of Jenkins' Ear 'was the result of a chronic state of friction between England and Spain, which developed into war in 1739 against the wishes of the responsible statesmen of both countries'. The War of the Bavarian Succession, between Prussia and Austria forty years later, was even more unintentional. 'Neither power wanted war,' we are told. Even the First World War is occasionally seen as unintended.

Perhaps many wars were like traffic accidents, the result of risky driving by nations rather than the result of a wish to crash into a rival. This analogy was offered in 1965 by a celebrated Dutch professor of international law, B. V. A. Röling. He suggested that there were two kinds of war: intentional wars, which had been much studied and unintentional wars, which had been much neglected. The unintentional wars were possibly becoming more frequent, but he thought that they were possibly less easy to prevent.

The idea of accidental war gained strength in the era of nuclear weapons. As the pressing of a button or the sending of a coded signal could send nuclear warheads soaring across oceans, accidental war became a terrifying prospect. A popular nightmare imagined a nuclear war beginning through a misunderstnding or an electronic error; and the nightmare aroused strenuous speculation among theorists of war. Mirroring the pessimism that inspired the debate was the emphasis on accidental war, not accidental peace. For if it were true that some wars were unintentional, then it was also likely that some wars came to an end – or some did not eventuate – through a similar kind of accident. Nobody mentioned however the idea of unintentional peace.

In the early 1960s the Berlin deadlock and the Cuban missile crisis fanned fears of accidental war. As the nation which fired first in a nuclear contest had an immense advantage, it was easy to conceive of a crisis in which one nation, thinking mistakenly that an enemy was about to attack, seized the initiative and attacked first. We can theorise on the danger of accidental war in the nuclear age until the missiles come home, but we can go no further. So far there is no precedent of how governments tend to behave at the start of a nuclear war. On the other hand history offers scores of precedents of how governments behaved on the eve of a conventional war. Just as the leader of a nuclear power knows the advantage of landing the first blow, so leaders even in the age of cavalry and camp-followers recognised the advantage of striking the first blow. Prussia tried to snatch that advantage when she invaded Silesia in the winter of 1740, England when she despatched Admiral Boscawen to intercept a small French fleet sailing to Canada in 1755 and the United States when she secretly prepared for war against England in 1812.

In the nineteenth century the quickening of links between nations increased the fear of surprise attack. The plan for a tunnel between England and France aroused the kind of fear which nuclear missiles now arouse. In London in 1881 the secretary of the Board of Trade, Sir Thomas Farrer, enquired whether the proposed tunnel between England and France could be used suddenly for a French invasion: 'is it probable that war would be declared against us, as we might say out of a clear sky (he really meant out of a dark tunnel), without any previous strain or notice that a quarrel was impending?'

Fear of a French army suddenly emerging from the tunnel was so strong in 1882 that the magazine *The Nineteenth Century* organised a petition of protest against plans for the tunnel. It was signed by the Archbishop of Canterbury and Cardinal Newman, by the poets Tennyson and Browning, and by 17 admirals and 59 generals. Sir Garnet Wolseley, who was adjutant-general and the hero of recent campaigns against King Koffee in west Africa and King Cetywayo in Zululand, wrote a strong memorandum in June 1882: 'a couple of thousand armed men might easily come through the tunnel in a train at night, avoiding all suspicion by being dressed as ordinary passengers, or passing at express speed through the tunnel with the blinds down, in their uniform and fully armed'. The attitudes to the tunnel exemplified the belief that a sudden attack could confer an enormous advantage on the attacker. A similar belief was probably held by the Japanese when they attacked Russia in 1904 and by the Balkan League, which attacked Turkey in 1912.

Two specialists in international affairs, Professor T. C. Schelling of Harvard and Morton Halperin of the United States' defence department, were uncertain whether a knowledge of the outbreak of earlier wars could really be a guide to the chance of accidental war in the nuclear age. Whereas today, they said, the first moments of a nuclear war could determine its outcome, in 1914 the nation which mobilised its armies half a day before the enemy gained a much smaller advantage. In one sense this is true. It is salutary however to read Field-Marshal Earl Wavell's description of the slow mobilising of the Austrian and Prussian armies on the eve of their war of 1866. 'Mobilisation arrangements', he added, 'had not then reached the nicety of timing that in 1914 made a delay of even a few hours dangerous.' It is even more salutary to read the peacetime prediction made by Sir George Reid to the Royal Colonial Institute in London on Empire Day, 1914. Whereas previous wars occupied tedious years the next war would be 'an affair of decisive moments, so overwhelming is the explosive force of the missiles that reach their mark first'. A sense of urgency is relative. Generals of the year 2000 may well look back to the 1960s and marvel that we measured urgency in yawning minutes. The impor-

tant point is not what we think were the advantages of a surprise attack fifty or two hundred years ago. Far more important is what leaders thought in those years. And since they
thought that the first shot could influence the course of the
war, they too must have been vulnerable to the danger of
accidental war. They too could have decided to harvest the
advantage of a sudden attack in the mistaken belief that they
were about to be attacked. Therefore a knowledge of the outbreak of past wars is perhaps the most useful way of testing
the idea that some wars are accidental or unintentional.

II

At Stanford University in California in the early 1960s two
political scientists, Robert C. North and O. R. Holsti, made a
bold investigation into the causes of war. They selected the
First World War, the favourite testing ground for war
theories; it was 'close to a prototype of crisis', they explained.
In analysing the minds of the leaders of the five main nations
which faced war in 1914, they said that they used the most
comprehensive evidence, including 'all verbatim documents
of unquestioned authenticity authored by key decision-
makers'. In examining these hundreds of documents, they
wondered whether the war was unintentional. Perhaps, they
suggested, the decision to wage war was based less on military
preparedness or confidence in victory than on the belief that
others were hostile towards them and anxious to hurt them. A
play-time experiment devised at Northwestern University
apparently gave them some support for their hypothesis.

Perusing the letters and memoranda written by European
leaders in the mid-summer of 1914 they counted how often
and how intensely the leaders perceived hostility or friendship in the attitudes of rival nations. They collected more
than 5,000 such 'perceptions' and apparently fed them to a
computer, which promptly provided a barometer of the feelings of European leaders in the five weeks between the assassination at Sarajevo and the start of the Great War. One conclusion from the 5,000 perceptions was that the leaders of all
the five powers – Germany, Austria, France, Russia and England – increasingly felt that their rivals were hostile. They

saw themselves as friendly but, alas, their friendship was not reciprocated. As the leaders of the nations in the crisis became increasingly tense, they became absorbed in the short-term rather than the long-term implications of what they discussed:

> More significant perhaps is the finding that each nation (through the nervous system of its key decision-makers) most strongly felt itself to be the victim of injury precisely at that time when its leaders were making policy decisions of the most crucial nature.

This statement is slightly puzzling, for it is contradicted by the index of injury which emerged from their computer. Both Germany and Russia, and they were the two nations which first mobilised for war, had a lower sense of injury at the crucial time when they decided on war than in the studied period as a whole. Nevertheless, even if leaders from St Petersburg to Whitehall – at the time when they chose war – had really felt most intensely slighted by the attitudes and actions of their potential enemies, their indignation would not necessarily have been evidence in favour of one theory of war rather than another. A sense of injury and hurt is quite consistent with all kinds of theories about the cause of the Great War.

Nearly all theories are based on the belief that the typical war was intentional: that at least one of the two sparring nations or coalitions wanted war. The Stanford team believed however that the Great War was not intentional. Germany initiated the war, they argued, but lacked confidence in her own military strength. 'Historical evidence', they said, 'revealed that Germany perceived itself as seriously unprepared for war in 1914 and essentially incapable of prosecuting a major armed conflict against other leading powers without risking national disaster.' Their blunt assertion is dubious. There is strong evidence that most German leaders were confident of their ability not only to win but win quickly. Some of the strongest evidence appeared in Fritz Fischer's massive book, *Germany's Aims in the First World War*, published in Düsseldorf in 1961 but unfortunately not translated into

English at the time when Holsti and North completed their research. It was not entirely their fault that a crucial leg of their argument wobbled.

Apart from measuring the frequency and intensity of hostility and friendship, Holsti and North tried to measure one of the factors which could help to explain oscillations in hostility. They tried to measure the various leaders' perceptions of their military strength or 'capability'. Holsti and North concluded that 'perceptions of capability appeared much less frequently in decision-makers' documents as perceptions of threat increased'. Unfortunately they counted only the frequency with which leaders mentioned military strength, and not how intensely they trusted in that strength. More important, their conclusions did not indicate that leaders perceived that their nation was incapable of military success if the crisis turned to war. The team's conclusion that nations went reluctantly to war were thus not justified by the tabulations which came from the computer. The computer had worked in vain: its two findings – on hostility and capability – were not accepted by its masters.

Holsti and North suspected that the Great War was an accident rather than an aggressors' plot, and that the accident possibly came more through imagined hostility. They argued positively that 'the major powers of Europe were drawn into a general conflict which none had desired and few had even foreseen, at least consciously'. Their research hinted at a warning for the 1960s. Military might, and victory in arms races, was no guarantee of peace.

Their research became celebrated among students of international relations. The exciting design of their experiment, the ravenous appetite for detail, and the enlisting of the computer deservedly won admirers. It may be that their conclusions were also acceptable because they supported the growing idea that accidental war was a neglected phenomenon that merited careful study. For one of the most prominent birth-marks of war theorising in the last decade is the assumption that some wars are accidental. The assumption is rarely illustrated by an example, but the rare and misleading example is the Stanford version of the First World War.

III

While political scientists have tended to accept the idea that some wars are accidental, historians have been wary. In history books the belief in accidental war does not often appear. In 1968 however a Harvard historian argued persuasively that the Seven Years War between England and France had hitherto been misunderstood. Neither nation had wanted it. That long war which evicted France from Canada and paved the way for the rise of an independent United States was apparently an unintentional war.

By the spring of 1754 the English and French colonies in North America were renewing the struggle for supremacy. According to Patrice Higonnet's new interpretation, those frontier scuffles should not have led to a wider and prolonged war between England and France. 'No one wanted to fight this war,' he argued persuasively. Both London and Paris were keen to negotiate, their leaders were 'well-meaning', their pleas for peace were sincere. 'Both the French and the English wanted to resolve the issue peaceably.' How then did peace slide from that friendly handshake? Dr Higonnet suggested that the English and French played brinkmanship, the one making threats in the hope that the other would negotiate, the other retaliating with its own cautious display of force. Thus England in September 1754 decided to send Major-General Edward Braddock across the Atlantic to organise her forces. He went with his reinforcements and in less than a year was killed by a force of Frenchmen and Indians and buried in the middle of the track to Fort Duquesne. Meanwhile in December 1754 France had despatched a fleet to protect Quebec, and three months later England retaliated by sending Boscawen to intercept the French fleet in the hope of winning command of the sea. War was now unavoidable: threats and diplomacy had failed.

An examination of this argument reveals one hitch. England and France wanted peace but they also wanted mastery in North America. The Duke of Newcastle, in advising the English ambassador to the French court, said that every effort should be made to preserve peace – so long as peace was consistent with attempts to strengthen the British defences across the Atlantic. For the English and French governments the colonies were the first priority and peace was second. And if there was a conflict between the two priorities the colonies won and peace lost. The sentences in favour of peace which filled the despatch boxes were sincere, but the employment of force which led to the final outbreak of war was even more sincere, for both nations ultimately believed that they could gain more by fighting than by negotiating.

The belief that some wars – whether the Seven Years or the War of the Bavarian Succession – were unwanted can always be supported by superficial evidence. Even Hitler pleaded for peace, at his price. But the notion of unintentional war usually relies on the setting up of a simple alternative – a nation either desired war or desired peace. Accordingly it is argued, if both nations showed a desire for peace but a war erupted, the war must have resulted either from a misunderstanding or from irrational twitches in the twilight of the mind. It seems unwise however to see peace and war as stark alternatives. In the minds of leaders, faced with an international crisis, war and peace are multiple alternatives.

England and France on the eve of the Seven Years War, or the giants of Europe on the eve of the Great War of 1914, faced so many alternatives – each involving preference for war or peace – that it is an over-simplification to reduce them to nine, let alone two. In a crisis the priorities for most nations might have run in this order:

1. To achieve its aims by peaceful means.
2. To achieve part of its aims by peaceful means.
3. To achieve its aims by a forceful action that is not itself war but creates some risk of war.
4. To achieve its aims by a short and small-scale war.
5. To achieve its aims by a long, large-scale war.
6. To sacrifice some of its aims by peaceful methods.
7. To achieve nothing by war.
8. To sacrifice most of its aims by peaceful methods.
9. To sacrifice most of its aims by war.

Any nation with these priorities could insist honestly that its first aim was peace. It is however peace at a price. Indeed every preference for peace or war is attached to a price.* It is probably sound to suggest that none of the five squabbling nations in 1914 wanted war, but to end the statement there, to add no more, is to portray only a fraction of their attitudes. The big powers wanted peace but only on their own conditions. By the start of August, Germany and Russia had decided firmly that their first set of peaceful priorities or alternatives was unattainable. Thus, by the elimination of their early priorities, war had become their first priority.

It appears that the desire for war or peace is always conditional. At scattered points of time in the last three hundred years a few nations have chosen peace at almost any price. Faced with the final alternatives – defeat by war or defeat by peace – they preferred to be defeated peacefully. Among that small band were Luxemburg in 1914 and 1940, Austria in 1938, and Czechoslovakia in 1938 and 1968. Even their desire for peace could perhaps be called conditional. They might not have preferred to surrender peacefully if they had believed that the all-powerful enemy intended to deport or kill tens of thousands of their citizens. As it was they decided that the price of peace was more favourable than the price of war.

IV

A war which was the culmination of an armaments race is sometimes seen as a kind of unintentional war. Rival nations, it is argued, had originally expanded their armaments simply to match those of a rival, but the competition progressively fomented fear and hatred. A leisurely race became in the end a vicious circle of death from which no competitor dared to withdraw.

The peril of an armaments race probably first caught the public attention in the 1870s. 'The continent', lamented *The*

* In reality the list of priorities would be longer and more blurred. Moreover they would not always be in the exact order set out here: priorities 5 and 6 are obviously interchangeable. It could reasonably be argued that my priority 1 may not always be the first priority. I have made it priority 1, however, partly to conform to the assumptions of the 'accidental war school' and thereby to test them fairly.

Economist of London in 1879, 'has been converted into a series of gigantic camps, within each of which a whole nation stands in arms.' The rising budgets of defence were deplored by hundreds of journalists and politicians and even by Tsar Nicholas of Russia who hoped that the international conference at The Hague in 1899 might limit the expansion of armaments. The belief that the armaments industry encouraged the rivalry spread from radical orators and pamphleteers to cautious scholars, and the two Balkan Wars of 1912–13 were sometimes blamed on the traffic in armaments. Even the Carnegie Foundation for International Peace, established by the Pennsylvania steel-maker Andrew Carnegie, issued in 1914 a report which denounced the armaments firms and the great powers for regarding the Balkans as simply a market to which they supplied munitions on generous credit.

The First World War remains the favourite example of a war which was promoted by an arms race. Professor Michael Howard of the University of London set out in 1962 a careful version of this argument: 'Since the preparations which each state made for its defence were seen by its neighbours as a threat to their own security, the great powers found themselves involved in an apparently inescapable competition which bore increasingly heavily upon public finance, inflamed mutual fear and suspicion, and was to play a considerable part – many historians would say the major part – in preparing the catastrophe of the First World War.' A more provocative version, placing much of the blame on the arms salesmen, was used by George Thayer in *The War Business* in 1969. 'It has happened twice in the Middle East in the last fourteen years, and the world is now witnessing a third arms race in the area that will inevitably culminate in yet another round of violent conflict.' The race in nuclear arms worries many scholars. They argue that heavy spending on nuclear arms indirectly increases the danger of the event which nations fear – a nuclear war.

That arms races tend to cause wars – unwanted wars – is not an easy idea to assess. It is one of those numerous theories of war and peace which we either favour or discard on intuitive grounds. It is usually a simple form of argument;

it does not consist of a series of steps, each of which can be examined. It is often strangely silent about the events in the last few months of peace and often assumes that the timing of the outbreak of war is a causal issue of no importance. It simply affirms that each step in the race provokes a retaliatory step from opposing nations until at last they stumble into the war.*

There are many reasons why we should be wary of the theory. It is popular partly because of our intuition that nations would not rapidly rearm unless they intended to fight. Why spend heavily on cruisers and field guns if they were not to be used? It is accordingly believed that Austria in 1900 was justifiably nervous if Russia were rearming, and Britain was justifiably nervous when the keels of cruisers were laid in German shipyards. But weapons could be useful even if they were rarely fired. That truth is appreciated by nightwatchmen and police constables as well as field marshals. In fact most of the warships, gun carriages and rifles built in Europe between 1870 and 1900 were probably never used in war, but they still served a function. Many writers who pointed to the danger of arms races implied that armed threats endangered the peace by fomenting suspicion. It is clear however that international relations had been marked by threats for centuries. Moreover threats – effective threats – were a vital characteristic of long periods of peace.

The emphasis on the danger of arms races arouses further unease because of its resemblance to other suspect theories of war. It is one of those theories which assumes that international relations since 1800 or 1900 can be explained only by invoking trends which are relatively new. It is like the Manchester theory of peace or the belief that advanced capitalism fosters war. As war however is an ancient institution, does its persistence into our era necessarily depend on new facets of society?

Even the haven of the theory, the First World War, does

---

* Most students of war who emphasise the dangers of arms races interpret the ensuing war as more or less unintentional. Those who concentrate more on the arms makers and salesmen, and see national leaders as merely their pawns, tend to argue that the unintentional component in the war was smaller.

not necessarily provide shelter. The war began as an Austro-Serbian war, and yet of all the major European nations Austria was probably the least energetic in rearming. In contrast Britain, which in the previous decade had rearmed most energetically, was the last of the big five to enter the war. Likewise one would expect that a sudden quickening of the armaments race would have occasioned the crisis that led to war, but in the previous few months not one of the major nations appears to have announced dramatic plans to increase its strength. Such war-eve evidence is inconclusive but it does not endorse the idea that the arms race was a vital cause of the war.

It is easy to imagine that arms races were the heralds of war but the evidence also suggests that they coincided with very long periods of peace. Between 1870 and 1914 most years were marked by increasing armaments in Europe but that was a remarkably long, even if jittery, period of peace. Likewise the absence of war between major powers since 1945 has coincided with strenuous armaments rivalry between Russia and the United States. Admittedly the Second World War came in 1939 after a spurt of rearmament, but it was a very short spurt; a strenuous arms race was not visible in western Europe before 1936. These facts do not dismiss the arms race theory; nonetheless they are inconvenient and unexpected.

Every newspaper-reader in Europe in 1914 knew that for decades the major nations had been spending more and more on armaments. In the democracies the soaring arms bills were often condemned, and the condemnation was most severe in Britain. In 1860 Britain spent about £25 million on defence, in 1885 the defence vote was £30 million, but by 1913 it had leaped to £75 million. In that year Britain, on the basis of population, spent more on defence than Germany and France and far more than Russia, Austria and the United States. As the main way of measuring the arms race was money, these statistics were influential. But what did they mean? While major nations spent more on defence they also spent more on education and on other services. As their population and revenue were rising, it would have been surprising if they had not spent more on defence. Indeed when successive British governments set out their budget – leaving aside those interest payments for which they had no choice – they chose to spend a declining proportion on defence even during those decades when naval rivalry with France or Germany was intense. Defence received 60 per cent of their expenditure in 1860, 50 per cent in 1885, and only 44 per cent in 1913. In the light of those figures the arms race in that era becomes less dramatic.

Nor did the increasing spending on defence in the era 1870 to 1914 simply reflect the rivalry and the step-by-step retaliation of the major powers. The shortness of European wars between 1859 and 1871 had taught nations to be prepared for war at short notice: it was no longer realistic to expect a long war during which an unprepared nation could tap its potential strength. As recent wars had been mainly fought on land, large standing armies and large reserves of trained militiamen seemed necessary. Likewise the expansion of navies late in the nineteenth century was partly a reflection of the rise of the German colonies in Africa and the Pacific Ocean, the spread of Russian colonisation to the fringes of the Pacific, and the rise of the Japanese, U.S. and Italian overseas empires. It may be significant that the murder of German missionaries in China and the punitive annexation by a German squadron of a corner of Shantung in 1897 coincided with one decision to enlarge drastically the German navy. It is deceptive to see the arms rivalry as simply a game of shuttlecock in which each hit depended on the preceding hit. The demands imposed on armies and navies by changing conditions, and the ability to meet those demands from rising revenue and population, would probably have led to higher spending on defence even if the era from 1870 to 1914 had been unusually placid.

That was also an era of rapid mechanical innovation in warfare as in so many industries. Drastic innovation is doubly expensive because it outmodes so much existing equipment and thereby calls for heavy spending on new equipment. Britain, during the undisputed height of her naval power, built costly warships that made her previous vessels seem impotent. 'The best ship existing in 1867 would have been more than a match for the entire British Fleet existing in 1857 and, again, the best ship existing in 1877 would have been almost if not quite equal to fighting and beating the entire Fleet of only ten years earlier.' So wrote the naval historian Sir William Clowes in 1903. Clowes, who followed the annual naval manoeuvres as excitedly as some of his countrymen followed the hounds, did not live to see at Portsmouth in 1905 the laying of the keel of H.M.S. *Dreadnought*, an 18,000-ton battleship which outmoded all previous ships and led to the virtual rebuilding of the British and German navies. On both land and sea the pace of innovation was fast, and was partly spurred by the small wars fought outside Europe. Smokeless powders were tested in the fighting in Chile in the early 1890s, heavy ordnance was reintroduced into the field armies during the Boer War, and the Russo-Japanese naval battle of Tsushima in 1905 illustrated the advantages of heavy, long-range guns and so influenced the design of the *Dreadnought*. The rising expense of defence was therefore in part the effect of lessons culled from a series of small wars far from Europe, in part the effect of rapid innovation, in part the effect of the growth of European populations and budgets, and in part the effect of increasing international rivalry.

For centuries there had been innovations in armies and navies, and rivalry in adopting them. What distinguished every generation after the mid-nineteenth century was the variety of new weapons and the speed with which they were adopted by rival nations. One may suggest that the accelerated tempo of innovation and the accompanying armaments races were simply a new version of an ancient form of rivalry. Armaments races were not a sign that hostility and misunderstanding had reached unprecedented peaks. They were more the mirror of a civilisation which was quick to mechanise every activity. They were not necessarily a cause either of war or peace.

Perhaps there are at least two kinds of armaments rivalry. The first is more the result of radical military innovations, the changing nature of warfare, higher government revenue, and a variety of other changes. For such rivalry the phrase 'armaments race' is misleading. The second kind of armaments race however is essentially spurred by intense rivalry between specific groups of nations: the Anglo-German naval rivalry in the decade before 1914 and the Russo-American nuclear rivalry of recent decades clearly resemble races. But even those races lack the characteristic commonly attributed to them. They are marked more by confidence than by fear. Certainly fear, irritation and tension are present but even more vital is the belief of rival nations that each can retain or improve its bargaining position.

The real armaments race is in one sense a substitute for war. It may seem a very expensive substitute, but compared to war it is cheap. It is commonly seen as an intentional preparation for war, a competition which brings war closer, but it may be rather a deliberate postponing of war, an attempt to use stronger threats in preference to war. Whether it ends in war depends not on accidents and misunderstandings; it depends ultimately on the rival nations' perceptions of their power to defeat one another.

v

Wars have been called accidental or unintentional by many political scientists and a few historians. It is difficult however to find a war which on investigation fits this description. This is not to say that an accidental war has never occurred. The likelihood of such a war however seems to be remote. It is remote partly because of the lack of evidence of such wars in the past but also because of the inherent confusion in the idea.

It is worth assuming for argument's sake that Japan, wrongly believing in 1904 that she was about to be attacked by Russia, decided to seize the initiative and attack first. In that situation Japan would presumably have declared war only because she was confident of victory or at least confident that she was in little danger of defeat: such confidence seems to be common to those nations which initiate fighting. If on the other hand Japan had doubted her ability to win or even to avoid defeat, would she have launched an attack? Presumably she would have offered concessions in the hope of avoiding war. To yield to Russia the concessions previously withheld might not have seemed very palatable to Japan's leaders but it was more palatable than the prospect of military defeat.

It is relevant too to ask why the Japanese leaders, in this

imaginary crisis, believed that they were about to be attacked by Russia? What convinced them an attack was imminent when in fact it was not? Let us assume that Japan received from her ambassador in St Petersburg copies of Russian documents which set out the plan for a Russian attack, and that Japan also observed Russian troop movements in Siberia. In fact the secret documents were forgeries and the troop movements were merely winter manoeuvres, but Japan was misled. Why did Japan so seriously misconstrue Russia's intentions? One cannot be sure of the answer, but it may lie in an observation made in 1929 by a Cambridge philosopher and literary critic, I. A. Richards. In reading his observation all we have to do is substitute 'diplomatic despatch' for 'poem':

Fundamentally, though this is an unfair way of putting it, when any person misreads a poem it is because, *as he is at that moment*, he wants to. The interpretation he puts upon the words is the most agile and the most active among several interpretations that are within the possibilities of his mind. Every interpretation is motivated by some interest, and the idea that appears is the sign of these interests that are its unseen masters.

If Japanese leaders completely misunderstood the Russian intentions, it was perhaps because they had already reached – not necessarily consciously – three vital conclusions. Firstly that Russia imperilled Japan's security, secondly that it was more advantageous for Japan to fight than to negotiate, and thirdly that Japan was ready to fight at a moment's notice. In such a situation the war was hardly unintentional.

It seems that an 'accidental war' becomes more likely in proportion to the presence of other conditions making for war. Ironically an 'accidental' war is more likely if the non-accidental factors are strong. Ironically an 'unintended' war becomes more likely if the intention of making war is stronger. Translated from war to law, the concept means that a murder is more likely to be called unintentional if the prisoner had strong intentions of committing murder.

VI

It could be argued at a pinch that certain kinds of wars were fought against the wishes of both governments. When sailing ships or diplomatic couriers were the fastest carriers of news, wars in remote parts of the world could continue for months after peace had been signed. In the Flemish town of Ghent on Christmas Eve 1814, the delegates from London and Washington signed an end to the Anglo-American War. On the same day – five thousand miles away – the rival armies fought outside New Orleans and, not knowing that peace had tentatively been signed, continued to prepare for a decisive battle. There, on 8 January 1815 an American army with a thick wood on one flank and the wide Mississippi on the other fired so accurately on the advancing British in the first light that the British commander, Sir Edward Pakenham, was fatally wounded and about 2,000 soldiers were killed, wounded or captured. A week later a British squadron fought a running battle with the great American frigate *President* which had evaded the blockade near the harbour of New York. And on 11 February, in ignorance of the news of the seven-weeks-old peace, the British captured the fort of Mobile and the garrison of 366 men. Five days later, in Washington, the treaty which had arrived from Ghent was ratified by the senate; and slowly the news of peace reached remote garrisons and ships far out to sea.

Just as wars could continue far from Europe even after both governments had signed the treaty of peace, so wars could begin far from Europe even before the home governments had decided whether to fight. Rival armies and rival men-of-war far from home had to be given some independence simply because they were far from home. Thus in Bengal in 1759 Dutch and British forces deliberately clashed along the Hooghly River, upstream from Calcutta, and a Dutch squadron was captured and the Dutch fort and trading post of Chinsura was occupied. Meanwhile, ten thousand miles away, Britain and the Netherlands were at peace and remained at peace. Indeed the British had attacked the Dutch without even the formal approval of their council in Bengal.

When Robert Clive, governor of Bengal, had received the message from the colonel in the field requesting an official order-in-council authorising the attack, he happened to be playing cards. Without bothering to summon the council he wrote on the back of a playing card: 'Attack at one; will send order in council.'

The events in North America and Bengal must have had scores of parallels in the era of slow travel. They can hardly be called unintentional wars; they certainly cannot be called accidental. That kind of war moreover was to be expected more when the pace of communications was slow than in an era when contact across the globe is almost instantaneous.

Occasionally a war was both begun and continued in defiance of the government of one of the fighting nations. When the Japanese army which controlled the railway zone in southern Manchuria took over the city of Mukden in September 1931 and then snatched the remainder of Manchuria from China, its campaign had not been authorised by the government in Tokyo. Indeed the commanders in the field ignored Tokyo's order to halt. Nevertheless the war, while not intended by the Japanese government, was fully intended by the Japanese Kwangtung army; and the army by its defiance had become in effect the Japanese govenment in Manchuria. To call such a war 'unintentional' would be also to call guerrilla warfare 'unintentional'. Guerrilla warfare frequently begins or continues without the sanction of the home government but is certainly a determined and intentional form of warfare.

VII

The idea of 'unintentional war' and 'accidental war' seems misleading. The sudden vogue for these concepts in the nuclear age reflects not only a justifiable nervousness about war but also the backward state of knowledge about the causes of war. One may suggest that what was so often unintentional about war was not the decision to fight but the outcome of the fighting. A war was often longer and more costly than each warring nation had intended. Above all, most wars were likely to end in the defeat of at least one nation which had expected victory. On the eve of each war at least one of the nations miscalculated its bargaining power. In that sense every war comes from a misunderstanding. And in that sense every war is an accident.

10: Aims and Arms

I

A culprit stands in the centre of most generalised explanations of war. While there may be dispute in naming the culprit, it is widely believed that the culprit exists.

In the eighteenth century many philosophers thought that the ambitions of absolute monarchs were the main cause of war: pull down the mighty, and wars would become rare. Another theory contended that many wars came from the Anglo-French rivalry for colonies and commerce: restrain that quest, and peace would be more easily preserved. The wars following the French Revolution fostered an idea that popular revolutions were becoming the main cause of international war. In the nineteenth century, monarchs who sought to unite their troubled country by a glorious foreign war were widely seen as culprits. At the end of that century the capitalists' chase for markets or investment outlets became a popular villain. The First World War convinced many writers that armaments races and arms salesmen had become the villains, and both world wars fostered the idea that militarist regimes were the main disturbers of the peace.

Most of these theories of war have flourished, then fallen away, only to appear again in new dress. The eighteenth-century belief that mercantilism was the main cause of war was re-clothed by the Englishman, J. A. Hobson, and the Russian exile, V. I. Lenin, in the Boer War and in the First World War; and the theme that manufacturers of armaments were the chief plotters of war was revived to explain the widening of the war in Vietnam. The resilience of this type of explanation is probably aided by the fact that it carries its own solution to war. Since it points to a particular culprit, we only have to eliminate the culprit in order to abolish war. By abolishing dictators, capitalists, militarists, manufacturers of armaments or one of the other villains, peace would be preserved. Indeed it is often the passion for the antidote – whether democracy, socialism or free trade – rather than an analysis of the illness that popularises many of these theories of war.

These theories assume that ambitions and motives are the dominant cause of wars. As war is increasingly denounced as the scarlet sin of civilisation, it is understandable that the search for the causes of war should often become a search for villains. The search is aided by the surviving records of war. So many of the documents surrounding the outbreak of every war – whether the War of Spanish Succession or the recent War of the Saigon Succession – are attempts to blame the other side. The surviving records of wars are infected with insinuations and accusations of guilt, and some of that infection is transmitted to the writings of those who, generations or centuries later, study those wars. Since so much research into war is a search for villains, and since the evidence itself is dominated by attempts to apportion blame, it is not surprising that many theories of war and explanations of individual wars are centred on the aims of 'aggressors'.

Most controversies about the causes of particular wars also hinge on the aims of nations. What did France and England hope to gain by aiding the Turks against the Russians in the Crimean War? What were the ambitions of Bismarck and Napoleon III on the eve of the Franco-Prussian War of 1870? Who deserves most blame for the outbreak of the First World War? The evergreen examination-question at schools and universities – were the main causes of a certain war political or economic or religious – reflects the strong tradition that ambitions are the key to understanding war.

The running debate on the causes of the Vietnam War is therefore in a rich tradition. Measured by the mileage of words unrolled it must be the most voluminous which any war has aroused, but it is mainly the traditional debate about ambitions and motives. The war in Vietnam is variously said to have been caused by the desire of United States' capitalists for markets and investment outlets, by the pressures of American military suppliers, by the American hostility to communism, by the crusading ambitions of Moscow and Peking, the aggressive nationalism or communism of Hanoi, the corruption or aggression of Saigon, or the headlong clash of other aims. The kernel of the debate is the assumption that pressures or ambitions are the main causes of the war.

II

The idea that war is caused simply by a clash of aims is intrinsically satisfying. It is easy to believe that historians will ultimately understand the causes of war if only they can unravel the ambitions held on the eve of a war by the relevant monarchs, prime ministers, presidents, chiefs of staff, archbishops, editors, intellectuals and cheering or silent crowds. Explanations based on ambitions however have a hidden weakness. They portray ambitions which were so strong that war was inevitable. It is almost a hallmark of such interpretations to describe ambitions – whether for prestige, ideology, markets or empire – as the fundamental causes, the basic causes, the deep-seated, underlying or long-term causes. Such causes merely need the provocation of minor events to produce war. The minor events are usually referred to as the occasion for war as distinct from the causes of war. Sometimes the incidents which immediately precede the war are called the short-term causes: the assumption is that long-term causes are more powerful.

This idea of causation has a distinctive shape. Its exponents see conflict as a volcano which, seeming to slumber, is really approaching the day of terror. They see conflict as water which slowly gathers heat and at last comes to the boil. The events which happen on the eve of a war add the last few degrees of heat to the volcano or kettle. It is a linear kind of argument: the causes of war are like a graph of temperatures and the last upward movement on the graph marks the transition from peace to war. If in fact such a graph were a valid way of depicting the coming of war, one would also expect to see the temperature curve move downwards in the last days of a war. One would also expect that if, on the eve of a war, minor incidents could convert the long-term causes of conflict into war, similar incidents could activate the transition from war to peace. No such explanations however are offered for the end of a war. If one believes that the framework of an explanation of war should also be valid for an explanation of peace, the volcano or kettle theories are suspect.

For any explanation the framework is crucial. In every field of knowledge the accepted explanations depend less on the marshalling of evidence than on preconceptions of what serves as a logical framework for the evidence. The framework dominates the evidence, because it dictates what evidence should be sought or ignored. Our idea of a logical framework is often unconscious, and this elusiveness enhances its grip. One may suggest that the explanations of war which stress ambitions are resting on a persuasive but rickety framework.

The policies of a Frederick the Great, a Napoleon and a President Lincoln were clearly important in understanding wars. So too were the hopes of the inner circles of power in which they moved and the hopes of the people whom they led. Likewise the aims of all the surrounding nations – irrespective of their eagerness or reluctance to fight – were important. It is doubtful however whether a study of the aims of many wars will yield useful patterns. There is scant evidence to suggest that century after century the main aims of nations which went to war could be packaged into a simple economic, religious or political formula. There is no evidence that, over a long period, the desire for territory or markets or the desire to spread an ideology tended to dominate all other war aims. It is even difficult to argue that certain kinds of aims were dominant in one generation. Admittedly it is often said that the main 'causes' – meaning the main aims – of war were religious in the sixteenth century, dynastic or mercantile in various phases of the eighteenth century and nationalist or economic in the nineteenth century. It seems more likely, however, that those who share in a decision to wage war pursued a variety of aims which even fluctuated during the same week and certainly altered during the course of the war.

One generalisation about war aims can be offered with confidence. The aims are simply varieties of power. The vanity of nationalism, the will to spread an ideology, the protection of kinsmen in an adjacent land, the desire for more territory

or commerce, the avenging of a defeat or insult, the craving
for greater national strength or independence, the wish to
impress or cement alliances – all these represent power in
different wrappings, The conflicting aims of rival nations are
always conflicts of power. Not only is power the issue at stake,
but the decision to resolve that issue by peaceful or warlike
methods is largely determined by assessments of relative
power.

III

The explanations that stress aims are theories of rivalry and
animosity and not theories of war. They help to explain increasing rivalry between nations but they do not explain why
the rivalry led to war. For a serious rift between nations does
not necessarily end in war. It may take other forms: the
severing of diplomatic relations; the peaceful intervention of
a powerful outside nation; an economic blockade; heavy
spending on armaments; the imposing of tariffs; an invasion
accomplished without bloodshed; the enlisting of allies; or
even the relaxing of tension through a successful conference.
Of course these varieties of conflict may merely postpone the
coming of war but serious rivalry and animosity can exist for
a century without involving warfare. France and Britain were
serious rivals who experienced dangerous crises between 1815
and 1900, but the war so often feared did not eventuate.

One may suggest that this kind of interpretation is hazy
about the causes of peace as well as war. Its exponents usually
ignore the question of why a war came to an end. They thus
ignore the event which would force them to revise their
analysis of the causes of war. Consider for instance the popular but dubious belief that the main cause of the First World
War was Berlin's desire to dominate Europe. Now if such an
explanation is valid, what were the main causes of the peace
which ensued in 1918? It would be consistent with this interpretation to reply that the crumbling of German ambitions led to peace. And why had those ambitions crumbled?
Because by October 1918 Germany's military power – and
morale is a vital ingredient of power – was no longer adequate. As the emphasis on aims cannot explain Germany's de-

sire for peace in 1918, it would be surprising if the emphasis on aims could explain Germany's decision for war in 1914. Indeed Germany's aims would not have been high in 1914 if her leaders then had believed that Germany lacked adequate power. Bethmann Hollweg, chancellor of Germany at the outbreak of war, confessed later that Germany in 1914 had overvalued her strength. 'Our people', he said, 'had developed so amazingly in the last twenty years that wide circles succumbed to the temptation of overestimating our enormous forces in relation to those of the rest of the world.'

One conclusion seems clear. It is dangerous to accept any explanation of war which concentrates on ambitions and ignores the means of carrying out those ambitions. A government's aims are strongly influenced by its assessment of whether it has sufficient strength to achieve these aims. Indeed the two factors interact quietly and swiftly. When Hitler won power in 1933 and had long term hopes of reviving German greatness, his ambitions could not alone produce a forceful foreign policy. Hitler's foreign policy in 1933 was no more forceful than his means, in his judgement, permitted. His military and diplomatic weapons, in his opinion, did not at first permit a bold foreign policy. A. J. P. Taylor's *The Origins of the Second World War*, one of the most masterly books on a particular war, reveals Hitler as an alert opportunist who tempered his objectives to the available means of achieving them. When Hitler began to rearm Germany he was guided not only by ambitions but by his sense of Germany's bargaining position in Europe. He would not have rearmed if he had believed that France or Russia would forcefully prevent him from building aircraft, submarines and tanks. In the main decisions which Hitler made between 1933 and the beginning of war in 1939, his short-term objectives and his sense of Germany's bargaining position marched so neatly in step that it is impossible to tell whether his aims or his oscillating sense of Germany's strength beat the drum. Opportunity and ambition – or aims and arms – so acted upon one another that they were virtually inseparable. The interaction was not confined to Berlin; it occurred in the 1930s in London, Paris, Warsaw, Moscow, Rome, Prague and all the cities of power.

A government's short-term aims, and its assessment of its ability to implement them, are always in some kind of harmony. This suggestion at first sight may seem preposterous. Throughout the centuries many nations, irrationally over-reaching themselves, were trounced in war. But those nations had entered the war in the belief that they were strong enough to win: otherwise they would have been less eager to fight. Thus in the early 1960s the war aims of the United States in Vietnam did not seem to exceed her overall strength, as measured by a majority of her leaders and advisers. The same was true of North Vietnam. This harmony is hardly surprising; a nation's policies and its perceptions of its own power are the products of the same minds. They reflect the same heightened or blunted sense of reality. The same men decide what should be achieved and what can be achieved.

Useful generalisations about causes of war are simply insights into the minds of those who had some say in the decision to make war. Headway, one suspects, will ultimately be made in understanding these mental processes, and how they vary from individual to individual, and perhaps how they vary subtly from century to century. And yet even with meagre knowledge one can suggest that in the last three centuries the decisions of hundreds of monarchs, presidents, prime ministers and chiefs-of-staff had much in common when faced with similar situations. If it were not so, there would be no patterns in the outbreak of war and peace.

The behaviour of those in power had much in common, because they were all specialists in power. Admittedly some hereditary monarchs, especially the young or demented, might have been apathetic towards some facets of power, but they thereby surrendered or leased their authority to ministers and advisers who, schooled in an arbitrary court, were undoubtedly specialists in power. It is therefore understandable that leader's perceptions of their nation's relative strength had strong and persistent effects on their foreign policy. If they believed that their nation was weak, their aims were tailored accordingly. If they believed that their nation was powerful, their aims were tailored differently.

IV

The writings of Lenin epitomise the frailties of those theories of war that rest on ambitions. During the first months of the First World War, while living in exile in the Swiss city of Berne, Lenin wrote what must be the most widely read of all explanations of that war. In emphatic essays and pamphlets that were smuggled into Russia, sold openly in Switzerland and clandestinely in Austria and ultimately extolled as dogma in many lands, Lenin asked the question: what did each country and class hope to gain from the war? The advanced capitalist countries had gone to war to win markets, colonies, monopolies, profits and loot. Russia, economically backward, had been driven to war less by the pressures of capitalism than by hunger for territory and power. 'Tsarism,' he added, 'regards the war as a means of diverting attention from the mounting discontent within the country and of suppressing the growing revolutionary movement.' Even the rulers of the industrial powers saw the war in part as a chauvinist circus, staged to quell tensions at home; and to Lenin's dismay the circus at first thrilled millions and even engrossed most socialists. Economic appetites and the quest for a scapegoat: such was the essence of Lenin's explanation of the First World War.

The man so observant of force, so convinced that force alone could create a classless paradise, said little about the reasons why Europe in 1914 had chosen force. While Lenin had expounded what he believed were the aims of European governments and pressure groups, he had not explained why they believed that they could achieve those aims by war. In his pamphlet of 1915, *Socialism and War*, Lenin had even affirmed the observant truism of Clausewitz that war is the continuation of politics by violent means, but he had almost forgotten to explain why violent means were chosen. Most of his essays and tracts devote only one sentence to that question. It is nonetheless a perceptive sentence. It argues that the German bourgeoisie had chosen a time favourable for victory: their military equipment was superior to the enemy's but, in the light of Russia's plans for massive armaments, the German forces might not long remain superior.

As Lenin tried to persuade working men, peasants and soldiers in the trenches that they could gain nothing from the war, it is not surprising that he emphasised the selfish goals of Europe's ruling classes. He was less interested in explaining why the war occurred than in explaining why the war was unjust. In his long exile Lenin was mostly a propagandist. Indeed nearly all explanations of war which overwhelmingly stress ambitions are propaganda. They are designed to pin the blame on one group, class or institution. Their selection of the target of blame rarely comes from a study of war but from deep convictions about behaviour in a wider context.

Lenin's famous theory claimed to see inside the minds of European rulers when they faced the alternatives of war and peace in 1914. Later the rush of events on the eastern front and in Russian cities was to give Lenin himself the opportunity to decide between war and peace. When the first Russian revolution broke out in Russia in March 1917, the German government realised that unrest could quickly force Russia to withdraw from the war. To fan the unrest it arranged for Lenin and a small party of Bolshevik comrades to travel in a guarded train from Switzerland to the Baltic whence they proceeded quietly through Sweden and Finland to St Petersburg. Renamed Petrograd during the wave of hatred against Germany in 1914, the city was soon to be renamed Leningrad, for there in November 1917 Lenin and the Bolsheviks seized power with the slogan 'Peace and Bread'. One of the first decisions of the new regime was to radio a message to the German Supreme Command proposing a cease-fire on the eastern front. The temporary armistice was signed on 5 December. At the railway town and fortress of Brest-Litovsk the German, Austrian, Turkish and Bulgarian delegates began their negotiations with the Russians on the terms of a peace.

Lenin and the committee of government now had to decide whether to make the severe concessions demanded by the Germans at the conference table or to resume fighting. In Petrograd, Lenin was thus personally confronted with the dilemma which he had written about in Berne three years previously. On 21 January 1918 he gave his views to a meeting of about sixty officials of the Bolshevik Party. He did not wish to surrender the territory and pay the indemnity which the German delegates demanded of Trotsky at the fortress of Brest-Litovsk. He wished to begin a new revolutionary war against Germany in the hope of spurring socialist revolutions in her industrial cities. These aims however were impracticable. He explained that the Russian army 'is absolutely in no condition at the present moment' to beat back a German offensive; in fact tens of thousands of peasant soldiers from the front were moving east, a rabble of individuals crowding the stations and trains and even crouching on the roofs of moving carriages where many were frozen to death. Lenin emphasised that most of the soldiers were exhausted and that many were hungry. The military horses were unfit to drag the artillery, presumably through shortage of fodder. Food was scarce and supply lines were chaotic. On the Baltic coastline east of Riga the German forces were so strong and the Russian defences so frail that if the war were to be resumed a German thrust could possibly capture Petrograd. In Lenin's mind it was therefore folly for the new Russia to launch a revolutionary war when the prospects of victory were frail. The Bolsheviks should instead seek peace in order to reorganise the economy and army, crush the 'frantic resistance of the wealthy classes', and make socialism invincible in Russia.

Lenin's was a sane and realistic survey of Russia's weakness. It reflected the assumption that a decision for peace or war rested ultimately on considerations of power. Like scores of leaders who over the ages had been forced to decide for peace and war, Lenin concluded that the central issue was whether his own nation was strong enough to enforce its will on the enemy. Thereby, perhaps unknowingly, he refuted the framework on which rested his celebrated interpretation of the causes of the First World War.

His plea for peace was at first rejected by zealous delegates from Moscow. Lenin regretted that 'they do not grasp the new socio-economic and political situation'. The Bolsheviks as a compromise tried to delay the negotiations at Brest-Litovsk. There on 10 February 1918 the People's Commissar for Foreign Affairs, Leon Trotsky, led his delegation from the

11: A Day that Lives in Infamy

I

Most explanations of wars assume that one nation should be totally or mainly blamed. Indeed the debate about blame usually begins before the first shot is fired; each nation insists that it is merely resisting the threat of the enemy. As the war persists, the debate circles the globe by satellite and short wave. At the end of the war the victor often tries to close the debate by affirming in the peace treaty that the loser caused the war, but that does not close the debate.

II

The idea that one nation must have caused a war intrinsically satisfies us. It is difficult to examine the outbreak of any war without searching for the warmaker. It is also difficult to resist the conclusion that if one nation started the war it must have caused the war. Moreover in most wars it seems easy to identify the nation which initiated the war. Thus one can suggest that in 1904 Japan initiated the war against Russia, that in 1914 Austria initiated the war against Serbia, and that in 1950 North Korea initiated the war against South Korea.

But when one examines more closely those wars in which the outbreak is clearly assigned to one nation, the clarity often vanishes. If the question is asked – why did they, rather than their enemy, fire the first shot – extenuating circumstances multiply. When Japan attacked Russia in 1904, it was partly in response to the despatch of Russian ships and troops to eastern Asia and the failure of diplomatic negotiations. When the United States attacked Britain in 1812 it was partly in response to many British attacks on neutral American merchant ships; in that sense open warfare had replaced intermittent warfare. When Britain declared war on Napoleonic France in 1803, she was partly replying to the French invasion of Switzerland. The British fleet which attacked French ships in the North Atlantic in 1754 responded to the crisis in North America where British and French colonists were already fighting intermittently. The Prussian attack on Austria in 1778 was provoked by the Austrians' annexation of part of Bavaria. When the French sent her invading legions to Algeria in 1830 they were answering countless episodes of Algerian piracy on the high seas. When Greece intervened in 1897 in the civil war in the Turkish island of Crete she was applying armed force to a situation where it was already the arbiter. And when France declared war on Prussia in 1870 she was responding to provocation. Here were eight different situations which preceded the outbreak of war, and those provocative situations applied to a majority of wars fought since 1700. Nor is it enough to trace back the retaliation or provocation only one step, for a series of threats or incidents usually preceded the beginning of wars.

The outbreak of war was usually not the abrupt step which we imagine. Moreover when two nations engaged in warlike acts, and one nation extended the conflict to that stage which is usually called war, that was not necessarily the end of the extension. In the eighteenth century most wars were divided into clearcut campaigns which ended with the onset of winter; and occasionally at the first green of spring one army renewed the war with such vigour that the transition to intense warfare was a more dramatic leap than the earlier outbreak of formal war. Similarly some conflicts began with isolated incidents at sea, broadened into a formal war at sea, and became intense only when one of the combatants began war on land. If for instance it could be shown that France had initiated the first step, Holland the second and France the third, how far can we blame Holland as the simple aggressor?

All wars arise from a relationship between two or more nations. An international war involving one nation is inconceivable. To argue that one nation alone wanted war and caused war is to assume that its enemy had no alternative but to fight in self defence. But before the war the enemy possessed various alternatives. It could peacefully withdraw its demands or offer concessions; it could enlist a powerful ally, though that would also have involved concessions; or it could launch its own surprise attack. If it rejected these alternatives, and found itself attacked, it could still offer those concessions which it had failed to offer earlier. Alternatively it could refuse to resist military invasion and surrender peacefully – a policy adopted by many small nations and large tribes in the last three centuries. If a nation rejected these alternatives, one can only assume that it preferred war. Wars can only occur when two nations decide that they can gain more by fighting than by negotiating. War can only begin and can only continue with the consent of at least two nations.

III

The leap from peace to war is usually seen as the most revealing event in the fluctuating relations between nations. The leap from war to peace is equally revealing. If it were logical to insist that one nation should bear the blame for beginning a war, then it would be equally logical to insist that one nation should be praised for ending a war. When a distinguished American professor of anthropology, Raoul Naroll, argued positively in 1969 that 'one must conclude that it takes only one nation to make a war', he perhaps did not realise that he was also arguing the corollary that it takes only one nation to end a war. If war is immoral and peace is virtuous the nation which terminates a war should be praised just as the nation which initiates a war should be blamed. This does not happen. The initiators of war receive an avalanche of blame, but the initiators of peace are neither identified nor praised.*

What usually terminates a war? Most wars since 1700 did not cease simply because the victor had shown overwhelming

---

* In several hundred books and articles on war I can recall reading one, and only one, such sentence of praise. Professor J. U. Nef, in his *War and Human Progress*, praised Napoleon III for wishing to end the war against Austria in 1859. The French emperor's motive, according to Nef, was his disgust at the corpses of men and horses on the battlefield of Magenta – a motive which incidentally is open to doubt.

superiority in battle. Most wars ceased at a time when the combatants were still capable of continuing the war. In Europe and North America since 1700 perhaps few wars have reached that decisive stage where the winners were in possession of much of the enemy's homeland and believed also that they were in a position to occupy the remainder: the most decisive wars were the Napoleonic, the American Civil, the Franco-Prussian and the Second World War. A group of other wars – for instance the First World War – ended when the victor was superior in the field, but it would be a mistake to suggest that those wars were terminated by sheer military superiority. Other influences, including the loser's internal dissension or the victors fear of outside intervention, helped to end them.

When we survey those more decisive wars, whom do we praise as the peacemaker? If might of arms has at last led to peace, do we praise the mighty or the weak? In the Franco-Prussian war do we praise France for her brittleness in 1870 or Prussia for her military feats? As the decisive outcome of a war must stem as much from the failures of the vanquished as the successes of the victors, it seems wise – if praise is to be offered to a peacemaker – to offer it to both. Alternatively should we praise the nation which, during the course of that war, was the first to negotiate seriously for peace? For instance, when the Prussian armies approached Paris in September 1870 the French ministry began to think of peace. On the night of 15 September Jules Favre, the vice-president and foreign minister of the new French republic, interviewed Bismarck in a Rothschild palace fifteen miles east of Paris. Alistair Horne describes the scene vividly in his book *The Fall of Paris*: Favre fidgeting and talking, Bismarck smoking and listening without sympathy until at last he replied that his main terms of peace were the French surrender of the eastern province of Alsace and part of adjacent Lorraine. They were in fact the terms of the peace which was to be signed months later, but the terms were unsatisfactory to Favre. He left the palace in tears, and France continued to fight. Other overtures for peace failed because France and Germany preferred to fight rather than to accept terms of peace which each thought were unfavourable. One can debate endlessly whether Bismarck demanded too much or Favre conceded too little, but there is no evidence to suggest that either the French or the German government were earnest peacemakers. The price of peace interested them more than peace itself, as indeed it always must.* What was true of the overtures for peace during the Franco-Prussian war was true of overtures for peace during the Second World War and those other wars which ultimately ended with decisive victory. During the course of those wars there is little to indicate that one nation was more a peacemaker than another.

Perhaps we could praise the nation which, in order to end a war, made concessions far greater than its military strength justified. But if we are to accept that definition, we should also apply it to the beginning of a war. And if applied there, a nation which started a war could often be praised. Germany, for instance, possibly could be exonerated for invading Poland in 1939 because on the eve of war she sought humbler concessions than her military might justified; Poland would thereby become the culprit for refusing those concessions. Any attempt to praise one nation for ending a war runs into hazards. The evidence seems strong that wars are ended through agreement. One nation cannot alone be praised as the bringer of peace.

Wars end when nations agree that war is an unsatisfactory instrument for solving their dispute; wars begin when nations *agree* that peaceful diplomacy is an unsatisfactory instrument for solving their dispute. Agreement is the essence of the transition from peace to war and from war to peace, for those are merely alternating phases of a relationship between nations. Admittedly the existence of that relationship is not easy to recognise when, as nationals, we have learnt since childhood to concentrate on one nation rather than on the relationship between nations. Moreover the mutual agreement which marks the dramatic turning points in that relationship – the move from peace to war or from war to peace – is not easy to detect because of the intense hostility which especially marks the beginning of the war. That two nations, by going to war, thereby agree to employ violent means of

* The idea of international peace, attached to no conditions, is meaningless. So too is the idea of war, attached to no conditions.

solving their dispute is obscured by the more conspicuous fact
that they disagree about the justice of their cause.

IV

War is so devastating, dramatic and cruel that it makes us
reject the idea that it has many similarities with peace; and
yet our rejection prevents us from understanding more about
peace and war. We deplore the visible assertion of military
power when it breaks the peace but we praise the quiet assertion of military power when it keeps the peace. We forget
that if war is immoral, the prizes of victory – whether territory or reparations or prestige or political power – are also
immoral. As the highest prize of victory is enhanced international power, and as that power is often utilised by the
victor to protect its own interests throughout the subsequent
period of peace, the peace can hardly be called righteous.

The character and conditions of peace, unfortunately, are
concealed beneath rhetoric and a façade of morality. Though
the methods and morality which initiated a war were virtually the same as those which ended a war, the one was declared immoral and the other was declared moral. Thus the
Congress of Vienna, the guardian of international morality in
1815, could pronounce judgement on Napoleon Bonaparte:
'as an enemy and a disturber of the tranquillity of the world
he has rendered himself liable to public vengeance'. The
victors likewise hired morality as their servant at the end of
the First World War. In the Treaty of Versailles, Germany
and her allies were formally condemned as the aggressors.
The treaty also called for a special tribunal – consisting of
judges appointed by the United States, Great Britain, France,
Italy and Japan – to try Kaiser Wilhelm II 'for a supreme
offence against international morality and the sanctity of
treaties'. In November 1918 however the German emperor
had left his headquarters on the western front and fled to
Holland, where the refusal of the government to surrender
him put an end to the tribunal. Nevertheless Germany's
leaders were forced to agree that the harsh conditions imposed on Germany were a punishment for her aggression and
a vindication of international morality. The overseas colonies

confiscated from Germany, the German territory which was given to five European neighbours, the reparations extracted, the ships scuttled and regiments disbanded, and the garrisoning of foreign troops on a long strip of German soil – all seemed to be just compensation for what the victors described in the Treaty of Versailles as 'the war imposed upon them by the aggression of Germany and her allies'. Under the treaty the last foreign troops were to be withdrawn from the Rhineland in 1934 but only if the victors deemed to be adequate 'the guarantees against unprovoked aggression by Germany'. In fact these were the penalties for defeat, not punishments for aggression. If Germany had won she would have imposed similar or even severer penalties, and imposed them too in the name of international morality.

As the victors at Versailles were the custodians of international morality, and as that morality rested on military superiority, it was vital that they should retain that superiority. They forgot that victory is mostly a wasting asset. They failed as custodians because, as if lulled by their own rhetoric, they continued to assert morality while they neglected armaments. The revival of German militarism in the 1930s owed as much to events in France and Britain as to events in Germany. It perhaps owed even more to the force of American opinion which made the United States – the most powerful of the victors of 1918 – turn away from Europe. As Dr A. Berriedale Keith of Edinburgh University argued in 1937: 'there can be no doubt of the gravity of the responsibility which thus fell on the United States for the subsequent developments of the European situation'. He wrote before that situation had been aggravated by German pressure on Austria and Czechoslovakia and Poland, and before the truth dawned that the custodianship of international morality was quickly passing to Berlin.

In essence the last months of the First World War had established a clear relationship between victors and vanquished, and both sides accepted that relationship. Most Germans must have disliked that relationship intensely, but they had no alternative but to accept it. Peace reigned so long as the relationship was accepted. What blunted and then confused that relationship was as much the decline or defection of the victors as the rise of two of the vanquished nations, Germany and Russia. In the background to the Second World War the isolationists of Washington were as prominent as the expansionists of Berlin; the defensive appeasers of Whitehall were as influential as the assertive appeasers of the Kremlin; and the opportunists in Paris were as influential as the opportunists in Rome. Nevertheless at the end of the Second World War the tribunals in Nuremberg and Tokyo were adamant that German aggression had caused the war in Europe and Japanese aggression the war in the Pacific. The United Nations endorsed the idea and later applied it to other wars.

v

The façade of international morality – and the belief that one nation is to blame for war – is almost hypnotic in the last days of peace and first days of war. The beneficiaries of the existing international order emphasise the sanctity of treaties and the solemnity of obligations between nations. Forgetting that some of the treaties most sacred to them had been bonded by armed force, they denounce those who break them with armed force. If the treaties are to be broken, formal notice at least should be given, If war is to begin, an official warning should be given. One advantage of a clear warning is that a last opportunity is offered for the peaceful settlement of disputes. Even more important to the beneficiaries of the existing order, a warning of war eliminates the danger of a surprise military attack. For a surprise attack is usually the weapon of nations which hope to change existing boundaries.

In the twentieth century the nations that began wars with surprise attacks were widely denounced even when the heat and partisanship had waned. The attacks were widely interpreted as evidence that one nation was to blame for the war. Japan has been singled out as the exponent of the aggressive, unannounced war. *The Encyclopaedia Britannica* refers to Pearl Harbor as 'the sneak Japanese attack'. Even *The New Cambridge Modern History*, which has remarkable standards of restraint and an admirable dearth of nationalist bias in its host of authors, remarked on the military advantages which Japan gained at Port Arthur in 1904 and Pearl Harbor in 1941 by the 'element of complete surprise without a declaration of war'. A trio of professors from North American military academies, writing of the Japanese raid on Pearl Harbor, suggested that a surprise attack, unaccompanied by a declaration of war, was 'in line with the practices of total warfare and was in the Japanese military tradition'. By total warfare they meant the all-out warfare practised in the twentieth century and visible in the earlier wars of religion. Another scholar hinted at deeper reasons; he wondered whether there was some ingredient in the national character of the Japanese that favoured this mode of starting a war.

Did the famous Japanese attacks take advantage of an unprepared enemy or were they no different from the launching of many other modern wars? In 1904, on the eve of the Russo-Japanese war, many Russian warships and regiments were travelling east. At the Russian garrison town and naval base of Port Arthur rumours of a coming war with the Japanese were plentiful. Early in January the Japanese freighters ceased to bring coal to the naval base where the stockpile of coal for the fleet was a high Russian priority. On 1 February military law had largely replaced civilian law in the port. On the same day the Russian commander at Vladivostock, Russia's other naval base in the Pacific, advised the Japanese commercial agent to warn his nationals to prepare to leave the town as a state of siege might be proclaimed at any time. Predictions of war between Russia and Japan could be read in scores of European newspapers. Their correspondents coming by the long overland railway to Port Arthur learnt on arrival that new security rules prevented them from transmitting messages by telegraph. On the morning of 6 February a Japanese warship three miles from the Korean coast apprehended a Russian cargo steamship bound for Colombo and Odessa and escorted her to a Japanese port; the cargo ship's armaments, we are told, were 22 rifles, 5 pistols and 3 boxes of cartridges. On the same afternoon the Russian mail steamer *Mukden* was detained by a Japanese warship in the Korean port of Fusan. Less than an hour earlier, in Tokyo, the government notified the Russian minister that diplomatic negotiations were severed. The Japanese warned Russia that they reserved 'the right to take such independent action as they may deem best to consolidate and defend their menaced position'.

Frederick McCormick was a foreign correspondent in Port Arthur, and at dusk on 8 February he was rowed by a Chinese coolie around the outer harbour where the Russian fleet was anchored. The evening was still, the bare hills enfolding the bays and inlets stood out sharply, and across the cold water came the sound of a band on a battleship and the voices of seamen singing the evening hymn. When he was rowed towards the shore the searchlights played on the water and electric signals were flashed from a nearby cruiser, but otherwise the scene was quiet. As Port Arthur was heavily fortified, as its approaches were well patrolled, and as it was perhaps six hundred miles from the nearest port in Japan, it seemed safe. Most inhabitants believed that, if war came, no attack would be attempted on one of the strongest bases in the Pacific. Later that evening, a quarter hour before midnight, McCormick heard a few shots, but like most of the townsmen he dismissed them as the sound of naval exercises. In fact they were naval exercises but the Japanese were conducting them. Their small destroyers had quietly torpedoed two Russian battleships and a cruiser.

Only after the war had begun did the enemies formally declare that they were at war. 'We, Nicholas II, Emperor and Autocrat of all the Russias', signed at St Petersburg his affirmation of how dear to his heart was the cause of peace but how necessary it was to wage war. From Tokyo was issued a similar declaration: 'We, by the Grace of Heaven, Emperor of Japan, seated on the Throne occupied by the same Dynasty from time immemorial, do hereby make Proclamation to all our loyal and brave subjects.' It would be valuable to know whether those loyal and brave subjects would have won the same victory at Port Arthur if, one hour before the torpedoes were fired, their emperor had formally declared war. One suspects that the surprise succeeded because the Russians at Port Arthur believed that surprise was almost impossible.

VI

Pearl Harbor, in 1941, was almost a replay of Port Arthur Months before the Japanese attack, diplomatic negotiations between Tokyo and Washington had almost reached a deadlock. While Japan was planning her attack, America was defensively increasing her forces in the Pacific. As a result of hostile edicts Japanese funds in the United States and American funds in Japan were frozen, thus ending commerce between the two nations. While Japan demanded a free hand in China, the United States demanded that Japan should withdraw her forces from China. Neither government seemed likely to yield. In these circumstances the war was not surprising.

Nor was the method of attack surprising. In January 1941 the United State ambassador in Tokyo, Joseph C. Grew, had warned that the talk about town pointed, if war should occur, to 'a surprise mass attack at Pearl Harbor'. At Washington however the Office of Naval Intelligence dismissed the possibility, and at Pearl Harbor the playing of war games suggested that a successful attack was unlikely. And so the base of the Pacific fleet lapsed into the same excessive sense of security which had trapped Port Arthur. For Peal Harbor was far from any Japanese base, was strongly defended, and in the eyes of its defenders was manned by superior men and weapons. Indeed Pearl Harbor seemed far more capable than Port Arthur of withstanding a sudden attack. The Americans had radar in Hawaii to watch the skies for approaching aircraft, they knew the secret Japanese diplomatic code, and they could even plot the movements of many Japanese warships in the Pacific.

At about 3.45 on the morning of 7 December 1941 the watch officer on a mine-sweeper thought he saw the periscope of a submarine near the entrance to Pearl Harbor. Not far away, at about 6.30, the conning tower of a strange submarine was sighted, and an American destroyer raced at full speed towards the submarine and fired the first shots of the long Japanese–American war. The destroyer's fire hit the conning tower, and depth charges were exploded close to the spot where the submarine had submerged. A coded radio message describing the engagement was transmitted ashore, but the vital warning was not exploited efficiently. 'Seven o'clock on Sunday morning', wrote Gavan Daws in his observant book *Shoal of Time*, 'was the low point of the Hawaiian weekend.' A few minutes later the radar-tracking station on the island sighted a large flight of aircraft about 140 miles away and approaching the island. They were the Japanese attackers; they had left their six aircraft carriers about half an hour ago, and in fifty minutes they would be over Pearl Harbor.

The radar warning was neglected. A Japanese attack on Pearl Harbor was clearly not expected; though war seemed likely it would surely not be a war near Pearl Harbor. At five minutes to eight however the war reached Pearl Harbor. Eight of the United States' battleships, three light cruisers, and three destroyers were sunk or severely damaged, and 188 aircraft were destroyed, mostly on the ground. President Roosevelt called it 'the day that will live in infamy'.

The spectacular way in which Japan began her wars against Russia and the United States raises two questions: why were her opening attacks so successful and why were they so denounced as infamous? The questions are related, for if the attacks had not been successful their 'infamy' would have been less obvious. The attacks on the enemy fleets at Port Arthur and Pearl Harbor owed most of their success to the complacency of the enemy. Both naval bases seemed relatively secure in peace and in war, for they were heavily fortified and remote from Japanese ports. As both Russia and the United States had considered themselves to be militarily superior to Japan, and as they were inclined to underestimate the military prowess of Asians, their feeling of security was enhanced. Their sense of security was boldly exploited by Japanese tactics. The incentive to exploit it was also high, for Japan faced nations which, militarily, were more powerful than herself. Above all, the opportunity for surprise at sea was higher than on land, and in the wars of 1904 and 1941 sea power was unusually vital.

Why were the Japanese attacks seen as the symbol of infamy? They were infamous partly because they were so successful. They were also deplored because their success seemed to depend on violating accepted rules of warfare. It is sometimes implied that the wars came as a surprise. In fact both wars came when negotiations had reached a deadlock. War, even to the enemy, had seemed highly likely. Even if Japan had declared war before attacking – even if her declaration of war had arrived, for instance, at seven o'clock on a Hawaiian Sunday morning – her attacks would almost certainly have been successful. Indeed they would have been psychologically more successful, for a prior declaration of war would have deprived the enemies of a morale-boosting excuse for the failure of their defences. As for the belief that Japan was taking unfair advantage of the enemy by not giving a warning, unfair advantages are a characteristic of war. In every war, it seems, at least one of the nations agrees to fight because it believes it is stronger than the enemy, because it believes that it possesses an 'unfair advantage' not merely for the first day but for every day of the war. Likewise in each period of peace larger nations peacefully exercise power in preserving their own interests simply because they possess that 'unfair advantage'.

Those who believe that the Japanese conduct at Port Arthur and Pearl Harbor was abnormal – and so should be explained perhaps by her national character or military tradition – have one final arrow to shoot. They can argue that it is irrelevant whether Japan gained or lost by her surprise attacks. They can simply argue that Japan knowingly scorned the accepted code of fair play when beginning those wars. One must doubt however the existence of that code.

VII

In 1882 a lieutenant-colonel in the intelligence department of the British war office investigated this reputed code of fair play. John Frederick Maurice, a son of the founder of the Christian Socialist movement, had served in the 1870s in the Ashanti War where he was Lord Wolseley's private secretary and in the Zulu War where he helped to capture the Zulu chieftain Cetywayo. Lord Wolseley once said that Maurice was the bravest man he had ever seen under fire; he was also brave in the face of hostile facts. When a tunnel under the

English Channel was planned, and the plans aroused fears in Whitehall that the tunnel might be used for a sudden invasion, Maurice was set to work by Lord Wolseley to decide 'whether a country living in peace with all its neighbours has any reason to fear that war may *suddenly* burst upon it'. Rather than theorise about the answer to the question, Maurice turned to the past wars of European and North American countries. He began to read a shelf of historians from Voltaire to Kinglake in the confident belief that he would find few wars which had been initiated without a formal warning or declaration. To his surprise he uncovered more and more. He began to realise that most wars had begun with fighting, not with declarations of war. He found forty-seven such wars in the eighteenth century and another sixty in the period 1800 to 1870, and he would have found even more if he had studied what he called European wars against 'savage tribes'. He also found that in forty-one of those wars which he studied one power appeared to have high hopes of taking the enemy by surprise. Pearl Harbor thus conformed to an old pattern. The stealth of the Japanese had been foreshadowed many times by France, Prussia, Britain, the United States and all the major powers. In contrast, less than ten wars since 1700 had been preceded by declarations of war, and many of those prior declarations were not designed to warn the enemy; they merely announced that a state of war now existed. To Maurice's knowledge only the French declaration of war against Prussia in 1870 had actually been delivered to the enemy as a warning before the beginning of fighting.

Maurice signed his report and went away to the Egyptian war. In 1883 his *Hostilities Without Declaration of War* was published as a thin book in blood-coloured cover and was sold for two shillings a copy. One of the most valuable investigations ever made of a facet of war, it had a short period of influence and then slowly floated away from the mainstream of knowledge. I have not seen Maurice's conclusions quoted in any book published in the last half century.

When the Japanese launched torpedoes at Port Arthur in 1904, their refusal to make a prior declaration of war violated neither the rules nor the practices of nations. The attack caused a sensation mainly because it was successful. There were cries that the attack breached the rules of warfare but those rules did not exist. Proof that the rules did not exist was provided in 1907 at the second international peace conference at The Hague, where the Russian military delegate pleaded for a rule prescribing how wars should commence. He was supported by the French delegation; France was Russia's closest ally. The conference finally agreed to a rule or convention which stipulated that wars should not begin until after a nation had issued either a reasoned declaration of war or an ultimatum containing a conditional declaration of war. The rule seems to have been designed more to save Russia's recent loss of face at the hands of Japan than to ensure that future wars began only after the enemy had been warned. The rule seems to have been supported primarily in the hope that the interests of neutral nations should be protected when two other nations suddenly went to war. The warning of war agreed upon by the nations at The Hague was in fact so designed that it would protect neutral nations rather than warring nations.

As a preventive of the sudden launching of war, The Hague convention of 1907 was not revolutionary. A country which declared war one minute before it attacked the enemy would conform to the new rule. A country which gave no warning could still conform to the rule if it insisted that it was merely repelling an attack or pacifying a disturbed region rather than beginning a war: to the surprise of the Chinese military delegate the conference had refused to define what kind of actions constituted a war. The new rule bound only those nations which signed their consent, and it did not bind them if they went to war with a nation which had not signed. Above all the rule adopted at The Hague represented not merely the first of many reforms in the manner of initiating a war but the peak of reform.

In the First World War nearly every nation conformed to the rule when joining in the fighting. At first sight this seemed a victory for the new code of warfare, but the victory was slight. The Hague stipulation gave only a faint warning. Moreover in Europe in July 1914 the tension and the expectation of war were so high that the advantage of a surprise attack would have been small. As foreigners were travelling freely in the main European nations until the outbreak of war, and as mobilisation and attack in 1914 depended on the massing of men and supplies at public railway stations, there was small opportunity for employing surprise methods. At sea the chance of surprise was higher; but as the war began between land powers, the sea powers received ample warning to be alert.

After the First World War the victors were more interested in banning war than in regulating the rules by which it should begin. The twelfth article of the Treaty of Versailles insisted that members of the new League of Nations should submit disputes to arbitration or the council of the League, and that they should not resort to war until three months after the adjudication of a dispute. The three-months' warning became meaningless, for most nations were not even interested in arbitration, let alone in the idea of a cooling down period. Even The Hague convention on a prior declaration of war was mainly ignored in the 1920s and 1930s. Most wars were not declared. Before invading Poland, Hitler conformed to the strong tradition of issuing no declaration of war: he merely issued a radio proclamation from Berlin fifty-five minutes after the invasion had begun. As Poland had begun to mobilise her army two days before the war began, and as Germany had also issued threats to Poland, Hitler probably gained nothing from ignoring The Hague convention. Surprise on the land in Europe in 1939 was as improbable as in 1914. Hitler gave his opinion on this question when he heard of Pearl Harbor: 'one should strike – as hard as possible – and not waste time declaring war'. He did waste time however to declare war on the United States in December 1941.

The shock felt by tens of millions of Americans when the Japanese, without declaring war, attacked Pearl Harbor is still visible in the writings of scores of able political scientists and historians. Again and again they go out of their way to notice or to deplore the way in which the Japanese had launched their wars: many have written their denunciations of Japan during years in which the United States was engaged in wars which were marked by no formal declaration either before or during the war. The contradiction is not surprising;

of all subjects international war is one of the most emotional, and we are all infected by its emotion. What is more surprising is the widespread belief in so many circles in so many nations that nearly all wars in recent centuries were only begun after the declaration of war.

The popularity of that belief is illuminating. It seems to imply that war and peace are tight compartments with nothing in common. To employ violence without warning when nations are ostensibly at peace is to break the walls of those compartments. A war, without clear warning, is therefore condemned as the intrusion into peace of the spirit and methods of war. An American specialist in international law, Ellery C. Stowell, discussing in 1908 the new Hague convention of declaring war, made the valuable observation that 'we must remember that public opinion has never given up those old ideas of the fair man-to-man fight'. War of course is not like a prize fight: it has no clear gong to sound the beginning of the fight, no rules of fair play to prevent one side from employing more soldiers or superior weapons, and no gong that ushers in an era of clear peace. War and peace are not separate compartments. Peace depends on threats and force; often peace is the crystallisation of past force. Admittedly the popular belief that war *should* begin only after an explicit warning is humane. It is also dangerous because it rests on a deep misunderstanding of the nature and causes of both peace and war.

VIII

Opportunism, and the veiled or open use of force, pervade every phase of the sequence of war and peace. They pervade the start of a war, the continuation of war and the end of a war. They pervade the start of peace, the continuation of peace and the end of peace. War and peace are fluctuating phases of a relationship between nations, and the opportunism pervades the entire relationship. Accordingly the popular contrasts of warmaker and peacemaker, of aggressor and victim, of blame and praise, do not fit this relationship. It seems invalid to argue that one nation caused a war or was responsible for war. All we can say is that one nation initiated or started or opened the war, but that is description, not explanation of the beginning of a war.

All nations, their leaders and those who are led, are not equally opportunist. They are not always incapable of restraint. But until we understand what conduct is normal or attainable on the eve of war or peace, our attempts to blame nations or praise nations will rest on standards that are either irrelevant or unattainable.

Book Four

The Varieties of War

12: Vendetta of the Black Sea

I

During a span of exactly two centuries – from 1678 to 1878 – Russia and Turkey fought one another ten times. They provided the regular fixtures of European war. They were prizefighters who fought for a few years, retired to their corners and after about two decades emerged fighting. In the space of two centuries the longest peace between them was twenty-nine years. After the defeat of Turkey in 1878 however they fought less frequently. In a period long enough – if they had adhered to their fixtures – to have accommodated four wars they met only once.

It is not quite true to say that the feud between Russian and Turk was unrelenting. When Napoleon invaded Egypt in 1798 the sultan and the tsar were briefly allies. Miracle of miracles, the sultan permitted a Russian naval squadron to leave the Black Sea and sail the narrow torrent past Constantinople, sail through the guarded Dardanelles, and so enter the Mediterranean; it was almost as if Egypt today reopened the Suez Canal to allow an Israeli fleet to pass. The Russians and Turks together drove the French invaders from Corfu and the Ionian Islands in 1799, but by the end of that year Russia had withdrawn from the alliance. The Bosporus and the Dardanelles were closed again to Russian men of war, and by 1806 the Turks and Russians were fighting again.

II

What produced repeated wars between two nations? Why did the Russians and Turks fight so often? Why was the European coast of the Black Sea the most fought-over ground in Europe – the grave in the eighteenth and nineteenth centuries for more soldiers than Flanders?* In addition to the questions of security and power which divide any two neighbours, no matter how much they have in common, Russia and Turkey were divided by persistent issues which were vital to both nations.

In religion St Petersburg and Constantinople were far apart. The Ottoman empire was Muslim but included several million Orthodox Christians who, Orthodox Russia believed, suffered from Turkish rule. Moreover the Ottoman empire included the Holy Land and Jerusalem, to which Orthodox Christians – unlike the Catholic or Protestant Christians of western Europe – still longed to make pilgrimage. The flow of pilgrims was a source of dispute and was often discussed in many of the end-of-war treaties signed by the sultan and tsar. 'Russian laymen and ecclesiastics', proclaimed the treaty of 1739, 'will be allowed freely to visit the Holy City of Jerusalem and other places that deserve to be visited.' Russian pilgrims passing through the long expanse of Turkish land or sea on their way to the holy city were to be charged no tribute or tax; and the right of pilgrimage was affirmed again in the peace treaty of 1774. As Tsar Nicholas I explained nearly eighty years later, on the eve of another Russo-Turk war: 'Our religion as established in this country, came to us from the East, and there are feelings, as well as obligations, which never must be lost sight of.' Successive tsars did not lose sight of them.

The Russian campaigns against the Turks resembled holy crusades. When in 1829 a Russian expedition besieged the Turkish fortified port of Anapa on the Caucasian coast of the Black Sea, and finally forced the Turks to surrender after bursts of bayonet-fighting, the Russian troops marched through the gates of Anapa in a procession led by an Orthodox priest in ecclesiastical robes and 'holding a cross in his hands'. Again in 1853, with the cross of Jesus marching on before, Russian troops entered European Turkey. In 1877, on the eve of the next Russian invasion the tsar reviewed his

---

* Flanders, as a fighting field, had many similarities with the European shores of the Black Sea. Both were plains, both were important lines of communication, both fronted strategic seas, and both lay near the borders of powerful nations.

assembled army in the town of Kishinev and heard a sabre-thrusting sermon from the Metropolitan of the Orthodox Church. 'Yours is the great destiny to raise the Cross of Christ above the Crescent in the lands of the Danube,' said the priest. 'Before thy face do I bless the army, beloved of Christ through thee ... May He crown thy hero deeds with glorious victory!' And to the west the Turkish army, beloved of Mohammed, were waiting to kill in the name of the True Prophet.

Commerce as well as the cross of Christ tempted the Russians to interfere in Turkish territory. Russia's main rivers flowed south to the Black Sea, which for long was a Turkish sea, and nowhere were rivers so vital as in empires of vast distances and rough roads. Although the rivers that flowed south were not so easily navigable as those that flowed to the Baltic, they floated many commodities from the Baltic region to the remote Black Sea ports. As early as the 1780s masts cut in the forests of Lithuania were sent to the distant Black Sea and shipped to many ports in western Europe. The Volga, Europe's longest river, an artery for territory as far north as the latitude of St Petersburg and as far south as the shores of the Caspian, meanders at one point only 45 miles from the River Don, and so goods from the far north could be shipped down the Volga, carted overland to the Don, and then floated in barges to the Black Sea. Of the three oceans which lapped European Russia, only the Black Sea was not blockaded by winter ice. It was therefore favoured by Russian strategists as well as by many merchants.

Rivers floated Russia towards the Black Sea, and the momentum did not end when the river mouths were taken from the Turks in the successful wars of the late eighteenth century. Once Russia had built her naval stations of the South – Kherson in 1778, Sevastopol in 1786, and Odessa in 1796 – and had launched a navy on the Black Sea, she was still at the mercy of the sultan. He controlled the narrow throat of the Black Sea. Whenever he wished he could block the throat. And so Russia, in capturing the mouth of the south-flowing rivers, was following a tantalising chase which could not end until she captured Constantinople or clipped its power.

Russo-Turkish enmity was at times sharpened by a third

issue. The Ottoman empire contained millions of Slavonic people, and from time to time the Russians championed their fellow Slavs. That Russia also oppressed Slavs in Poland and tried to dominate Slavs who won independence in the Balkans makes one wary of over-emphasising this loose linguistic bond. Nevertheless the Slavs of the Balkans – Serbs, Croats, Bulgarians and Macedonian Slavs – often invited Russia to liberate them from Turkish domination, and Russia at times saw their liberation as almost a divine mission. Dostoievsky and Tchaikovsky were in the 1870s two of the most fervent Russian preachers of the Pan-Slav ideal, and the mission gave wars against Turkey wide popularity on Russia's home front. Just as Russians had a bond with the Slavs in the Ottoman empire, so Turkey had a bond with the Muslims in Turkestan and other provinces of Asiatic Russia. But the belief in Constantinople that the Muslims in Russia were oppressed was not always shared by the oppressed ones. That Muslim dignitary, the Emir of Bukhara, was so perturbed by Russia's losses in the war against Japan in 1904 that he sent money from his ancient inland town to pay for a torpedo-boat destroyer, to be used against the Japanese. So, with the blessings of the Muslims of Bukhara, the Christian cross was forcibly raised in some Korean bay.

III

Geography and religion, and to a lesser extent the Slavonic cement, were issues which for centuries linked the Russian and Ottoman empires. Those linking issues formed a bridge which had to carry heavy emotional and commercial traffic, but it was the sultan who normally had the power to regulate the traffic because the bridge lay in his territory. He ruled the narrow waters between the Black Sea and the Mediterranean, he ruled the Holy Land, and he governed the Slavs in the Balkans. If Russia usually seemed to be interfering in Turkish affairs, and if Russia seemed to initiate the fighting in most of their wars, it was largely because Turkey otherwise would have had the power to regulate completely those issues which were so important to Russia. The prized goldfish swam in the sultan's pond, and he normally fished alone.

These issues were perhaps as divisive as those which any other pair of nations faced in the eighteenth and nineteenth centuries. Nevertheless the issues would not have provoked wars and might not even have been so contentious if both nations had been able to agree on their respective military strengths. They were unable to agree. Successive sultans who occupied the walled palace on the hill above the Golden Horn do not appear to have doubted their military strength. But that doubt was held in St Petersburg and in nearly every other European capital. Predictions that Turkey had come to the end of its long era as a great power seemed sensible to all who thought that national power relied on economic advancement, willingness to experiment, and technical efficiency. Turkey, by all these criteria, was backward. Her leaders were notoriously backward. One sultan believed that the success of Frederick the Great in battle came from the advice of his astrologers. When Turkish delegates met Austrians on the Danube to negotiate a peace in 1791, it transpired that the Turks thought that Gibraltar was a town in England.*

The imminent collapse of the Ottoman empire became the great cliché of international politics. 'This vast, ill founded, and unwieldy empire, seems indeed nodding to its fall,' reported the Annual Register of London in 1770. The fall might be delayed, it added, because western nations preferred to see the rich trade routes of the orient under Turkish rather than Russian rule. An English military engineer reported in 1810 that during the previous half century 'almost every traveller' had predicted the immediate downfall of Turkey. Napoleon Bonaparte and successive Russian tsars agreed that with the aid of a slight push the empire would topple. Russia applied that push again and again. In February 1853, on the eve of the eighth push, the tsar confided to the British ambassador that Turkey at last would topple: 'I repeat to you that the Bear is dying.' A year later an Anglo-French expedition helped to keep the bear alive in the Crimean War. The next

---

* The Turks, of course, were not alone in their ignorance. More than a century later the famous United States politician, William Jennings Bryan, was farewelled at the railway station at Constantinople with the wish that he would have an interesting trip through the Balkans. 'What are the Balkans?' asked Bryan.

Russian attack on Turkey, in the 1870s, was highly successful, but Turkey still held one of the world's most valuable empires. As late as 1900 Turkey held all or part of the present territories of Greece, Albania, Jugoslavia, Bulgaria, Libya, Tunisia, Syria, Lebanon, Israel, Jordan, Saudi Arabia, Iraq and several pocket states along the Persian Gulf. The Ottoman empire in fact lasted almost as long as the younger Spanish, Dutch, French, British, German and Italian empires. Many observers equate technical civilisation and economic progress with military success, but the equation is often deceptive.

Russia's belief that Turkey was about to collapse, and Turkey's refusal to share that belief, was merely a prolonged reflection of the fact that they rarely agreed on their relative military strength. The issues that divided them were therefore difficult to solve diplomatically. Both Russia and Turkey demanded too much and conceded too little. Ironically some of the contentious issues contributed to their contradictory bargaining positions. The religious issue was difficult to settle peacefully, for Turkey's and Russia's sense of military might was enhanced by the belief that Allah or Christ was their flag-bearer. The racial issue had a similar effect. The uprisings of the Slavonic or Orthodox Christian minorities within the Ottoman empire, by weakening Turkey, gave Russia an incentive to pounce. At the same time these minorities were more likely to rebel if they believed that Russia would aid them. The contentious issues were hopelessly entangled with the means – military or peaceful – of solving those issues. The contentious issues could be solved peacefully only if Russia and Turkey agreed on their relative power and yet some of the issues tended to make them disagree on who was strongest.

So Russia and Turkey fought because each believed that she was stronger and could gain more by fighting than by negotiating. At the close of each war they agreed on their strength, but the agreement was temporary. After one or two decades the loser recovered confidence, regained financial strength, perhaps reorganised its army and enlarged its fleet, forgot the dangers and aches of war and explained away its previous military defeat with one of those ubiquitous national myths that restored self-respect. The accession of new rulers and military leaders aided the fading memory of defeat. The terms of the previous peace treaty were chains which could now be thrown away. Revenge became attractive, for it now seemed attainable.

IV

The essence of their recurring wars was the inability of one side to defeat the other decisively. Russia usually won but her victories did not weaken permanently the military power of the Ottoman empire. Russia's victories did not weaken Turkey's grip on the narrow straits – a goal which was vital to successive tsars. Only in 1877, in the tenth of their wars, did the Russians almost reach the walls of Constantinople, and there they were halted by the fear of British intervention. Not once did a Russian fleet force its way through the narrow waters of the Bosporus.

Unusual facts prevented decisive victory. Both nations were powerful with large armies: if Turkey had been small in area and population their series of wars would soon have ended. During a period of nearly two centuries the strength of neither nation was seriously sapped by defeat at the hands of other powers. Russia and Turkey, with the aid of allies, might have had a greater chance of decisive victory in their wars; but they rarely enlisted allies. When allies did join in Russo-Turkish wars, moreover, they were usually on the side of the weaker nation. Thus Russia had allies in the eighteenth century and Turkey in the nineteenth century. But the indecisive outcome of these wars stemmed mostly from geography. The narrow Straits, fortified by geology and Turkey, formed a magnificent defence for the Ottoman empire. The vast plains on the European shore of the Black Sea and the wild Caucasian mountains on the eastern shore formed defences for both empires. In most of their wars the theatre of fighting was so far from the capital or heart of the rival empires that even a decisive victory in battle did not endanger the heartland of the losing nation.

Distance was the greatest enemy of the opposing armies. For Russia the transporting of supplies and troops to the coast near the Black Sea was slow and costly; even when by the

1850s the transport within Russia was more efficient, her armies in the Crimean Peninsula were hampered by inadequate supplies and reinforcements. In marching across the coastal plain towards Constantinople the Russian armies faced the same hurdle which thwarted European invaders of Russia: the further they advanced, the more inadequate became their supply lines. At least the Russian armies advancing near the Black Sea could use ships to carry in supplies and reinforcements, but that was feasible only if Russia controlled the sea. Control of that sea was extremely difficult for Russia to achieve, because her main fleets lay in the Baltic and could never force a passage through the Dardanelles and Bosporus in order to reach the Black Sea. Russia thus needed a separate fleet in the Black Sea, and that called for shipbuilding yards in a region which was not economically advanced. As seapower was vital in all the Russo-Turk wars, and as that power usually favoured the Turks, it was one of the most effective restraints on Russia's increasing superiority in land warfare after 1750. A century later Russia also had a powerful fleet on the Black Sea, and fear of that fleet largely promoted the intervention of the English and French on the side of Turkey during the Crimean War of 1854. As the most famous event of that war in English memory was the charge of the Light Cavalry Brigade, the war's naval aims have largely been forgotten; but the Light Brigade was charging the Russian cavalry not far from the great Russian naval base and dockyard of Sevastopol, the destruction of which virtually ended the war.

Distance dominated the Russo-Turkish wars, preventing that decisive victory which could have imposed some order on the relationship between the two nations. The main conqueror of distance was the railway. By 1877 the existence of a few trunk railways in western and southern Russia enabled the Russians to assemble troops and artillery and horses and supplies at the south-western frontier. The Rumanian railways carried most of the invaders and supplies to the banks of the Danube, where they were only two hundred miles from Constantinople. While Prussia's use of railways to assemble her troops for the invasion of France in 1870 is usually seen as the great demonstration of how railways were revolutionising warfare, Russia's exploitation of railways in 1877 was probably even more essential to her crushing victory over the Turks.

That war established Russia's decisive superiority. Russia at last commanded the Black Sea. Moreover she saw herself as the protector of the small Balkan states which had been carved from the Ottoman empire. The government in Constantinople henceforth seemed to recognise its military inferiority to Russia; even after the Japanese victory over Russia in the far east in 1905, Turkey did not take advantage of Russia's temporary weakness. Turkey was now so weak that in the generation after her crushing defeat of 1878 many nations nibbled at her territory and influence. Russia for her part had less incentive to interfere in Turkish affairs because Turkey was more compliant. Moreover Russia now realised that the Balkans could never again be insulated from western Europe and that any armed Russian interference would almost certainly arouse major powers. Thus the most likely explanation for the thirty-six years of Russo-Turkish peace – their longest peace for more than two centuries – is that both nations accepted the hierarchy of power established in the war of 1878. Contentious issues still divided them; Russian warships for instance could still not sail the Bosporus. But those issues were far more negotiable if both nations believed that they could gain at least as much by diplomacy as by war.

The last battle which Russia and Turkey fought was in the First World War. It was symptomatic of their new relationship that Turkey went to war as much because she was ally of Germany as enemy of Russia. The Turks and Russians between 1914 and 1917 fought mainly on the rugged Asian shore of the Black Sea and their battles were merely a sideshow of the wider war in which Russia was engaged. Ironically in their last war both Russia and Turkey were the losers, and the long history of the Russian monarchy and the Turkish sultanate came to an end.

13: Long Wars

Over the last three centuries international wars have tended to become shorter. The months of war have tended to become fewer but deadlier. In the eighteenth century the War of the Bavarian Succession was probably the shortest, lasting only ten months, but in 1866 came the Seven Weeks War and in 1967 the Six Days War. While the duration of wars had dwindled, the pattern is neither neat nor predictable. In 1900 it had been widely believed that the world had seen the last of the long wars that ran for four or eight years, but two world wars punctured that optimism. The innovation of nuclear weapons revived the idea that future international wars would be short, terrifyingly short, but the strongest nuclear power was to fight in Vietnam a war which, by the most frugal measurement, was a nine years' war. Obviously it is not easy to predict, nor even to know through hindsight, why some wars are long and others short.

II

The long war was typical of the eighteenth century. Between 1700 and 1815 Europe experienced seven wars which lasted for seven years or longer, but thereafter no war in Europe was so long. In the eighteenth century the long wars crowded the calendar of combat. In the first quarter of the century only about three years were free from war, and in the last quarter no more than three years were peaceful in Europe as a whole. It is unlikely that as many as twenty years in the period 1700–1815 were peaceful.

Time is only one way of measuring the severity of a war; some wars were long partly because the fighting was not severe enough to achieve a result. In the eighteenth century war tended to stop and start, to flame and smoulder. The tempo of war also fluctuated with the seasons. On the approach of winter most fleets retreated to their home harbours and regiments usually entered winter quarters, though the winter siesta had dramatic exceptions; one was in the 1790s when a Dutch fleet, seemingly safe in an iced harbour, was captured by a squadron of French cavalry. In the warmer months the tempo of fighting was also lulled by the patient processes of siege and blockade so common in the eighteenth century. And yet the wars still had bitter battles and long passages of savage fighting, and even the years of peace had intermittent scuffles – particularly on the high seas, which were not easily regulated. Even if allowance is made for the intermittent fighting in so many wars of the eighteenth century, the wars were still conspicuously long.

It has long been known that those long wars coincided with a period when the defence was in the ascendant. Wars were unusually difficult to win. A version of the deathly deadlock which dominated the western front in the First World War had occurred again and again in the eighteenth century. During most of that century an army could not rely on patriotism in order to enlist recruits or inspire them in the field. Nor could an army rely on a rush of recruits when its homeland was invaded. Even peasants with a small plot of land knew that if their province were permanently annexed by an enemy, they themselves would retain their land. When their province was invaded they were neutrals more often than nationalists; their grain and eggs and meat were bought or plundered by both armies. Warfare frequently respected private property. The Austrian army in the Netherlands in 1793 even paid rent for the fields in which its men camped. In the following year Austrian troops, fleeing from the French at Mainz, reputedly lacked the cash to hire ferries that would carry them to safety across the Rhine: penniless and calm, they surrendered.

Perhaps the Austrians on the banks of the Rhine had surrendered merely under the guise of honesty. Troops which lacked enthusiasm for a war were only too happy to desert or surrender. Desertion was so widespread that it influenced military tactics and helped to make wars indecisive. When Tallard led a French force consisting mostly of fresh recruits through the Black Forest in 1704 he lost most of them through desertion. Half a century later, in the Seven Years War, the armies of France, Austria and Prussia lost more than 200,000 men through desertion. Soon after that war a British general, Sir John Burgoyne, reporting privately on the Prussian army at a time when it was 'the stupendous machine' of Europe, claimed that desertion in peacetime equalled one-fifth of Prussia's forces. During a Prussian defeat on the field of battle, he added, the lists of soldiers who deserted were usually treble those who were killed or captured. The phrase, 'soldiers missing in action', obviously had a different meaning in the eighteenth century.

Many regiments could not be trusted to forage for food in the countryside – they might forage out of sight and vanish. An army was therefore usually chained to its lines of communication and its own supply wagons which moved slowly forward on poor roads. Professor Harold Temperley, a Cambridge historian who wrote a masterly book on the War of the Bavarian Succession, argued that an army of the era of Frederick the Great 'was like a diver in the sea, its movements strictly limited and tied by the long, slender communicating tube which gave it life'.

Unreliable soldiers also led to cautious tactics. Generals whose main problem was to maintain discipline naturally favoured the massing rather than the dispersing of troops when they attacked; the skirmishers and sharpshooters whom France from the 1790s was to use so effectively in the prelude to many battles were considered too risky, too untrustworthy, by most earlier commanders. The straitjacketed tactics probably restricted the chances of winning a decisive victory on the formal field of battle. They certainly restricted the chance of exploiting a victory. One reason why an army could rarely pursue a retreating enemy was fear that part of the victorious army might not only reach the enemy but run past them. Marlborough provided a rare example of a successful pursuit in 1706 when, following the Battle of Ramillies, he captured most of Flanders and Brabant from the retreating French in barely a fortnight. It may be significant however that Marlborough had already shown in his long march from the Netherlands to Bavaria that he was one of those rare commanders who lost surprisingly few men through desertion. Foreign mercenaries, because of their morale and loyalty, were often preferred to national troops. The small state of Hesse-Cassel, in the hills of central Germany, was famous for the mercenaries which her landgrave hired to foreign monarchs. She hired out soldiers just as Italy and Greece today hire out labourers; indeed soldiers probably were her main source of export income during war years. In the war of the Austrian Succession one Hessian contingent of 6,000 men was fighting for Austria under British pay, and another Hessian contingent was fighting against Austria. Britain alone signed seventeen contracts with Hesse for the supply of troops. In one transaction involving £3,000,000 Britain hired 20,000 Hessian soldiers in an attempt to quell the revolt of the American colonies in the 1770s; the dark Hessian Fly which was long a pest on the wheatbelts of North America is said to have migrated in the straw bedding of these mercenaries. Even Russia supplied mercenaries, and Britain came close to sending troopships of Russian mercenaries to Boston and New York to quell rebellion in the 1770s.

The military deadlock tended to be tightest in the western parts of Europe. There the land was more closely settled, and the towns were often richer and were fortified more substantially. A strong fort also gained strength indirectly from the cautious warfare of the times and was not easily captured. Moreover a cautious enemy was usually not willing, in his advance, to bypass the forts and so endanger his own lines of communication.

Fighting in eastern and northern Europe tended to be less static. On the plains which often served as the theatre of war for Prussia, Sweden, Poland, Russia and Turkey, the war-horse had the space in which its mobility could sometimes prove decisive. Frederick the Great possessed, in the opinion of one military expert, 'the two finest cavalry officers a single army has ever known'; and he won at least fifteen battles through the power of his cavalry in co-operation with muskets and artillery. On the lightly settled plains warfare was less deadlocked. During all the wars of the period 1700–90 the only capital city of a major power to be captured by an enemy was Berlin, a city of the northern plains. Berlin was penetrated during the Seven Years War when Prussia was fighting the united might of France, Russia and Austria and several smaller powers. Berlin, it should be said, was additionally vulnerable because it lay less than twenty miles from Prussia's southern border.

The sayings of two of the most observant strategists of the eighteenth century illustrate the frequent indecisiveness of war on land. Both Marshal de Saxe and H. H. E. Lloyd believed that an able general could succeed for long periods by avoiding battles; he could select such strong positions that the enemy would not dare to attack him. This was the advice not of tin soldiers but of men of steel; and a glance at their careers perhaps elucidates their advice. Maurice, Count de Saxe fought as a boy and a young man for the Austrians against France and for the Russians against Sweden and Turkey before he joined the French Army. When the French fought the English at Fontenoy in May 1745 Saxe was suffering so much from dropsy that he had to direct the battle from a wicker chariot. A commander directing a battle from the equivalent of a wheelchair is unusual in any century. Perhaps more unusual is a commander who is an alien; Saxe was not a French citizen when he led France to victory at Fontenoy. Similarly Henry Lloyd, the son of a Welsh clergyman, appears to have been a lieutenant-colonel in the service of France, a major-general in the service of Austria, and commander of a Russian division at the siege of Silistria in the Turkish war in 1774. It is even possible that he fought for Prussia; it is certain that he did not fight for Britain, though he claimed that duty to his native land made him write his military treatise of 1779, *A Political and Military Rhapsody on the Defence of Great Britain.*

Saxe and Lloyd were mercenary generals, the counterparts of the mercenary troops of that age. Their dictum – that an able general should avoid battles unless the chance of victory on the battlefield seemed overwhelming – possibly reflected the futility of so many battles in an era of military deadlock. And perhaps one of the reasons why warfare became more mobile in the 1790s was the rise of ardent nationalist armies which had less place for the foreign general or the hire-purchase troops of Hesse and which believed that the intelligent exploitation of fervour and force could flatten the enemy.

III

Of the naval commanders of the eighteenth century, perhaps the most successful was Edward Boscawen. In April 1744, in the English Channel, he made the first capture of a French frigate in the War of the Austrian Succession. Three years later he was the senior captain in Anson's squadron which, waiting in the busy sea lane off Cape Finisterre, fell on a French fleet and captured ten ships and about £300,000 of specie. In 1755 Boscawen was promoted to the rank of vice-admiral and given command of eleven sail of the line and instructions to attack the French in the west Atlantic. Six weeks out from England he captured a French ship of sixty-four guns and one of two large transports conveying reinforcements to Canada.

Boscawen won his most decisive victory in 1759 – the high tide of English naval power. A French squadron of twelve of the line had sailed from Toulon with the aim of slipping through the Straits of Gibraltar and joining the French squadron in Brest, thus forming a mighty naval force that could escort the invasion transports across the English Channel. On 4 August Boscawen's fleet was anchored in Gibraltar Bay when an English frigate patrolling the Strait saw the approaching French squadron. That evening Boscawen put out to sea. His pursuit was fortunate, for his fourteen ships eventually fell in with seven of the French ships off the coast of Portugal. One French ship of seventy-four guns was pounded into a virtual wreck and four others were chased into the Portuguese port of Lagos. Boscawen however was no respecter of neutrality. In Portuguese waters he attacked the four French ships, captured two and would have captured the others if the French had not set them alight. Soon the English navy virtually ruled the coast of France. So strong was the English grip that Boscawen anchored his fleet in Quiberon Bay and even planted a vegetable garden on a nearby French island. It was almost as if a French fleet grew vegetables on a headland of the Isle of Wight.

Not everything was decisive in the naval career of this terrier of a man who permanently cocked his head to one side. Boscawen had taken part in at least four attempts to capture enemy forts or fortified harbours – Cartagena in the West Indies, Mauritius and Pondicherry in the East, and Louisburg on Cape Breton Island – and only in the latter assault were the English successful. Moreover his famous victories at sea were against smaller fleets which did not constitute a large part of France's navy. Nevertheless his career illustrated the decisive side of warfare in a century when inconclusive battles at sea were normal.

In the second half of the eighteenth century the war at sea tended towards deadlock. The Frenchman, Bigot de Morogues, wrote in 1763: 'there are no longer decisive battles at sea, that is to say battles on which the end of the war absolutely depends'. John Clerk, a grizzly-haired Edinburgh merchant who turned in his forties to private study, complained in 1781 in his Essay on Naval Tactics that in Britain's naval wars of the last half century only the minor encounters ended in victory. When large English and French fleets met in line of battle, the fight usually ended without 'anything memorable achieved, or even a ship lost or won on either side'. John Clerk and many others attributed these futile battles to the straitjacket of contemporary naval tactics. A battle at sea had become almost as formal and ritualistic as ballroom dancing, and rival fleets were like dancers who formed two lines and swung down the centre of the ballroom, except that instead of holding their partners' hands they fired inaccurate broadsides. In the British navy a popular description for parallel lines of battle was 'to take every man his bird'. It sounds like a sentence snatched from a smoky discothèque rather than a battle at sea but the meaning is similar.

Only six of the fifteen battles which Britain fought at sea in the ninety years from 1692 could be called decisive in the opinion of the naval historian, Professor Christopher Lloyd. And they were decisive mainly because the formal line of battle was fragmented into a series of individual chases. Even in those conclusive battles there were limits on the extent of a victory since many ships of the defeated squadron usually escaped.

The phrase commonly used to describe war in the eighteenth century is 'limited war', but it was not completely true of war at sea. A kind of guerrilla warfare was conducted by hundreds of armed privateers which preyed on merchant ships of the enemy or on neutral ships carrying contraband. In the War of American Independence the British government issued letters of marque to more than 2,100 private ships, of which some were merchantmen and others glorified pirates. In one year of the war the port of Liverpool had 120 privateers employing nearly 9,000 sailors; in the last year of that war the new United States had only seven naval ships but a grand total of 327 privateers. The privateers which swarmed the seas from the English Channel to the coast of Nova Scotia spray doubt on one popular explanation: that warfare in the eighteenth century was restrained because the spirit of the age favoured restraint rather than passion. If moderation was the breath of the age, then it did not breathe on the sails of privateers which crept out of Dunkirk, Liverpool and Boston.

IV

Wars were prolonged partly by frugal tactics which were in part the effect of financial strain. Decades of warfare drained several royal treasuries almost dry. Many nations became reluctant to begin fighting or to continue fighting in certain wars unless they received subsidies from wealthy allies. The most prolific paymaster was Britain, and in the Revolutionary and Napoleonic Wars her circle of allies received 65 million English pounds. In 1813 for example Austria, Prussia, Portugal, Russia, Sicily, Spain and Sweden received British gold or war stores; and in the following year Denmark and Hanover joined the queue. The nations which received subsidies usually had to pay even greater sums from their own revenue in order to keep armies in the field and fleets at sea. As the taxes which they levied on their own citizens could not supply enough revenue, they also had to borrow at home as well as overseas.

One country, Prussia, was famous in the eighteenth century for her ability to wage war without incurring crushing debts. When Frederick the Great became king in 1740 he inherited a treasury of 9 million thalers, and when he died in 1786 his treasury held over 50 million thalers; and yet even that paragon of good housekeeping would probably have lost the Seven Years War but for British subsidies. Most other nations which engaged in the long wars of the eighteenth century incurred heavy public debts. Adam Smith, who was usually a brilliant observer of the economics of war, deplored 'the enormous debts which at present oppress, and will in the long run probably ruin, all the great nations of Europe'. The monarchs of Europe had learned the value of hire-purchase or time-payment long before there were department stores or car salesmen, but their willingness to 'fight now and pay later' was for them expensive. The revolutions in the United States in the 1770s and in France in the 1790s were partly spurred by resentment at the high taxes which the previous wars had made necessary.

The cost of keeping large armies and navies, let alone the cost of replacing men and armaments lost in battle, had become a burden. The monarchies possessed in their armed forces an enormous array of capital equipment which, if it were destroyed, they could scarcely afford to replace. And yet their military equipment could not serve its function if it did not run the risk of being destroyed. The outcome was a breed of commanders who often were instructed to win without running the risk of losing.

'There is', wrote the brilliant Prussian military writer, Carl von Clausewitz, 'no human affair which stands so constantly and so generally in close connection with chance as War.' Of all the branches of human activity, he added, war was 'the most like a gambling game'. If this is true, the gambling game of warfare in the eighteenth century was distinguished by a widespread desire to minimise the gamble.

v

Warfare on land and sea was blunted partly by the kind of weapons and tactics employed in the eighteenth century, and they in turn were influenced by the social and economic structure of the monarchies. Then came a series of events and innovations which rejuvenated the power of the offensive. In revolutionary France in the 1790s, as in the rebelling American colonies two decades earlier, men from the streets and lanes became for a time enthusiastic participants in war. Napoleon the commoner commanded armies larger than any monarch had commanded, and his armies had a fervour such as few armies had displayed in the eighteenth century. Many armies found a new flexibility and striking power, once they were unshackled from the caution and tight discipline necessary in the mercenary armies. French armies usually foraged their food from the lands through which they marched; and so they moved with a speed that seemed devastating to earlier soldiers. Napoleon's armies also used sharp-shooting skirmishers in the first stage of an engagement. Skirmishers and foragers would have both been risky in earlier armies because they would have frequently deserted.

The overthrow of the old regime in France enabled the rise of young officers of varied background in place of the gentleman generals. The new commanders were not so bound by military or class traditions and profited from an atmosphere favourable to new ideas. Napoleonic France became the symbol of an imaginative approach to war; and this symbol pervades a note written by a powerful British official on the hundredth anniversary of the battle of Waterloo. The writer was Lord Esher, who was conducting a confidential British mission in France at the very time when a great war had become deadlocked. Great wars, he wrote in his diary, cannot be won without 'imaginative passion', and that quality belonged to youth. It belonged to the young Napoleon and not the tired Napoleon of 1815. Esher regretted that in France and Britain in 1915 about forty able gentlemen were in command of the government and the fighting forces, but were unable to provide inventiveness and enthusiasm. They were unable 'to do something which long life, sedentary occupations, leisurely habits of mind render ludicrously impossible'. Lord Esher, who was himself in his sixties, was adamant that if only the leaders could be replaced by men as young as those pinned down in the trenches, the Germans would be driven back. Perhaps Lord Esher was too adamant. It was not only youth but also the fall of the previous ruling caste and their locked portmanteau of ideas – in short it was civil revolution – which helped Napoleon and, much later, Hitler and Mao Tse-tung to revive the stalemated game of military chess which each had inherited.

The Napoleonic Wars marked a swing from the defensive to the offensive, a swing which may have been faintly visible before 1790 but was pronounced thereafter. Tactics and strategy often became bolder; enthusiasm and ardour often supplanted restraint; and the slow campaigns which typified warfare of half-a-century previously were replaced by a war of movement which quickly spanned long distances. The more energetic approach filled the average year of war with more warfare than in the days of the mercenaries. The new spirit however did not seem to shorten wars. The French Revolutionary War lasted ten years, the Napoleonic War lasted twelve years. It is clear then that conditions which prolong or shorten a war are complicated.

There must have been other influences which could shorten or prolong wars. One influence was so conspicuous that it seems to have escaped observation. The long wars between 1700 and 1815 were general wars in which many nations participated. Of the seven wars which each lasted at least seven years, all were general wars.* In contrast the only general war in the northern hemisphere during the ninety-nine years from the defeat of Napoleon to the start of the First World War was the Crimean War: significantly it was the longest European war in that period.

Why, at a given time, were general wars usually longer

---

* The phrase 'a general war' is loose and has no accepted definition. I have defined a general war as one in which at least five powers, of which three are major powers, participate. By that definition 1700–1815 had nine general wars, and 1815–1930 had two. With a more rigorous definition of 'general war' (say a war involving eight states, of which at least four were major states) the distinction between the nineteenth and eighteenth centuries becomes sharper; by that test period 1700–1815 had six and the period 1815–1930 one general war (the First World War). For those who may argue that it is too difficult to define a 'major state' and who suggest that the only test is the number of states which participate in a war, the period 1700–1815 had six wars, each of which involved eight or more states: in contrast the period between 1815–1930 had two such wars, the Austro-Prussian and First World War.

than wars involving only two or three nations? At least four reasons can be offered. Firstly, in a war in which many nations participated, military strength was more likely to be distributed evenly between the two sides, and the more even distribution tended to prevent an early result to the war. Secondly, in a general war fighting was usually on several fronts and on sea as well as land, and therefore one alliance was less likely to be winning simultaneously in all theatres of war; this tended to prolong the fighting. Thirdly, a war alliance of many nations did not usually co-ordinate its campaigns efficiently; its members could not so easily be enticed to a conference to negotiate peace, nor could they so easily come to agreement on the terms of a peace.

A fourth fact tended to prolong general wars and to shorten wars between two nations. In a war between two nations the winning side was often willing to seek an early peace because it feared that another nation might intervene and so remove the advantage which it had painfully won. In contrast the nations that were winning in a general war were not likely to cease fighting through fear that another nation would intervene; understandably the danger of decisive intervention was small if nearly all the adjacent nations were already participating in the war. In Europe since the 1790s ruthless aims have been characteristic of general wars whereas moderate aims have been more characteristic of two-sided wars. Every general war from the era of Napoleon and Pitt to the era of Churchill and Hitler was probably prolonged by the refusal of the winning side to be satisfied with a moderate victory.

The Battle of Waterloo marked the end of an era of general wars in Europe. The long duration of wars between 1700 and 1815 had come partly from the more intermittent tempo of warfare and partly perhaps from the prevailing techniques of warfare and the economic and social structure of states. But the main influence which had prolonged warfare was the tendency for wars to involve many nations.*

* The causes of general wars, as distinct from wars between two or three nations, are discussed in Chapter 15, 'The Mystery of Wide Wars'.

VI

In the century after Waterloo the longest wars were fought outside Europe. Colonial wars began to dominate the calendar of fighting. While the casualties and cost of one year of a colonial war were often less than those of one month of a European war, many colonial wars were serious wars and were unexpectedly difficult to win. It is therefore useful to ask whether those long colonial wars were affected by the same factors which prolonged war in Europe.

Perhaps the longest international war in the nineteenth century was between France and Algeria, and in some ways it foretold the long wars which France was to fight in the middle of this century in Algeria and Indo-China. Algeria, on the eve of the French invasion of 1830, was an independent republic stretching from the fringes of the Sahara to the rugged coast of the Mediterranean. For generations the Algerian pirates had sailed from rocky harbours to attack European ports and ships at the western end of the Mediterranean, and these pirates of Barbary survived a long line of European naval expeditions. As late as August 1816 Admiral Pellew with five English sail of the line and the support of Dutch frigates bombarded the port of Algiers for almost eight hours and released about 3,000 European slaves. His display of power was soon forgotten. An Anglo-French expedition appeared off the Algerian coast in 1819, but piracy still flourished. These naval expeditions, stretching back decade after decade, were like fox-hunters who went hunting every few years but never disturbed the fox-holes.

In May 1830 the French government sent a powerful expedition to capture the fox-holes. From Toulon sailed nine French ships of the line, fifty-six frigates and corvettes and brigs, eight steamboats, and a flotilla of smaller craft. In the fleet were 37,000 men, 4,000 horses and France's minister of war, Marshal de Bourmont, who commanded the invasion. A few miles from Algiers a French steamboat terrified armed parties of Arab horsemen and the French regiments were landed. Within three weeks Algiers had capitulated, and soon the powerful Dey of Algiers was escorted into exile in Italy and most of his soldiers were shipped away to Asia Minor. All that the French now required was the occupation of the smaller ports long the coast; piracy would vanish and, increasingly important, France would possess one of the strategic areas of the Mediterranean. But French regiments could not safely hold ports such as Oran and Bona and Algiers unless they also held the surrounding countryside which supplied the ports with foodstuffs, forage and articles of commerce. And the ring of villages around the ports could not be held efficiently unless the outer arc of countryside was relatively peaceful. As the rocky terrain favoured snipers, and as the Algerians were fearless horsemen, the French conquest of the Algerian coastline was slow and expensive. In 1833, three years after the capture of Algiers, French forces held only three ports, and even their suburbs were not secure. By 1835 they held six coastal towns.

The occasional victories of the French armies were punctuated by indecisive campaigns and dismal defeats. In the summer of 1835 a French force from Oran suffered heavy losses while pushing through a mountain defile, and then began a retreat which Algerian sharp-shooters turned into a rabble; in the retreat the French lost 570 men through death or wounds and all baggage and wagons. From France came a reinforcement of 10,000 troops and the heir apparent, the Duke of Orleans, hungry for glory. His large French army and twenty-six pieces of artillery rolled inland from Oran towards the mountain slopes and destroyed the town of Mascara which had been hastily abandoned. No sooner had the French force and the victorious duke returned to Oran than the Algerian horsemen rode down from the mountains to resume control of the countryside.

The Algerians captured a town south west of Oran, so in January 1836 another large French force was sent to recapture it. They arrived only to find the town had been evacuated. When the tents of thousands of Algerian horsemen were seen in the interior the French cavalry gave chase, but the Algerians outpaced them. The French placed a garrison of 500 soldiers in the captured town, but the main force had no sooner returned to Oran than the Algerians occupied the road down which the French regiments had marched. In

April 1836 a French force again marched from Oran; and after a long campaign, which called for another 4,000 men from France, they drove the Algerians into the mountains. It was easier to drive them there than to hold them there, and soon they returned. Meanwhile, late in 1836, a force of 7,000 French soldiers left Bona to capture the ancient inland town of Constantine. Snow and rain set in, the heavy artillery was stuck in mud so deep that even the axles of the wheels were buried, men fell out or died from sickness and exposure, the assault on the walls of Constantine failed as soon as the ladder-carriers were shot and the retreating French army was harassed by Arab horsemen. 'The expedition against Constantine', wrote the French marshal, 'has not had complete success.' So the campaigns thundered and fizzled, year after year.

The Algerian resistance was led brilliantly by Abd-el-Kader, a direct descendant of Mohammed. He had returned from a pilgrimage to Mecca and Baghdad not long before the French began their invasion; and in 1832, when he was aged no more than twenty-five, he was elected the emir of Mascara. He made Mascara the eye of the Algerian resistance. For the best part of ten years his mobile forces harried the French, and he was nearly always able to avoid a pitched battle except when the odds were heavily in his favour. A talented tactician and horseman (author of a book on the Arab horse as well as a philosophical treatise), persuasive in ideology and spartan in the field, he had some of the characteristics of the recent nationalist leaders in eastern Asia – Mao and Ho. Only when Marshal Bugeaud, the French governor-general of Algiers from 1840, copied the mobile tactics of the Algerians and employed pack animals in place of slow-moving wagon trains, and adopted quick cavalry thrusts in place of the cumbersome movements of infantry, did Abd-el-Kader ultimately lose the initiative. He finally surrendered in December 1847 and passed into exile.

An explanation of why the French spent more than seventeen years in conquering Algeria should illuminate other long colonial wars. A small land with a sparse population was more easily conquered than a wide land with millions of people. As Algeria stretched about 600 miles from east to west and extended about half of that distance southwards towards the silence of the Sahara, and as its population was perhaps three million, it was not an easy prey for an invader. The hot summers and the rocky terrain of Algeria also favoured the defenders and so helped to prolong the war. Similarly a land which was relatively united – Algeria was bonded by faith in Islam – had more hope of resisting European rule than a land where racial and religious allegiances were seriously divided.

The power of an invading army depended not on its superiority in a variety of techniques of warfare but on its superiority in that narrow range of techniques which could be applied efficiently to colonial fighting. Reluctance to accept that humiliating lesson helped to prolong many colonial wars. Thus France's strength in artillery – vital in so many wars in Europe – was far less devastating in Algeria where the dragging of gun carriages into the interior was not only arduous but a loud announcement to the Algerians of the French plan of attack. Similarly the swiftest means of transport in Algeria was the horse, and the Algerians often surpassed the French cavalry in rugged terrain. Likewise in Vietnam in the 1960s airpower did not give to the United States the sweeping advantages which would have come against an enemy whose transport system was funnelled along a few crucial railways and whose war effort relied on vulnerable pockets of heavy industry – North Vietnam's main pockets of heavy industry were in the Soviet Union, eastern Europe, and China, and thus invulnerable. Nuclear weapons – ostensibly the hallmark of military might – were of no advantage in American field operations in Vietnam, just as England's possession of the world's mightiest navy was no aid in pursuing Boers in the interior of South Africa at the turn of the century. The value of these idle insignia of military power was rather their ability to warn other nations not to interfere in the fighting.

Thus one fact which tended to prolong colonial wars was the inability of the stronger state to use some of its superior weapons. Indeed some of these wars resembled a European war between a seapower and a landpower: they could not adequately come to grips. The elusiveness was intensified when guerrilla warfare was practised by the Algerians in the 1830s, by the Cubans against the Spanish in the 1870s and

1890s, by the Boers against the British at the turn of the century, by Vietnamese against French and Americans since 1945, and by the home forces in other wars of colonisation or liberation. The western answer to guerrilla warfare was invariably to send out reinforcements, but the despatch of troopships and supply ships was always costly and often slow. Long colonial wars required ultimately many more regiments than had originally been envisaged.

All the long colonial wars proclaimed that the expectations of at least one, and perhaps both sides, had been too optimistic. France for example had begun the Algerian war for a limited goal. She believed that by quickly capturing the main harbours she would control Algeria. She was slow to realise that parts of the interior had to be occupied in order to safeguard the ports: when that truth was at last accepted, inadequate forces were sent. The war was therefore prolonged because a succession of French ministries were slow to realise that victory demanded more money and men. It is understandable that a European power fighting a colonial war – a war where the prizes of victory, though attractive, were not usually glamorous – should hope to devote only part of that effort which would normally be given to a war against a major power. Whereas defeat in a war against a major power could be disastrous, defeat in a colonial war was simply humiliating. Indeed ultimate defeat at the hands of races regarded as backward was often difficult to imagine; and that disbelief helped to confine the scale of the forces employed against a colonial race.

The capacity of an 'advanced nation' to conquer quickly was often retarded by its liberalism and its respect for human life. When the French in 1830 captured the city of Algiers, they issued a manifesto of toleration:

'The exercise of the Mahometan religion shall remain free. The liberty of the inhabitants of all classes, their religion, their property, their commerce, their industry, shall be inviolate; their women shall be respected: the General-in-chief promises this upon his honour.'

Although a nation professing these principles often failed to honour them entirely, these principles thwarted campaigns against an unorthodox enemy. France's relative tolerance towards Algerican civilians who aided Abd-el-Kader or who engaged in terrorist activities in French-occupied towns enabled the enemy to resist more effectively. The same restraint is visible in Indo-China in the last quarter century. If the French and the Americans, in their governing of occupied areas, had applied the more ruthless methods adopted by Germany and Japan during the Second World War, the war in Vietnam might have been more decisive. In South Vietnam in the 1960s the smaller forces of South Koreans were more efficient – in other words more ruthless – than the Americans in eliminating enemies from occupied zones;* and their success pinpointed indirectly one reason why the United States had difficulty in restoring order in South Vietnam.

Some colonial or imperialist wars were prolonged by the crusade of critics who hoped to shorten the war. In France an anti-war party became vocal in the 1830s, and when the French campaign in Algeria was frustrated the critics of the war called for peace. They simply enquired whether the war was worth the expense. Their opposition to the war tended to be loudest in those frustrating times when the ministry hoped to despatch more troops in the hope of forcing a quick victory. If the opposition was strong, and if the ministry, like so many French ministries, was tottering, reinforcements were less likely to be sent. The war controversy which was so audible in Paris in the 1830s and 1840s was to be heard again when France fought unsuccessfully in Indo-China a century later, and was to be even louder in Washington when Americans suffered similar reverses in the same territory. It seems that much of the homeland opposition to wars in faraway lands is more an aversion to the lack of success of the military expedition than an aversion to war itself. Ironically this

* The significance of the massacre of unarmed Vietnamese civilians at My Lai in 1968 and the subsequent investigation was two-fold. It was firstly a revelation of the methods which American troops sometimes employed against insurgency, and secondly an indication that these methods were not officially approved.

opposition, by lessening the prospect of reinforcements, sometimes prolonged the war.

In contrast when Britain fought the two Boer Republics between 1899 and 1902 she was aided by a high level of support and even of jingoism at home. Though an anti-war party flourished in Britain it was far from as vigorous as the similar parties which harried the French and United States' governments when their forces fought in Algeria or Indo-China. Popular enthusiasm for the Boer War was high in Britain and in many parts of the British Empire: from the Australian colonies went an army of volunteers consisting of one in every fifty men of military age; the support for the war was also reflected in the size of the British armies which sailed to South Africa. In the history of modern warfare it is doubtful whether any invading army was so large in relation to the enemy's population, both military and civilian. Thus in the final phase of guerrilla warfare Britain's army was large enough to master the Boer commandos. If that mastery, however, had come more slowly, the anti-war party in Britain would have become more influential.

One other clue to the forces prolonging certain colonial wars is clear. The long overseas wars were fought when peace prevailed in Europe. One may enquire whether the European peace helped to prolong colonial wars or whether colonial wars helped to prolong the European peace. Both arguments are feasible. France for instance was so heavily committed in some years to the war in Algeria that she possibly was reluctant to take risks in European diplomacy. At the same time the peace in Europe enabled France to continue fighting in Algeria. If a major war had come to Europe when a western nation was absorbed in a costly colonial campaign, that campaign almost certainly would have been terminated.

A long list of conditions seems to determine whether a colonial war will be short or long. If to the list are added the vital intangibles – morale and leadership and the unforeseen events which sway battles – the complication increases. Nevertheless one observation may help to simplify the list. The long colonial wars, though usually involving only two contenders, had the characteristics of general wars fought in

Europe.* The factors which tended to prolong many-sided wars in Europe resembled those which prolonged two-sided wars outside Europe. In the long colonial wars fighting was on many fronts – this is almost a definition of guerrilla warfare – and so neither side was likely to be winning simultaneously on every front. Similarly, unexpected causes equalised the effective military strength of the two sides, though one side was enormously more powerful on paper. Agreement on the terms of a peace was also difficult to reach because in colonial wars the aims of the two sides were utterly incompatible. What was at stake for one side was the right of national independence – a right which in Europe was disputed only in bitter general wars such as the Napoleonic Wars and the Second World War.

Above all, the long colonial wars, like Europe's general wars, were insulated from outside interference. They were insulated partly by the remoteness of the theatre of war but more by the strength of the western power which engaged in each of these long wars. When France fought in Algeria between 1830 and 1847 her army was widely respected as the foremost in the world; when Britain fought the Boers her navy was all-powerful; when the United States intervened in Vietnam her air force had no equal. Thus, when a western nation fought in a colonial war, rarely was it opposed directly by another western nation. One of the rare exceptions was when the United States intervened on behalf of the Cubans in 1898 and went to war against Spain. Significantly that intervention was unusually easy, for Spain was a second-ranking power and moreover the theatre of war was closer to the United States than to Spain. Thus the Cuban war lacked that insulation which helped to prolong other colonial wars. In Europe wars between two sides were often cut short by fear that a stronger power would intervene; outside Europe some colonial wars were prolonged partly because there was no such fear.

* They also had the characteristics of long civil wars in large countries: for instance the Taiping Rebellion in China 1851–64 or the Chinese civil wars of 1916–36 and 1946–49.

14: And Shorter Wars

In Europe in the ninety-nine years between the Battle of Waterloo and the First World War, most wars were short. The Seven Weeks War was one of the most remarkable events of that century but it was only one of a growing list of short wars. In the 1880s came an even shorter war, a fierce fortnight of fighting between Serbia and Bulgaria. In the 1890s Greece and Turkey fought near their hilly border, and many foreign correspondents barely had time to reach the battlefront before they were cabling home the news that the thirty days war had ended. If the average European war of the nineteenth century had been as long as the average war of the previous century, few people who lived through the age of Darwin, Bismarck, Marx, and Edison would have hailed it as peaceful. A vital part of the explanation of the relative peace of those fortunate generations is simply that wars in Europe were short.

To Europeans one of the astonishing facets of that age of mechanical marvels was the speed of warfare. Indeed the swiftness of wars was largely seen as the belated result of the industrial revolution. The new machines, it was argued, had transformed fighting. In men-of-war the steam engine was replacing sails, and iron was replacing wood. On land the railways were replacing baggage carts, and the electric telegraph superseded the despatch courier. The organisation of armies was more efficient and their equipment was transformed by breech-loading rifles, machine-guns and enormous cannon. The weapons had been so sharpened that by 1900 most European observers believed that the long war belonged to the past, to the age when soldiers carried powderbags and officers wore lace cuffs.

Even before the lightning victories of Prussia in her wars of 1864, 1866 and 1870, the innovations of the machine age seemed to be favouring quick victory. The war between Austria and France in 1859 encouraged the idea that a few decisive battles would constitute a modern war. Colonel Charles Chesney, professor of military history at the Staff College at Sandhurst and sometimes acclaimed as England's finest military critic, welcomed the new type of warfare with the sense of wonder of an archer who had just seen his first rifle. He viewed the new technology not only as labour-saving but as life-saving. From 'the prolonged horrors' of a Thirty Years War, he wrote, the world at last had been delivered. The new warfare now decided the fate of nations 'in the first few days of conflict'. Even in January 1866 he was certain that 'with advancing civilisation, increased wealth, more rapid and certain communication, strategy will increase its sphere and become bolder and more decisive'. His argument was almost a Sandhurst version of the Manchester prophesy; whereas many merchants thought that technological civilisation was weakening the appeal to war, many soldiers thought that it was fostering swifter and less-dislocating wars.

The Seven Weeks War between Austria and Prussia seemed to confirm Chesney's optimism. The Prussian invasion of Austrian territory began in mid-June, 1866; on a modern map it was a southwards thrust from East Germany and Poland on to the Czechoslovak plains. In less than three weeks more than 200,000 Prussians and more than 200,000 Austrians and Saxons faced one another at Sadowa, near the river Elbe. Probably the two largest armies that had ever met on the one field, they began battle in the rainy morning of 3 July, and by 4.30 in the afternoon the Austrians were retreating, leaving behind as captives or corpses more than one fifth of their men. Three weeks later Austria and Prussia accepted peace.

While Prussia's war of 1866 showed the speed of the new breech-loading rifle over the Austrians' muzzle-loader, Prussia's war of 1870 showed how meticulous organising of a railway system could rush a great army to the front. The speed with which Prussia launched her attack shocked the French and astonished military observers throughout Europe. In about seventeen days Germany railed to the front 440,000 men, 135,000 horses and 14,000 vehicles and guns: a clockwork procession of 1,200 trains. The Prussians celebrated the end of the second month of the war by beginning the siege of Paris. One of the most decisive wars fought in modern history, it seemed to hammer the message that the new military techniques were deadly.

The succession of short wars continued; between 1860 and 1914, the nine wars in Europe were all virtually over in a year. The same half century witnessed longer wars, but they were fought in the Americas. In the 1860s three wars – the American Civil War, the Paraguayan War, and the French expedition to Mexico – had each lasted for at least four years, and in 1879 Chile and Bolivia and Peru began their War of the Pacific which flared and smouldered for four years. As these wars had been fought outside Europe, and as only the Mexican war involved a European army, they unfortunately did not disturb the widening belief that wars would become shorter and shorter. They were often dismissed as wars in which the new military technology had not been sufficiently applied. Nevertheless they offered at least one unnoticed lesson. They were insulated by ocean or by political circumstances from interference by outsiders. They lacked those pressures which in Europe were tending to terminate wars.

While many wars in Europe illustrated the decisive effect of new weapons and means of transport, it was easy to exaggerate those effects. In at least half of the European wars after 1815 the losing nation, when the armistice was signed, was still capable of continuing to fight vigorously. The victors however offered them moderate terms partly in the fear that an outside nation might interfere and snatch away their gains. In 1859 France was content with a minor victory over Austria because the Prussians seemed likely to side with Austria if the war went on. Even Prussia and Austria, in their swift war against Denmark in 1864, knew the dangers of French or British intervention on the side of the vanquished. And Prussia in 1866 was alert to the danger that France might come to the aid of the Austrian forces which were

withdrawing towards Vienna. As Bismarck told members of
the Prussian lower house:

> You all know what I mean. Nobody could expect us to
> carry on two wars at the same time. Peace with Austria had
> not yet been concluded; were we to imperil the fruits of
> our glorious campaign by plunging headlong into hostil-
> ities with a new, a second enemy?

Those who attempted to explain the shortness of European
wars were inclined to forget Bismarck's words and to remember only the speed of the needle-guns, or the neat procession
of Prussian troop trains. They therefore did not observe a
more important reason why the short war had become normal
in Europe.

III

The belief that future wars would be short became a dogma,
but it was not completely ascendant. The most withering
attack on the dogma was made by, of all people, a banker who
lived in the Russian-ruled city of Warsaw. When Ivan S.
Bloch issued in 1897 and 1898 a six-volumed work on war, his
voice at first seemed like a frog in a backwater, croaking at
the hoot of a passing steamer. Here was a businessman, telling
strategists what to expect. He suggested that the next major
war in Europe would be a long and murderous siege. He envisaged huge unwieldy armies spread along an enormous
front and firing with such speed and accuracy that the sur-
vivors had to find shelter in trenches. 'It will be a great war of
entrenchments,' he said. 'The spade will be as indispensable
to a soldier as his rifle. The first thing every man will have to
do, if he cares for his life at all, will be to dig a hole in the
ground.' The gap between the two entrenched armies would
be so pierced by bullets that no army could hope to storm the
enemy's trenches. In the words of a French captain he
quoted, the front line would be a 'belt of a thousand paces
swept by a crossfire of shells which no living being can pass.'
Neither side would win that monstrous battle. While the
stalemate continued in the trenches, the civilian population

would suffer. Food would become scarce, prices would rise, morale in the cities would quake. Peace would eventually come, Bloch predicted, through famine and socialist or anarchist upheavals, leaving no nation with victory.

As a scholar of warfare Ivan Bloch was a genius. His must have been one of the most remarkable predictions ever made in the field of human behaviour. So many events of the Great War – the muddy trenches of Flanders and Galicia, the millions of casualties, the socialist revolutions in Russia, the overthrow of the Russian and Austrian and German monarchies, the scarce victories on the battlefield – were consistent with his predictions. Above all he predicted a calamitous and long war: that he should have designated a war lasting at least two years as 'a long war' was a sign of the prevailing faith that future wars would last only a few months.

In making these predictions Bloch culled his evidence from the same recent wars which had persuaded others to see the short war as inevitable. Whereas others had plucked from the Franco-Prussian war the simple lesson that modern wars were decisive and swift, Bloch observed more the revolution which broke out during the indecisive siege of Paris in 1870–1. Whereas others simply marvelled at the swiftness of the Russian victory over the Turks in 1877, Bloch observed how the hasty Turkish entrenchments at Plevna, near the Danube, had thwarted the Russian invaders for several months. But there were sharper differences between Bloch and most other analysts of war. He did not believe that past wars were a reliable guide to a future war between major European powers. A major war in Europe, he believed, would probably involve Russia and France on the one side and Germany, Austria and Italy on the other. As each alliance had about five million fighting men and as their armaments were similar and as their frontiers were heavily fortified and as military techniques now favoured the defenders, neither alliance would have sufficient strength to break through the opposing defences. 'The war of the future, whatever may be said, will be a struggle for fortified positions, and for that reason it must be prolonged.' Bloch also believed that another set of influences would ultimately intervene and terminate the war. Those influences were economic. Famine and inflation would set in more quickly and devastatingly than in previous wars, for the economy of Europe had changed. The economic changes would be most effective, he argued, in a general war, for nations would be unable to borrow gold and food because of the lack of lenders. In the Europe of mass armies, he argued, 'you cannot feed your people and wage a great war'.

W. T. Stead, the London journalist who wrote the preface for Bloch's only volume that was translated into English, gave a quick sketch of the man in 1899. Bloch was of benevolent appearance, middling build, and 'between fifty and sixty years of age'. Did he shoot deer, play the harpsichord or take snuff? The only other snippet we learn about the man whose head was a card index of armaments is that in Paris he stayed at the Grand Hotel and in St Petersburg at the Hotel d'Europe.

The Boer War, which began late in 1899, offered a testing ground for the rival predictions of the future of warfare. At his home in Warsaw or in the reading room of his favourite hotel, Bloch followed the prolonged fighting on the faraway veldt. The short-war school explained away the length of the Boer War by pointing to South Africa's isolation and terrain – conditions not relevant to future fighting in Europe – or to the inadequacy of a British army which had not fought a major war for more than forty years, or to Britain's difficulty in fighting far across the sea. Bloch, his theory at stake, replied in 1901. He deplored the reluctance of military observers to cull the correct lessons from the Boer War. The lesson, to his mind, was overwhelming. Here was the first war in which the new smokeless powder and the small-bore rifle had been employed on a large scale. British and Boer soldiers knew only too clearly that the trajectory of bullets fired from those rifles and the invisiblity of the men who fired them – for the absence of smoke disguised the source of the firing – made firepower devastating. In Bloch's opinion success now favoured the defenders even when outnumbered by four to one. The defender, by digging trenches for his own protection and by erecting barbed wire in order to expose the attacker even longer to his firepower, could halt those swift advances which had marked the final stages of recent wars. What was happening to small forces on the grasslands of

South Africa would be more visible, he predicted, in European wars. He reaffirmed that economic rather than military strength would decide future wars, but even the economic strength of the German Ruhr and the Russian wheatlands was not adequate 'for the length of time that a war under present conditions must last'.

Ivan Bloch died in 1902, before the Boer War ended. He was very much a debater and, deprived of the right of reply, his arguments became less compelling. Certainly they did not die. They were translated into many languages, and a version reached a wide audience in the English-speaking world through H. G. Wells, a novelist who felt the pulse of applied science. Many soldiers now agreed that war had ceased to be an efficient way of settling disputes. Bloch himself had liked to quote the opinion of General von der Goltz because an officer's opinion, and especially that of a German officer, had more punch than a civilian's opinion. 'One may safely say', said von der Goltz, 'that wars cannot end otherwise than in the utter annihilation of one, or the complete exhaustion of both belligerents.'

The Russo-Japanese war of 1904-5 suggested that trenches and barbed wire entanglements and the deadly firepower of new machine-guns and quick-firing artillery were tending to halt mobility, but they did not prevent an early and victorious outcome to the war. The Italo-Turk War of 1911-1912, and the two Balkans wars which were fought on European soil by large armies with powerful weapons, were even shorter. The wars since 1900 had offered a contradictory set of lessons, one of which favoured Bloch's warning of the increasing power of the defensive, and the other favouring the belief in short wars. As Bloch's prediction concerned only a war in Europe between the rival alliances of great powers, it had been neither proved nor disproved.

On the eve of the Great War the faith in the warhorse epitomised the prevailing opinion of the future of warfare. A cavalry charge was most effective when the defenders' fire-arms had a small range, dubious accuracy and sluggish methods of re-loading. In 1840 the smooth-bore Brown Bess had an effective range of only two hundred yards, and that length of ground could be quickly crossed by the oncoming cavalry. By 1900 the danger zone for cavalry was four or five times as long, and so for several minutes the approaching cavalry was exposed to the slaughter of rifles and machine-guns. As the number of rounds which could be fired in a minute had increased from about two in a Brown Bess to 700 in a Maxim machine-gun, and as accuracy had improved, the cavalry was running a lethal gauntlet.

During the Boer War the British cavalry sensibly discarded the sword and the lance, but after the war the lance edged back into cavalry training and, when so ordered, even into field service. Britain's *Cavalry Training Manual* of 1907 still sang a hallelujah to the warhorse: 'the rifle, effective as it is, cannot replace the effect produced by the speed of the horse, the magnetism of the charge, and the terror of cold steel'. Britain's faith in the warhorse waned slightly in the following seven years, but many of her military leaders envisaged the charge of cavalry against infantrymen who were low in morale as one of the events which would determine victory in a coming war. In 1914 cavalry was highly favoured in Austria and France, strongly favoured in Britain, and less enthusiastically favoured in Germany.

Of those European generals who tried to predict the future role of cavalry, few doubted its value even in an era of devastating firepower. Some argued that the warhorse was more important than for many decades. Colonel F. N. Maude, who lectured in military history at Manchester University and reached a vast audience through his military writings, believed the warhorse would triumph in the next major war. To the argument that machine-guns and rifles would decimate the oncoming cavalry, he replied optimistically: 'great though the increase of range of modern infantry weapons had been, the speed and endurance of cavalry has increased in a yet higher ratio'. He explained that in Napoleon's day the advancing lines of cavalry were expected to trot for 800 yards and gallop the last 200 yards. Now, however, they could trot for 8000 yards – or nearly five miles – and then gallop for more than one mile in their final assault on demoralised foot soldiers.

Colonel Maude predicted a short and dashing war. Battles would be won by the nation which managed to amass its big guns in long lines and so would rout the enemy with superior firepower. Cavalry, in escorting its own artilley or harrying the enemy's, would determine which side succeeded in massing its artillery most favourably. On the collisions of cavalry in the early stage of battle 'will hang the fate of the battle and ultimately of the nation'.

Many of these arguments were familiar not only to generals but to thousands of the soldiers who would be called upon to fight the war. Europe's bookshops increasingly sold a kind of science fiction which prophesied that the next major war would be short. In England the first of the new forecasts was written by Sir George Chesney who, returning from those Indian parade grounds where cavalry pranced, was surprised by the way Germany defeated France in 1870. In the following year *Blackwood's Magazine* published his anonymous article, the 'Battle of Dorking', which imagined a German invasion of England. That was the forerunner of scores of books which depicted future wars, especially Anglo-French wars, in which scientific weapons quickly crushed armies. The intermittent war-scares in Europe spurred authors to write vivid timetables of what each feared war would be like, Thus the Tangier crisis of 1905 filled a shelf with German and English books, of which William Le Queux's depiction of a German invasion of Britain was the most popular; *The Invasion of 1910* was bought by more than one million readers and was translated into twenty-seven languages. These futuristic books on the coming First World War have been analysed by I. F. Clarke in his recent *Voices Prophesying War*; he concluded that most of these books 'reflected the general view, based on the experiences of 1870 and the Balkan wars, that a decisive battle or two would quickly end hostilities'.

IV

The optimism was also kindled by economic arguments. Many bankers and businessmen thought that a scarcity of gold or credit would soon end the war. Edgar Crammond, addressing the London Chamber of Commerce in 1911, was inclined to foresee warfare lasting a mere six months. An editorial in the London magazine *United Empire* in September 1914 reminded readers that gold served as the sinews of modern war: 'The amounts of coin and bullion which were in the hands of the continental Great Powers at the outbreak of hostilities is a matter of great importance, not only in determining the intensity with which operations may be carried on, but also the probable duration of the war.' *The Times* of London had already issued the same warning in the first week of the war by pointing out that an Englishman who hoarded gold – thus reducing the nation's effective stock – did more to help the enemy than if he had actually enlisted in the enemy's army. The emphasis on gold reads a little strangely today, but in 1914 gold was respected as the indispensable disciplinarian of economic life. In wartime an ample stock of gold could facilitate the importing of essential supplies and, above all, check inflation. In many eyes gold was the enemy of economic and social chaos.

Even those who did not emphasise the importance of gold saw financial factors – in a wider sense – as a guarantee that the war would soon be over. A best-selling book of 1910, written by an English journalist named Norman Angell, had described large-scale war as *The Great Illusion* because it seemed to be no longer profitable. Many readers of his book accepted his pessimistic premiss but optimistically believed nations would end a war before destruction became enormous. In September 1914 *The Economist* of London, perhaps the most respected journal of finance, discounted Lord Kitchener's prediction of a long war by stressing 'the economic and financial impossibility of carrying on hostilities for many months on the present scale'. That doubt was repeated again and again in the early months of the war. *The Economist* hopefully detected financial strain in Vienna and Berlin; it reported that the Reichsbank had issued so many banknotes that their value was diminishing, and that the huge public loans raised in Berlin to meet the soaring cost of the war were no sooner collected than they were spent. The journal predicted the collapse of the German financial system and an early end to the war. In 1915 an Englishman, F. W. Hirst, writing one of the few studies on the economics of war since Adam Smith, reiterated the financial predictions. Though collapse might not come as quickly as had been expected, it would still come, and the effects would be terrible: 'What will be the condition of Europe, when peace comes through exhaustion, after the continental states have used up all their credit and borrowed all that can be borrowed, may be left to the imagination.'

With the experience of two world wars behind us, these financial predictions appear misguided. In 1914, however, the gloom was understandable. Banking and finance were viewed as a delicate mechanism which worked best when interfered with least. For a government to interfere too often was said to be perilous; heavy borrowing and taxing were hazardous. And yet the war was to prove that the mechanism was tougher and more versatile than had been predicted. The war showed that most people could tolerate unbalanced budgets, huge government loans, rising prices, the rationing of food, high taxes and all those economic dragons so dreaded in 1914. The fracturing point of society came much later than those reared in the long peace of the nineteenth century could envisage.

Other prophets expected the war of 1914 to be terminated less by monetary bedlam than by a breakdown in production and commerce. European nations, in their pre-war commerce, depended on one another more than ever before. They also relied heavily on importing much of their food and raw materials from the new world. War would tear these neat patterns of trade and the regular shipment of goods from the Atlantic, Pacific and Indian Oceans. It was expected that some of the warring nations would soon be knocked out by shortage of food, munitions or arms. In Russia at the outbreak of the war the fear of dislocation almost caused panic. As one contemporary observer of Russia noted: 'Everywhere a world-wide economic collapse was regarded as inevitable, and the supposition was that it would occur in a matter of only a few months.' When it occurred, the war would almost certainly cease.

As it later became common to deride high-ranking soldiers for not foreseeing the long duration of the First World War – as if 'soldier' is a synonym for stupidity – it is sobering to discover that so many economists and financiers could not foresee a long war. Optimism even seems to have flavoured the war predictions of surgeons. 'It is indubitable', wrote the medical scientist Sir Almroth Wright, 'that if before the outbreak of war a consensus of surgical opinion had been taken on the question as to whether grave and universal infection of wounds was in prospect, it would in view of the experience gained in the South African War and in the accident wards of civil hospitals have been confidently asserted that such sepsis was a thing that belonged to the past.' Instead the manured farmlands which were fought upon, the mud and excreta of the trenches, and the velocity of bullets and shrapnel fired by powerful weapons at close quarters, combined to confound such predictions. 'In this War', wrote Wright in 1915, 'practically every wound is heavily infected.' Most of our predictions are simply projections of recent experience; they are assertions that recent history will repeat itself. Most predictions of war follow that pattern.*

v

In 1914 Germany's military leaders were not disciples of Bloch. They did not envisage deadlocked warfare. Their plan of attack, a more cautious version of the plan made by Count Alfred von Schlieffen before he retired as chief of the general staff in 1906, envisaged that a section of the German forces would hold Russia on the eastern front while the main German forces made a lightning thrust on the western front. According to Schlieffen's plan the spearhead of that western thrust was to be a great wheeling movement through Luxembourg, Belgium and northern France, and so past Paris itself. Meanwhile the left wing of the German forces – a mere 15 per cent of those engaged in the great wheeling movement on the right wing – were to fight a rearguard action against the French in Alsace and Lorraine where ultimately, it was hoped, the French would be overwhelmed from the rear by the completion of the great wheeling movement of the armies that passed through Belgium and northern France. Schlieffen's successor, General Helmuth von Moltke, thinking – perhaps wisely – that the plan was too risky, preferred

* So much of this chapter was devoted to the long debate on the likely duration of the next world war because this seemed the easiest way to crystallise the factors which were believed to shorten or prolong wars.

to strengthen the left wing at the expense of the right wing. The right wing was therefore weakened. When the war began and the Germans commenced their wheeling movement through Belgium and the north of France, they lacked the strength to make the thrust really decisive; their strength was further sapped by Moltke's decision in the first month of the war to rush reinforcements from his right wing in France to the eastern front against the Russians. Nevertheless the German advance was so powerful that it almost reached Paris before it was halted and even pushed back in places.

In the first month the fighting had displayed the mobility which most military leaders had anticipated. That countryside through which the German army had advanced and then, in the face of the French revival, had retreated, resembled engravings of the battlefields of Italy after the short war of 1859. Here were the same scenes which had inspired the early prophets of the short war to argue that warfare henceforth would be like passing thunderstorms which left the landscape – once the corpses had been buried – relatively unscathed. Visitors to the Marne at the end of September 1914, observing a landscape which had been twice crossed by two great armies in the previous month, could see French villages wrecked by shellfire and bridges blown up, a dead horse slightly covered by straw and dead soldiers here and there, but overall the impression was one of peacefulness and life. The crops stood high, the trees were heavy with apples and pears, the grapes were ripening on the vines, and the bodies of thousands of dead lay beneath the earth.

Further north and east a new landscape was gardened. The ebb and flow of attack and counter-attack ceased as armies dug trenches and gained that protection which they could not obtain in open fighting. Spades and coils of barbed wire turned the western front into long fortified pits. The opposing lines of trenches ran almost continuously from the North Sea to Switzerland. Temporary defences, they became permanent. Between October 1914 and March 1918 – a period of three and a half years – the mammoth attempts to break through the entrenchments pushed the front no more than a few miles this way or that. Whenever troops tried to storm forward they were exposed to such a whirlwind of fire that casualties were prodigious. In 1916 the German offensive along twenty miles of front at Verdun advanced five miles – a mere kink in the long line of entrenchments. Those five miles cost the German and French an average of more than 120,000 casualties for each mile. In the same year the Battle of the Somme along a thirty-mile front achieved a maximum penetration of seven miles; but the price of that devastated strip of land was almost one million British, French and German casualties.

A war which was expected to illustrate the decisiveness of mechanical weapons – machine-guns, artillery, mortars and quick-firing rifles – quickly subsided into the trenches that typified the vanished era of sieges. Ironically, trench fighting often called for primitive weapons; the Imperial War Museum in London displays a strange collection of the trench clubs roughly shaped by soldiers for hand-to-hand fighting on the western front. There are batons with nails protruding from the head, clubs studded with iron rivets, and wooden clubs that resemble the top half of a baseball bat. If they had been displayed without a label, visitors would probably have regarded most of them as weapons of Charlemagne's or Caesar's armies.

The cavalry was not the dramatic influence which so many had prophesied. On the Russian front and in Mesopotamia the wider spaces made cavalry useful and often vital. On the western front mounted troops were often employed, especially to hurry to sudden gaps in the defences, but overall they had become a minor arm of warfare. The western front experienced no great clashes of cavalry; there were few retreats in which the cavalry could act as the terrifying pursuers or as defenders of the pursued. Once the trenches had been dug for the best part of 500 miles, no space remained in which cavalry could outflank the enemy. Once the tangles of barbed wire had been erected, the frontal assault by cavalry was futile. Even the task of reconnaissance passed from horses to aircraft. Meanwhile hundreds of squadrons of cavalry waited behind the opposing lines, in readiness for the pursuit that might suddenly begin. Of the huge tonnage of munitions and supplies shipped from England to France in the four years of war, the main item was horsefeed. And yet at the war's end faith in the value of cavalry was revived in some quarters. Sir Douglas Haig's last despatch, written on the morning of the armistice in 1918, described two British cavalry divisions pursuing the Germans east of the River Scheldt when suddenly they were told that the war had ended. Their morning of trumph, lamented Haig, had been snatched away:

> 'There is no doubt that, had the advance of the cavalry been allowed to continue, the enemy's disorganised retreat would have been turned into a rout.'

On the eastern front the trenches and wire did not appear so quickly nor was the fighting deadlocked month after month. The long frontline, running about 650 miles from the Baltic Sea to the frontiers of neutral Rumania, perhaps gave more space for flanking movements by Russian and Austro-German armies. There the war swayed backwards and forwards until the winter of 1915–16 when most of the troops settled into trenches. Warfare flowed again when the Rumanians joined the Russians in 1916, and on that elongated front that linked the Baltic and the Black Sea decisive advances were made until the Russians sought their armistice in 1917. The massive casualties on the eastern front were partly a reflection of the more intense winters and the absence of the protective shield which trenches provided.

Politicians as well as generals were blamed for the indecisive warfare on the western front. Many politicians had not realised the importance of an adequate supply of munitions: and after one month of fighting the artillery at many points of the western front lacked shells at the very time when heavy shelling might have aided momentum. Politicians retaliated by blaming military leaders for their inability to end the deadlock. 'Confronted with this deadlock', wrote Winston Churchill, 'military art remained dumb.' Churchill's was one of the voices which sought a partial solution to the deadlock by proposing a new theatre of war against the enemy. In April 1915 a British fleet and an Anglo-French army tried to break through the Dardanelles: the only result of the Gallipoli campaign was the loss through death or capture or illness of 252,000 British, French, Australian and New Zealand soldiers, and perhaps twice as many Turks. In another corner of the Balkans an attempt to open a new spearhead had little success until the last months of the war when the Bulgarians were suddenly defeated, exposing Constantinople to the danger of a quick overland thrust.

Back on the western front the Germans, in an attempt to break through, released chlorine gas against the enemy's trenches in 1915 and mustard gas in 1917. Of the casualties suffered by the Americans one in every four was inflicted by gas; but only one of every fifty Americans who were gassed died from the effects. 'Contrary to common belief', wrote Major-General J. F. C. Fuller, 'gas was the most humane weapon used in the war, and one of the most effective.' When the Germans in March 1918 made the first deep bulge in the lines of trenches, pushing back the British almost forty miles in one section of the western front, they relied heavily on the avalanche of gas shells fired by their artillery. And when the British made their great drive through the entrenchments later that year they relied heavily on tanks; here at last was a moving shield which gave the attacker that protection which accurate firepower made essential. The tank and the gas bombardment had eased the stalemate; but when the war ended in November 1918, the opposing lines on the western front were still continuous for three hundred miles, and only a few of those miles were on German soil. Perhaps the war had been ended less by grave defeats on the battlefields than by collapse and rebellion within Germany and Austria.

VI

For half a century before the First World War students of war had discussed – more than ever before or after – the conditions which prolonged or shortened wars.* After 1918 the

---

* This discussion, it should be said, was more academic and impartial than discussions that went on within national palaces and ministries on the eve of wars. The academic discussion, of which Chesney of Sandhurst and Bloch of Warsaw were opposite flagbearers, centred on general principles. On the other hand the discussions within a ruling group on the eve of war were characterised more by the belief that their nation was a principle to itself and so somewhat exempt from the operations of

post-mortems cemented the conclusions. Among those who asked why that war had been so long, the answer was almost unanimous. The stalemate in the trenches had prolonged the war; the long swing in technology had swung back to the defensive. That was the verdict of gifted soldiers and military historians who scanned the First World War for the more accurate lessons it might offer. As some of these lessons – culled by the Englishmen Sir Basil Liddell Hart and Major-General J. F. C. Fuller – were to influence Germany's successful offensives in the Second World War, their interpretation of the previous great war gained additional respect with the passing of time.

In essence these soldiers and military historians argued that the pattern of fighting in the first World War could have been predicted or avoided by studying earlier wars. General Sir Ian Hamilton, writing in the 1920s, regretted the refusal to learn lessons from the Boer War in which he had fought and the Russo-Japanese war in which he had been an official observer with the Japanese army. He recalled that Lord Kitchener, who directed the British forces from 1914, was more fascinated by ancient porcelain than by new firearms:

> On his way home from the Manchurian campaign in March 1905, the British officer who had been attached to the Japanese Army was ordered to break journey at Calcutta, so that the Govt. of India might learn the latest developments of war at first hand. But once Lord Kitchener realised that there was no blue china in Feng-hwang-cheng he lost interest in the subject; it was Lord Curzon [the Viceroy of India] who wished to hear about the 11-in. howitzers, the barbed wire and the trench mortars.

Hamilton summed up the failure to see the impact of new weapons in one memorable sentence. 'Never, in the history of the art of war, has the world been treated to so much war and so little art as in the conduct of the World War.' Similarly

---

those factors which were believed to prolong or shorten wars. Germany or Russia in 1914 had faith in their military superiority and, as suggested in a previous chapter, the expected dividend of their military superiority was a short war.

Field-Marshal Earl Wavell, Field-Marshal Lord Montgomery and Major-General Fuller believed that if European soldiers of 1914 had studied more closely the field operations of the Russo-Turk war of 1877 or the later Boer or Russo-Japanese wars they might have expected a long war. And Sir Basil Liddell Hart suggested that if they had studied carefully the actual field campaigns of the American Civil War they might have learnt 'to expect and prepare for a long war, even if hoping for a short war'.

Through the generosity of Fuller and Liddell Hart the name of Ivan Bloch, now almost forgotten, was resurrected. It is not clear however whether they knew – or we know – why many of Bloch's military predictions had come to pass. Bloch had not plucked his predictions simply from the field operations of earlier wars, though he used those wars as supporting evidence. He had had the imagination to sense that a major war in Europe would be deadlocked because of the greater armies available, the defences that could be dug, and the lack of space for the outflanking of defenders. These peculiarities of a major European war, when combined with the deadliness of modern weapons, made him predict a stalemate.

It is not detracting from Bloch's genius to suggest that the stalemate in the trenches may also have come from events and facets of war which he did not probably envisage. He had predicted that Germany and Austria and Italy would form one alliance and Russia and France the other; but many additional nations – some of them great nations – were actually involved in the war. One cannot be certain that the stalemate in the trenches would have been so widespread or so prolonged if the war had been confined to five nations. A war confined to five nations might have taken different turning points and exhausted its manpower more quickly. Certainly the distribution of military strength would then have favoured more strongly the German alliance and perhaps produced a more mobile and more decisive war. Nor could Bloch, when he wrote, possibly envisage the rise of German naval power, nor could he foresee the effects on the First World War of German superiority under the water. Germany's power on the Baltic and, through the Turkish alliance, her command of the narrow Dardanelles, blocked the outer flanks and heightened the importance of the existing western and eastern fronts, and so increased the prospect of deadlock. All these are speculations – their influence is open to endless debate and the weighing of many alternatives of what might have happened. To my mind stalemated warfare, in the light of the soundest evidence available on 1 August 1914, was a strong possibility rather than a probability.

Furthermore, warfare between 1914 and 1918 was not quite as indecisive as Bloch had predicted* nor as his later admirers assumed. To most citizens of France, Britain and the United States the centre of fighting in the war was the western front, and since that was static for almost four years they tended to believe that fighting everywhere was static. The fact that the British and French forces were also pinned on the hills of Gallipoli increased the idea that the whole war was stalemated. Outside those two fronts however the fighting was more mobile. Thus the German and Austrian armies in the east pushed back the Russians several hundred miles in Poland and White Russia, and over 100 miles along the Baltic. They also quickly overran Serbia and Rumania. In Asia Minor the Russians won a wedge of Turkey extending some 300 miles south-east of the Black Sea towards the Persian Gulf, and the British won wedges of territory from the Turks in Palestine and Mesopotamia. These advances seem slow and the distances covered seem small to those who remember the advances during the Second World War, but they were still considerable. It is worth remembering that an advance of 200 miles against an opposing army was an unusual achievement in the main wars between 1815 and 1914. In that century the famous thrusts – the Prussian march to Paris in 1870, the Russian drive towards Constantinople in 1877, or the Japanese thrust into Manchuria in 1904 – covered a distance no longer than some of the slower advances of the First World War. Except for that terrifying ordeal on the western front, the First World War would not have been remembered for its static warfare. Nor would those techniques

---

* Even on the western front storming troops often crossed that no-man's-land of death which Bloch predicted would be impassable, and they accordingly defied his belief that 'the day of the bayonet is over'.

of warfare have been selected as the main cause of the long duration of that war.

Even if the chiefs of staff of Europe had prepared for a different kind of war, and even if soldiers had resorted only briefly to the shield of trenches and earthworks, the war would probably still have been long; it might even have lasted more than four years. That can be said with some confidence. Indeed the one principle which seems to have remained outside the debate that preceded and succeeded the First World War is the principle that general wars tend to be long wars. In Europe, in every age, wars involving many states have been longer than international wars involving only two or three states. Even when warfare was decisive, even when the long swings in techniques and tactics of warfare favoured the attack, general wars tended to be longer. Thus despite the swing to the offensive, the Revolutionary and Napoleonic wars were long. Despite the swing back to the defensive, the First World War was long. Despite the swing back to the offensive, the Second World War was long. That was a war of swift movements, and they were dramatically illustrated in 1940 when the German armoured divisions raced to the Channel across those French fields in which the armies had been bogged for four years during the previous war. Although the Second World War avoided stalemate it was even longer than the First World War.

VII

In the half century between 1920 and 1970 most international wars were short. A careful list, compiled by David Wood of London's Institute for Strategic Studies, suggested that at least thirty wars were fought between sovereign states during that half century; and most of them were terminated in less than a year. Many, however, were violent incidents rather than wars. Thus the war between Honduras and Nicaragua, which killed about forty soldiers in 1957, was perhaps short because it was an isolated skirmish rather than a war.

Since 1920 most wars confined to a few nations have been short and, in casualties, slight. Between 1920 and 1945 there were three clear exceptions: the bitter war in the early 1920s between Greece and Turkey which killed about 50,000 soldiers and many more civilians in Asia Minor; the Chaco War which, fought in the humid lowlands of the interior of South America between 1928 and 1935, killed about 130,000 Bolivian and Paraguayan soldiers during the three years of serious fighting; and the Sino-Japanese War which began in 1937 and raged for eight years with enormous military and civilian casualties.

Why was the war in China a belated echo of the long eighteenth-century wars? Part of the answer must lie in conditions peculiar to each war, but part of the answer can be generalised. The strength of Japan and China was so great and the theatre of war was geographically so quarantined, that the threat of strong interference by other nations was small, even when in its fifth year the war became part of the Second World War; indeed the war ended in China only when Japan in 1945 was defeated outside China. Similarly the expanse of China was so large that long supply lines impeded any invader; China was so large that the war was often fought on many fronts, thus limiting the chance that one side would be winning simultaneously on every front; and the war had an additional front – guerrilla warfare – which always tends to prolong a war. In effect the kind of influence which prolongs general wars was at work in the Sino-Japanese war.

In the last half century the world has experienced only one general war, the Second World War. It was a long war, and its 17 million military deaths were double those inflicted in the previous world war. Another modern war, the Korean War, could by some definitions be called a general war; it involved eighteen states, but most fought under a common organisation. Lasting for three years and killing nearly 600,000 fighting men, it was certainly serious and, by some measurements, long.

Little has happened since 1920 to disturb the conclusions which could have been drawn then about the factors which prolong wars. This applies not only to the orthodox international wars but also to colonial wars. Nearly all the reasons offered for the long duration of the French war in Algeria in the nineteenth century seem relevant to the French war in Indo-China (1945–54), to the Algerian War of Independence against French rule (1954–62), and to the War of American Intervention in Vietnam which began in 1962. The four wars contain ingredients similar to those visible in long general wars. This does not mean however that one could have confidently predicted, at the beginning of those four wars, that they would be so prolonged.

The influences which prolong or shorten warfare seem similar over a long span of time. While the mechanisation of warfare is perhaps the one exception it has been an uneven influence. Indeed part of the shortening effect of mechanisation is an illusion. It merely reduces the years of fighting by waging war more intensively and by filling more hours with fighting; mechanical warfare enables phases of the war to continue at night as well as day, in winter as well as summer. In the last century and a half those short wars, which seemed most dramatically to proclaim the value of mechanised methods, were shortened only in part by new techniques of warfare. Thus the Seven Weeks War of 1866 was ended quickly, less by the decisive battle of Sadowa than by the realisation of each side that if they continued the war other powers might intervene and so worsen their position. In 1967 the Six Days War between Israel and the Arab states was probably ended by similar fears and preferences. Those two swift wars have been seen as classic examples of the decisiveness of mechanised warfare. More important they are classic examples of wars which, lacking quarantine, were particularly susceptible to outside interference.

The hope, so widely held between 1860 and 1914, that mechanised methods of warfare were making long wars an impossibility, has not been fulfilled. That hope was revived in 1945 when the first nuclear bomb was dropped on a Japanese city, but so far it has not been fulfilled. Even if two main nuclear powers went to war, the web of their alliances would probably turn it into a general war; and present knowledge offers no strong probability that a general war would be short. Even if it began with nuclear attacks there is no strong probability that it would end quickly. Although there seems a chance that a general war could end in a month, a disastrous month, there also seems a chance that it could continue for years.

15 : The Mystery of Wide Wars

One vanity of the twentieth century is the belief that it experienced the first world wars, but at least five wars in the eighteenth century involved so many nations and spanned so much of the globe that they could also be called world wars. To explain why some wars touched such a huge expanse of sea and land is at first sight easy. The world-wide wars reflected the spread of European colonisation and civilisation and the mechanical shortening of space and time. And yet most wars in every generation since 1700 were not general wars or world wars. It seems clear therefore that those influences confining war to a few nations and a small theatre of war were usually stronger than global influences.

Why were some wars confined to two nations and why did other wars embrace ten or twenty nations? Some scholars imply that a great war must have had great causes: that what provokes a war between only two nations must have been present in greater intensity on the eve of a war involving many nations. Thus those who see the breakdown of cultural values, the decline of war-immunity, or widespread internal strife as the major cause of war will argue that those factors were present in higher degree on the eve of a major war than on the eve of a minor war. It is a precept among many political scientists, sociologists and theorists of international relations that one can learn more about the causes of war by studying a great war than a small war. There may be a tinge of truth in the precept though possibly that tinge is faint. Would scientists necessarily have learnt more about the causes of malaria by studying a large outbreak or would economists necessarily have learnt more about the main causes of economic fluctuations by studying a serious depression?

An alternative explanation of why some wars became

general wars* is that they were preceded by a network of alliances. Hence when two nations started a war, their alliances automatically drew in many other nations. This interpretation has been often applied to the First World War but it is doubtful whether it fits many general wars. It does not fit the Revolutionary and Napoleonic Wars, slightly fits the Second World War, and loosely fits some but not other wars of the eighteenth century. Moreover a peacetime alliance between major nations did not necessarily mean that a war involving one member automatically embraced other members of the alliance. Certain alliances seemed firm before a war, but when tested they were shown to be fragile. Some alliances, on the outbreak of war, had no more force than a flapping sheet of paper.

For a long time I was unable to see any influence other than alliances which might explain why some wars became general wars; and yet alliances seemed to offer only part of the explanation. They were a valuable clue rather than a solution. A survey of the outbreak of general wars seemed to offer no further light. In the end it seemed sensible to turn the question upside down, and analyse those wars which failed to widen. If one could detect barriers which confined certain wars to two nations, one would expect those barriers to be absent from general wars.

II

An examination of wars which were confined to two nations reveals one immediate clue. Nearly all were fought on the geographical fringes rather than in the core of international power. Europe was indisputably the centre of power in the eighteenth and nineteenth centuries and in those centuries wars confined to two nations were rare in the centre of Europe, more frequent on the margins of Europe, and normal in places far from Europe.

The United States illustrated the pattern. In the century

* A general war, by my definition, involves the main forces of at least five states including three major powers. In the last three centuries most general wars have been world wars; the three exceptions are the Great Northern War, the War of the Polish Succession, and the Crimean War.

and a quarter after she had won independence she engaged in no war that involved more than two participants. In succession she fought France (1798–99), Tripoli (1801–05), Britain (1812–14), Algiers (1815), Mexico (1846–48), the breakaway Confederate States (1861–65) and Spain (1898). Though her short wars against the French and then the British were in one sense episodes in the Revolutionary and Napoleonic Wars, she did not declare war against the allies of France or Britain nor did she form her own alliance with the enemies of France or Britain; thus these two short wars were isolated wars on the fringe of the serious wars being fought in Europe. Why were foreign wars involving the United States so insulated? Her wars were insulated not only by the Atlantic Ocean but by her own strength. She was strong enough to require no allies, and her enemy was usually so weak militarily or so isolated geographically that it too could attract no allies to its side. The traditional insulation of the United States from general wars was also visible in her late entry into the two world wars of this century.

On the far eastern flank of Europe, as on the far western flank, most of the wars in which Japan engaged were confined to two nations. After the Meiji Restoration, Japan fought three wars against China and two against Russia. With the exception of the last half of the third Sino-Japanese war, they were two-nation wars. Moreover in the First World War the Japanese fought only in the minor Pacific theatre and they were a late-comer to the Second World War.

The common kind of two-nation war in the nineteenth century was the colonial war that dotted the maps of Africa and Asia. The ability of other European powers to interfere in these wars was obviously restricted by the remoteness of the theatre of fighting. Moreover the incentive for France to interfere in an Italian colonial war, or for Britain to interfere in a Spanish colonial war was usually small, because the result of the fighting rarely seemed likely to affect the distribution of European power. Likewise the African or Asian state or tribe was usually unable to attract allies from among its neighbours. When the Zulus fought the British in the 1870s and the Ethiopians fought the Italians in the 1890s, they had no neighbours who were either powerful enough or willing enough to become allies.

Inside Europe most of the Russo-Turkish wars were fought without allies. Russia and Turkey fought one another four times with virtually no aid or interference from an outside nation in the period 1750 to 1900, and they were opponents in two other wars in which only one or two outsiders participated. During those wars the Black Sea and its approaches seems to have been a barrier against intervention. For most of the time Turkey and Russia were the only nations which occupied the shores of the Black Sea; moreover the sea's narrow throat at Constantinople prevented the sea-powers of Western Europe from interfering in a war unless Turkey consented. Another facet of geography quarantined Russo-Turkish wars. Both Russia and Turkey were major powers occupying huge territories, and most of their neighbours were weak. Their only strong neighbours were in Central Europe. One was Poland, and she had vanished by the end of the eighteenth century. The other was Austria, and several times she was a third party to Russo-Turk wars. So their wars were relatively well insulated. Indeed, even if nature had drained the Black Sea and the dry bed had become the favoured battlefield of Russia and Turkey, their wars would still have been partly insulated by the absence of strong neighbours on seven of the eight points of the compass.

If one marks on a map the specific theatres in which two-nation wars were fought in Europe during the last century and a half, the location of warfare confirms the previous observations. Of the fourteen wars eleven were fought close to the sea – in only three was the main theatre of war more than one hundred miles inland. Ten of the fourteen were fought in south-eastern Europe or on the opposite coast of Asia Minor. And none of those wars involved two major states from central or western Europe.

The parallel between the geography of two-nation wars and the geography of neutrality is at once obvious. The kind of influences which localised a war were similar to those which aided some nations to remain neutral in global wars. The only European nations which remained neutral in the two world wars of the twentieth century were Sweden, Switzerland and Spain. They were geographically isolated by mountains or sea and so were less vulnerable. Being relatively small they had less incentive to intervene in the wars. While these were not the only reasons why the three succeeded in remaining neutral, they were vital reasons.

III

The tentative explanation of why some wars involved only two nations can be turned upside down. It then offers an explanation of why some wars involved many nations. One can therefore suggest that a war was more likely to widen if it began near the hub of Europe and first involved at least one major European power; no general war since 1700 was originated as a war between two minor or middle-ranking powers. A war was more likely to widen when a major nation won decisive victories or was expected – unless opposed – to win decisive victories; a war was most likely to widen if it threatened to make a radical reshuffle of the hierarchy of national power. In those situations outside nations had an incentive to intervene and an opportunity to intervene.

General wars began simply as wars between two nations. Other nations were later drawn in. A general war was thus a series of interlocked wars happening simultaneously. In the growth of a general war the entry of additional nations was often like the fisherman who intervened while the waterbirds fought, or waterbirds who pounced while the fisherman slept. This is revealed by a survey of general wars in the last two hundred years.

The War of American Independence started as a colonial war in 1775 and probably would not have become a many-sided war but for Britain's increasing difficulty in suppressing the rebellion. A series of British reverses culminating in the Battle of Saratoga in 1777 emboldened France to attempt to reverse the results of the previous Anglo-French war. From 1778 France and Britain were at war. In the following year Spain was persuaded to enter the war, probably in the belief that she could recapture Florida and the Mediterranean island of Minorca. A year later the Dutch became Britain's fourth enemy.

The French Revolutionary War began in April 1792

simply as a war between France and Austria, though the chance that Prussia would fight as Austria's ally was high. Within four months Prussia had entered the war, and the invasion of France was about to begin. If the invasion had been successful the war would probably not have widened into a general war. The invasion failed, and before the close of 1792 French armies had occupied the Austrian Netherlands to the north, crossed the Rhine to the east, and captured Nice and Savoy in the south-east. France's sweeping victories, rather than shortening the war, widened it. France's own war aims became bolder: a clear sign of her boldness was the decision at the end of 1792 to impose her own revolutionary institutions on the territories she captured. France's early military triumphs challenged the independence of neighbouring nations which had remained neutral; her triumphs also encouraged, within those nations, a fifth column of radicals who sympathised with revolutionary ideas. Those nations had a strong incentive to join in the war against France, and because they were so close to France they could easily intervene. In the first three months of 1793 Britain, the Dutch Republic, Austria and Spain joined in the war against France. The war continued to widen until it embraced most European states. The last of the peace treaties was signed in 1802, and a year later the Napoleonic Wars began as simply an Anglo-French war. By the same ricochet process the decisive French victories on land widened it into a general war, and indeed a world war.

For the following hundred years only the Crimean War approached the dimensions of a general war. It began as a war between Russia and Turkey, but the destruction of a division of the Turkish fleet at the Black Sea harbour of Sinope in November 1853 aroused fears that Russia might crush Turkey and so penetrate at last into the Mediterranean and become more powerful than ever before. Britain and France entered the war against Russia early in 1854, and the small kingdom of Sardinia in January 1855. But the theatre of war was remote, and furthermore no decisive military events provoked or tempted other European fishermen to intervene.*

* In Asia, Persia seized the opportunity in 1856 to poach on Britain's sphere of influence, leading to a short Anglo–Persian war.

On the other hand, if Turkey early in that war had won decisive victories over Russia, the intervention of other powers would have been less likely; Turkey had long ceased to be viewed as a danger in Europe.

Among the cluster of European wars of the period 1848 to 1870 three others held some danger of becoming general wars, for they involved major powers in the centre of Europe. Two of those wars – the Franco-Austrian of 1859 and the Austro-Prussian of 1866 – did not last long enough to establish a decisive superiority on one side. Austria lost both wars but remained a great power; it had not lost by such a margin that the ladder of European power seemed likely to be altered drastically. The third war, the Franco-Prussian war of 1870–71, ended with one of the most crushing defeats in the military history of Europe. But because France had been seen as a greater danger than Prussia, the Prussian victory did not arouse immediate fears that Prussia could dominate Europe. It may have been good fortune that when the war was in its decisive stage, and so likely to involve other nations, any neighbour which thought of intervention was checked by the outbreak of violent revolution in Paris itself.

Fear of popular revolution, and the belief that it was a contagious disease that could race through Europe, was probably an insulator of warfare for much of the nineteenth century. In 1848, the year of revolution, three European wars began in those central regions where war was not easily insulated, but the wars did not spread. The fighting was insulated partly because so many leaders saw international war as a disturber of internal stability. On the eve of the Franco-Austrian war of 1859 the Earl of Malmesbury, the British foreign secretary, warned that a long and indecisive war 'would give new life to that dreaded class who look in anarchy alone for a realisation of their avarice or ambition'. The revolutions in Paris in 1870 and 1871 kept alive these fears. The revolution in Russia towards the end of the Russo-Japanese War in 1905 revived them. One of the widespread beliefs of 1914 was the faith that governments would end the war if hardships and famine seemed likely to provoke internal revolution. While fear of anarchists, socialists or militant rebels fluctuated widely in the heads of governments, at times it may have helped to end wars quickly and on moderate terms. Clearly war was a less attractive way of adjudicating international disputes if it increased the danger of provoking serious internal disputes.

IV

At first sight the First World War defies the suggestion that general wars are two-nation wars which multiply. But in the background to that war, and in the first week of fighting, the ricochet process is visible. The two Balkan Wars of 1912–13 made Serbia bolder and doubled her territory. Though a year elapsed between the end of the Balkan Wars and the beginning of the First World War, the first stage of that war was almost a ricochet off the Balkan Wars. It began on 28 July 1914 simply as a war between Austria and Serbia. Russia then mobilised her armies to aid Serbia, realising that Serbia unaided would be defeated. On 1 August Germany, believing that Austria unaided would be defeated by Russia and Serbia, declared war on Russia. On 3 August Germany, knowing that France would ally herself with Russia, declared war on France. Thus in the space of six days the war embraced Russia and France and Serbia on the one side and Austria and Germany on the other and was virtually a general war, though curiously it was not until 5 August that Austria and Russia were formally at war and not until the 10th that France and Austria were at war.

It could be argued that the lag in the sequence of events is misleading: that the war of 1914 was from the beginning almost certain to be a general war because of the alliances which bound major European nations together. This is probably true. And yet what did the alliances signify? Firm alliances existed only because nations believed that an absence of allies would weaken them in diplomacy and in war. In 1914 two alliances were cemented tightly because of the widespread belief that the war would be short. An ally was useful only if it had pledged itself to enter a war quickly; an ally that arrived weeks after the war had begun was expected to be of little aid.

Whereas in most general wars the formation of alliances had been largely a reaction to decisive military events in the opening campaigns, the alliances of 1914 were a reaction to military events before they had occurred. The alliances of 1914 were based on a prediction that if war came, decisive military events would come swiftly. So France and Russia were allies because they believed that if war occurred Germany would be too powerful for any one nation. Germany and Austria were allies for fear that if war occurred France and Russia together would otherwise be too powerful. The speed with which the Austro-Serbian war of July 1914 became the general war of August 1914 was largely a reflection of these beliefs. Only in speed did the transition to general war in 1914 differ from the transition experienced by earlier general wars.

The existence of firm alliances on the eve of the war did not alone dictate which nations would enter the war. Britain did not belong to an alliance in July 1914. Though she was much closer to the Franco-Russian alliance than to the opposing alliance, she was not firmly committed. But when the Germans, on 3 August 1914, invaded Belgium in the first stage of their curved march into northern France, the British cabinet decided to intervene.* Britain's entry into the First World War was thus similar to her entry into the French Revolutionary War in 1793 when France's occupation of 'Belgium' had aroused British fears. The only difference was that in 1914 Britain did not wait for the enemy army to reach the Channel ports before entering the war. In the speedy warfare anticipated in 1914 the British believed they could not afford to wait. While Britain, which was not a firm member of one of the rival alliances, quickly entered the First World War, Italy remained neutral for nine months though she had been the third member of the German-led Triple Alliance. Italy was in no way endangered by the first phase of the war. When she did enter the war in May 1915

* Britain gave as her reason for declaring war the German violation of the neutrality of Belgium, of which Britain was one of the guarantors. But Germany had two days previously violated the neutrality of Luxembourg, of which Britain was equally a guarantor, and Britain had not threatened war over that violation. There was one vital difference; Belgium faced the English Channel. The violation of geography rather than neutrality was probably the crucial issue.

she declared war against her former ally Austria; not until August 1916 did she declare war against Germany.

As the war went on it continued to widen, much as earlier general wars had widened by the process of ricochet or rebound. Of the major late-comers Japan and Turkey entered the war in 1914, Italy and Bulgaria in 1915, Rumania and Portugal in 1916, the United States and China in 1917. Nonetheless the war remained a chain of separate wars loosely strung together. Significantly, for eight months of 1917 the United States was at war with Germany but at peace with Germany's main ally, Austria.

v

The Second World War began simply as a war between Germany and Poland on 1 September 1939.* As Britain and France were allies of Poland they went to war with Germany on 3 September; on that and the following days four British dominions entered the war. Russia invaded eastern Poland on 14 September but remained at peace with Britain and France. Thus by the end of September 1939, with Poland crushed, the war had been reduced to a simple contest in which France and the British empire fought Germany with the minimum of fighting.

Whereas in 1914 the widespread expectation of decisive victories had quickly widened the fighting into a general war, in 1939 the expectation that the war would be decisive was far from universal among neutral nations. The quick victories of 1940 then temporarily widened the war. In April the Germans occupied Denmark and Norway; in May they occupied Belgium and Holland. In June 1940, four days before the German advance reached Paris, Italy entered the war on Germany's side. By the end of June 1940, Hitler had won such a triumph that his only remaining opponent was Britain and her overseas dominions. Ironically the war by the summer of 1940 was less a general war than it had been in the first month of the war.

* The name Second World War is a misleading name for this war until December 1941. Hitherto it was much less a world war than the six general wars of the eighteenth century.

The crisis in western Europe gave Russia a free hand in the east. In the winter of 1939–40 she fought Finland, and in the week that the Germans occupied Paris the Russians quietly occupied the three small Baltic states of Latvia, Lithuania and Estonia. At the end of that month the Russians occupied parts of Rumania. Other wedges of Rumanian territory were passed to Hungary and Bulgaria. None of these events in eastern Europe involved Russia in war with the main combatants in the west.

The rebound of military events was visible month after month. The entry of Italy on what seemed to be the winning side transferred the centre of the war to the Mediterranean where both Britain and Italy had bases and colonies. Likewise the defeat of France led to a struggle for possession of French colonies on the African and Asian shores of that sea. On the European shore the neutral nations of Jugoslavia and Greece were now vulnerable, and by May 1941 they had been defeated by German thrusts. The two Axis powers, Germany and Italy, thus virtually held the outer coast of Europe stretching all the way from the Norwegian–Russian border to the Aegean and the Black Sea: the only gap was the Iberian peninsula where Spain and Portugal remained neutral.

A European war which was decisive sometimes brought face to face two countries which previously were far apart. Just as France's successes in the Napoleonic wars had transformed Russia and France into neighbours, so the first phase of the Second World War drew Germany and Russia to a common frontier. Between 1919 and 1939 they had been kept apart by a barrier of six states stretching from Estonia on the Baltic to Rumania on the Black Sea, but by 1940 those six states had been swallowed, and the swallowers – Germany and Russia – now shared a common boundary running from the Baltic to the Black Sea. Hitler's triumph in western and central Europe now emboldened him to attack the Soviet Union. Germany had just won the most brilliant victories since the time of Napoleon, whereas the Soviet Union in its short war against the small state of Finland had been far less impressive. That war, announced Winston Churchill, just before the Russians finally penetrated the lakes and forests and man-made fortifications of Finland, 'had exposed, for the

world to see, the military incapacity of the Red army'.
Hitler's confidence – not shared by his military advisers – that
Russia's armies were brittle was written into the first sentence
of his secret document on 18 December 1940: 'The German
armed forces must be prepared to crush soviet Russia in a
quick campaign before the end of the war against England.'
The phrase 'quick campaign' is revealing; it echoed scores of
forecasts made on the eve of previous wars. In June 1941 the
Germans began their quick campaign against the Soviet
Union, and the mechanised spearheads reached the forests
enclosing Moscow and the outskirts of Leningrad and the
Black Sea river-port of Rostov before the winter – an early
winter that year – halted the advance. The Germans had
neither the equipment nor the clothing for winter warfare in
the heart of Russia. How close they had gone to defeating
Russia will never be known. What is known is that from the
onset of winter the war in Russia began slowly to erode Germany's overall power.

Soon after the invasion of Russia, the Soviet Union and
Britain and the British dominions became allies. But in
another sense the Russian war remained a separate war. Finland and Hungary and Rumania had joined in the attack on
Russia but Britain waited almost six months before she declared war on this trio which was attacking her ally. Similarly
when Japan at the end of 1941 became the ally of Germany
and Italy, she did not go to war against Russia. For almost
four years – until the last month of the war – Japan and
Russia remained at peace with one another though they were
central members of rival alliances.

The German conquest of western and central Europe and
the German invasion of the Soviet Union were enormous
events that ricocheted around the world. In East Asia their
effects were soon visible. Japan and China had been at war
since 1937; and in 1940 huge Japanese armies were attempt-
ing to end the war and Japanese aircraft were pouring bombs
on to the new capital city of Chungking. The conquest of
Holland and France and the dangerous plight of Britain suddenly enhanced Japan's bargaining position. The three great
colonisers of south-east Asia were now vulnerable. Japan's
first bargain in June 1940 was to persuade Britain to sever.

temporarily the road from Burma into western China and to persuade the falling French government to sever the railway from Indo-China into southern China. China's only two supply routes from the outside world were now blocked, though the road through Burma was later opened again. French Indo-China was particularly vulnerable; Thailand forces attacked the western provinces and Japan won the right to use northern provinces as a base for aircraft attacks on China.

Hitler's invasion of Russia in 1941 removed another danger to Japan's flank. A month later the Japanese troops invaded the southern part of French Indo-China and so won a springboard from which they could attack other western possessions in south-east Asia and the adjacent islands.

On 7 December 1941 Japanese aircraft bombed Hawaii and British Malaya, and her fleets and armies began one of the most astonishing ventures ever attempted in island warfare. Britain and the United States promptly declared war on Japan; China declared war on Germany and Italy, though it is doubtful if China and Germany exchanged one shot during the war; and China also declared war on Japan with whom she had already exchanged hundreds of millions of shots. Four days after the bombing of Pearl Harbour, the United States and Germany became formal enemies. The war had at last become global though it was to remain more a set of spliced wars than one great war.

VI

The six general wars fought since the 1770s had much in common. They began as wars between two nations and then were multiplied by power-shaking victories; the First World War differed only because the decisive events were clearly anticipated before the war. On the eve of each of these wars nobody could have logically predicted how many nations would ultimately take part in the fighting. Only on the eve of the First World War was it reasonable to predict that the coming campaign would probably be a general war, though few predicted that it would embrace so many nations.

The entry of a new nation into a running war is really the beginning of another war. A general war is a series of wars happening simultaneously and entangled with one another. The kind of reasoning which can explain why two countries begin to fight will also explain why a third, fourth or even tenth country join in the fighting.

War began when two countries had contradictory ideas of their own bargaining position and therefore could not solve peacefully an issue which vitally affected them. The spread of that war to other countries was the result of the same kind of conditions which began the war. For the fighting often raised issues vital to countries which were adjacent but aloof: it endangered their independence or it offered the opportunity to increase their independence. Decisive fighting in the early phase of some wars not only raised issues that were vital to adjacent nations but it led to contradictory perceptions of military power. A country which was decisively winning the first phase of a war – France in 1792 or Germany in 1940 – usually became more confident and enlarged its war aims. But its heightened sense of power was not shared equally by adjacent nations. Some agreed with this perception and either became fighting allies of the temporary victor or offered peaceful concessions. Some disputed the assessment and, confident of their own might, declared war on the temporary victor. In effect the first phases of what became a general war created those same contradictory expectations which had been created slowly during many periods of peace.

The process which widened a war, converting it into a general war, was reversed in the final stages of a war. Two dramatic events of 1917 reveal how much the widening and narrowing of warfare had in common. In April 1917 Germany and the United States disagreed on their bargaining position and signed declarations of war: in December 1917 Germany and Russia agreed on their bargaining position and signed a truce of peace. While one event widened and the other narrowed the First World War, both events fit into the same causal framework. Whereas the aims which drew the United States into the war seemed attainable by force, the aims which had originally drawn Russia into the war were now unattainable by force. Whereas Washington was confident of its military strength, Petrograd had lost confidence in its military strength.

VII

The same framework and the same set of causes should be employed to explain each dramatic turning point in relations between nations. The same set of factors should be examined in order to explain the outbreak of a war, the widening of a war by the entry of other nations, the narrowing of a war by their withdrawal, the ending of a war, the surmounting of crises during an era of peace, and the closing of that era of peace. The same causal factors, though they appear in different combinations, explain both war and peace.

16: Australia's Pacific War

In seeking the causes of a war, historians and political scientists have tended to conclude that one nation is largely or primarily to blame. It is nearly always a large nation on which blame rests. And yet in many major wars a cluster of smaller nations share, to some degree, in the decision to go to war. Australia since 1899 has fought in six international wars and in most of those wars she fought from the outset, but in the histories written of Australia she receives virtually no blame for her decision to fight nor is she seen as in any way contributing to the causes of those wars. The outbreak of the Japanese war in the Pacific in December 1941 is, therefore, worth scrutinising because it shows how a smaller nation may be fitted into the framework of causes. It also shows how Japan viewed the prospect of a war which, in hindsight, is usually seen as unwinnable and morally unjustifiable. Hindsight, however, is not the same as insight.

II

An Australian judge, Sir William Webb, presided over the international tribunal which tried Japanese leaders for violating the peace in 1941. The Japanese were pronounced guilty of causing the war which began at Pearl Harbor, and their guilt as warmakers was pronounced again and again in the following decades. In contrast Australia emerged as blameless. The widespread belief that Australia was blameless was aided by our knowledge – I write as an Australian – that the war had begun with the Japanese attacks on Pearl Harbor and Malaya. The belief that Australia was blameless was entrenched by the assumption that we had no alternative but to follow the decisions of our powerful allies. But Australia was neither a minor ally of Britain in the first two years of the war against Hitler nor a minor ally in the last year of peace in the Pacific Ocean. On the eve of the war in the Pacific, Australia had considerable influence in shaping the policies towards

Japan. The main British defences against a possible Japanese thrust were in Malaya, and there the Australian forces were as numerous as the British soldiers. The Australian government, in confronting Japan in the last months of peace, was not a sleeping partner of the Allies but a vociferous partner, eager to influence events.

We could also plead our innocence by pointing out that we, unlike the Japanese, had no ambition to conquer territory. As we were satisfied with the might of the British Empire and the red-splashed map of the world of the 1930s, we could side theoretically with the peacemakers. We could claim that the present colours on the map were indelible and that any nation which tried to repaint the map would be an aggressor. And yet the vast European empires in the Orient — with all their virtues and vices — had been won by force or threats, and were held by force and threats. The Dutch and French colonies stretching from Hanoi to New Caledonia, the red patchwork of British colonies, Australia and her own New Guinea possessions, Portuguese Macao and East Timor, the United States' satellite in the Philippines, the Dutch East Indies, and the sweeping Russian empire in east Asia — they had been captured by Europeans and most had been conquered after 1800. If it were true that the conquerors of lands were entitled to retain them in the name of international morality, then morality was obviously a sliding principle. It was not completely logical for Australia and Britain to argue that any Japanese annexations would be immoral if at the same time they insisted that their own past conquests were decidedly moral. Admittedly many historians in the British Empire had long argued that their empire had expanded unintentionally. There was some truth in this belief, but many strategic parts of the empire, including South Africa and the St. Lawrence Estuary and Gibraltar, had been won by formal war and many other parts had been captured or defended by informal war.

Australia had enlarged her own empire 'unintentionally' in the First World War. A small naval and military force captured German New Guinea in 1914, and at the peace conference in 1919 Australia clung tightly to the seized territory. During the Munich crisis in 1938, the idea arose that Germany might be pacified if she were given several of those colonies which she had lost in the previous war. Would Australia therefore return the mandated territory of New Guinea embracing the north east of New Guinea, New Britain, New Ireland, and the Solomons? The Australian government in Canberra expressed the strongest hostility to the idea. It would seem that any territory won in the Pacific in the First World War was permanent, but any territory won in a new war in the Pacific would represent an act of aggression.

Each nation sees history through its own eyes. The weight of war-time propaganda and national emotion makes a people see a war as simply a fight between good and evil or between war-makers and peacelovers. It is true that in one sense Australia did not wish to fight Japan in 1941, but it is equally true that Australia did not want peace in the Pacific if a continuation of peace entailed the erosion of Australia's security and independence. Likewise Japan did not necessarily want a war in the Pacific in December 1941. Her leaders would have preferred peace; but they believed that if peace were to prevail, Japan's power would be curbed or her independence would be whittled away.

This argument in no way denies the patriotism and courage of the tens of thousands of soldiers who were to fight in the war. Nor does it suggest that Australia should have avoided the war. In an international system that emphasised the independence of each nation, Australians were right to believe that ultimately it was in their nation's interest to fight the Japanese. While they saw no point in initiating a war and much point in avoiding a war, they knew that Australia's independence and interests would suffer if they made those concessions which alone might forestall a war.

III

For half a century Australian governments had tended to treat Japan with a mixture of suspicion and mild contempt. In most Australian eyes, after 1900, Japan rather than China personified the Yellow Peril. Even in the First World War, when Japanese vessels helped to escort the convoy carrying the first Australian contingent of soldiers from Albany to

Suez, most Australians remained wary of Japan's territorial ambitions. Indeed, Australia justified her own territorial ambitions in the tropics by pointing to the danger of Japanese expansion. That was one argument with which W. M. Hughes, as prime minister, justified Australia's retention of the captured German New Guinea after the ending of the First World War. Likewise, at the peace conference in France in 1919, Hughes opposed Japan's request that the covenant of the new League of Nations should expressly recognize racial equality. Hughes ceased to be prime minister in 1923 but continued to preach that Japan was a menace in the Pacific.

The growth of Japan's land empire was observed with concern by many Australians but was observed more nervously by the Russians and Chinese, at whose expense Japan grew. Japan's empire grew as the result of victory in short wars against China in 1895, Russia in 1905, and the North Pacific colonies of Germany in 1914. Persistent disputes with China led to the occupation of Manchuria and Jekol in the early 1930s. Japan's territory on the mainland of east Asia now ran, at its greatest elongation, over 1200 miles from the Yellow Sea to the Amur River in eastern Siberia. Further disputes between China and Japan led in 1937 to war on a wide front. By 1940 Japan controlled the main ports in China, forcing the Chinese government to import war materials by the long road from the British colony of Burma or by railway from the French colony of Indo-China. Without those supplies China's resistance, in the opinion of many Japanese leaders, would collapse.

It was understandable that Japan should resent those western powers which tried to aid the Chinese. And when Hitler in 1940 overthrew most governments in western Europe, Japan understandably took advantage of Europe's weaknesses. She promptly demanded that France and Britain should cease to allow military aid to enter China through the back door. From July to September 1940 the road through British Burma to China was closed, and in September the French railway running from Haiphong to south China was taken over by the Japanese.

Japan was now in a strong position to invade the fragile European empires in south-east Asia. The British Navy no longer ruled any seas except the Indian Ocean and the South Atlantic. The United States Navy could not necessarily be expected to intervene if the Japanese invaded European colonies in south-east Asia. As late as October 1940 President Roosevelt was privately confiding that a Japanese attack on the Philippines might not necessarily draw the United States into war against Japan.

For a few months after the fall of France, the vulnerability of Australia to Japanese pressure was acute. The Australian government had to face the fact that if Japan invaded Thailand or the Netherlands East Indies, Australia might have to remain neutral rather than risk offending Japan. When Japan placed pressure on the British Empire to halt the trucking of supplies along the Burma Road to China, Australia agreed that the safest policy was to yield temporarily to the demand. Sir Paul Hasluck, writing in the official Australian history of the Second World War, accurately described Australia's policy towards Japan as an attempt 'to tiptoe past the danger'.

Australia also decided in August 1940 to appoint her first ambassador to Japan. As the post was vital Sir John Latham, the chief justice of the high court, was appointed. Latham now suggested that Australia should offer to buy Japanese military aircraft, and for a few months promising negotiations with Mitsubishi proceeded. Thereby he showed towards Japanese technology a respect which, had it been equalled in high places in Washington and Whitehall, might have prevented or delayed the Pacific war.

The tiptoe policy towards Japan did not last long. As a German invasion of Britain now seemed less likely, Australia became less nervous of Japan. Similarly, in high military and political circles in England late in 1940, the prospect of a Japanese attack on British possessions in the Far East was seen as a possibility rather than a strong probability. Moreover the prospect of Japan winning such a war was seen as unlikely. Because Japan was seen as a relatively minor threat, she became a major threat. Ironically, if the British defences in Singapore, especially the aerial defences, had been strengthened in the fifteen months after the fall of Dunkirk, Japan might not have made war in south-east Asia in 1941.

IV

Even after Hitler had conquered France, Holland, Belgium, Denmark and Norway, Australia had many of the signs of a nation at peace. Though arms and munitions were being manufactured vigorously, football and racing and spectator sports were flourishing. Strikes, especially on the coalfields, were curbing output more than in many peace-time years. Crowds of people preferred to spend their savings in brightly-lit shops than to lend money for the war effort, and the Christmas of 1940 was a shopping spree. While many commodities in Britain were severely rationed, or too scarce to be worth rationing, Australia had rationed only one commodity – petrol – by the end of 1940. Australian soldiers had sailed to Egypt in 1940 but had not yet entered the fighting. To the end of 1940 the most conspicuous Australian action in the war had been H.M.A.S. *Sydney*'s sinking of an Italian cruiser in the Mediterranean. The closest approach of the war to the Australian coast had been the unseen arrival of a German sea-raider which quietly laid explosives on shipping lanes.

In 1941, Australia had a strong opportunity to influence the British policy towards Japan. At many meetings the Australian war cabinet had to choose between sending a further contingent of soldiers to the Middle East or strengthening the defences of Singapore and areas nearer home. On the information available, the choice was always thorny. As Churchill argued strongly in favour of intensifying the fight in the Middle East rather than preparing defences against Japan, and as resources were inadequate for both projects, the Australian government usually put its weight behind Suez rather than Singapore.

In the event of a Japanese attack on British colonies in south-east Asia, it was always understood that Britain would quickly move ships and aircraft from Suez to Singapore. This armoured sprint from the Mediterranean to Singapore was one of the hallucinations of the defence policy of both Australia and Britain. A drug which always brought on that hallucination was labelled 'Made in Japan'. Japanese technology, especially the technology of war, was treated as so inferior that Japan was seen more as a dangerous nuisance than a serious threat in the far east. The speed of the Japanese thrust towards the equator in 1941-42 is now history but was then unimaginable.

Meanwhile the Japanese remained wary of the Soviet Union; the two nations had already fought briefly in 1938-39 near the border of Japanese Manchuria and Outer Mongolia. As the Soviet Union was not fighting against Hitler, she was still free to turn her attention to the far east and to fight against Japan if the need should arise. This uneasy stillness was ended in June 1941; Japan's flanks were suddenly freed when, thousands of miles to the west, German forces moved swiftly towards Leningrad and Moscow and Odessa.

In the week of Hitler's invasion of Russia the Japanese government toyed with the idea of joining in the attack. The Soviet Union was a permanent threat, in the eyes of most Japanese. The nearest Soviet territory was only 80 miles across the water from Japanese Sakhalin and even the great Soviet naval base of Vladivostock was not as far from Japan as Melbourne is from Sydney. The alternatives facing Japan were discussed at a secret conference in Tokyo on 26 June 1941. To the navy chiefs the solution was to push aggressively south towards the tropics. On the other hand — according to transcripts of the conversations — the foreign ministry and the army favoured an attack on the Soviet.

The Soviet Union seemed to invite attack, for her forces were in retreat in the first weeks of Hitler's invasion. One impediment, however, to a prompt Japanese attack on the Soviet Far East was the lateness of the season: in the cold latitudes the effective warfare ceased with the approach of winter. Moreover the Japanese navy could not be ready for a war against the Soviet until the end of August, too late for that year. A war against the Soviet could also be unexpectedly long, and in a long war Japan might run out of petroleum and other essential materials, thus inviting defeat. Six of every ten tons of oil consumed in Japan in 1940 had been shipped from the United States. Could those American supplies be relied upon if Japan was to side with Hitler against the Russians?

While the debate continued in Tokyo, the Japanese quietly edged south. They resolved to extend their influence to the remainder of French Indo-China, including Saigon and the coastline facing the Gulf of Siam. That colony was still governed by a French admiral, who took orders from the puppet Vichy government in France. In the event of war the French forces isolated in Indo-China could expect few reinforcements, and indeed Thailand had recently snatched part of French Laos and Cambodia. On 21 July 1941 France and Japan signed a mutual security pact, by which Japan was permitted to occupy strategic points in the southern part of Indo-China. The Japanese were authorized caretakers; but to Australia and Britain and the United States, the Japanese were invaders.

In quietly occupying the French colony, the Japanese at first sight strengthened their own security. War with China could be prosecuted more vigorously, or a future war against the Soviet could be commenced with a more assured supply of war materials and food. Indo-China could now supply natural rubber to Japan for aircraft and truck tyres, conveyor belts, and for dozens of military needs; Indo-China could also supply tin, zinc, coal, iron, manganese and other metals of war. More important, she was the world's third largest exporter of rice, whereas Japan no longer grew sufficient rice for her own needs. The occupation of Saigon and the southern part of Indo-China also provided launching pads which might someday be used for invasions; and many of the Japanese forces which later invaded Thailand, Malaya, British Borneo and the Dutch East Indies actually sailed from Indo-China.

Japanese leaders were inclined to predict that their peaceful occupation of French Indo-China would not lead to retaliation by the United States and by the British Empire. The prediction proved false; and yet perhaps they were entitled to conclude, on the weight of the evidence available, that their occupation of the French colony would be treated with no more seriousness than similar occupations by British forces of weak colonies or nations. Within the next few months Britain was to occupy Persia without the Shah's consent, and Australia was to invade eastern Timor without the consent of Portugal.

The reply to Japan's southward move was swift. Britain and the United States declared economic warfare, though they did not call it economic warfare. Late in July all the Japanese assets in the United States, Australia and Britain, and British colonies were frozen. Exports from the British Empire and the United States to Japan virtually ceased. Likewise shipments of petroleum from the Dutch East Indies to Japan ceased, thus ending months of patient negotiations by a Japanese economic mission which had sought to buy oil and other strategic minerals in Djakarta. Australia, in declaring economic war, placed an embargo on virtually all exports to Japan, including zinc, lead, wool and foodstuffs. These edicts in Washington, London, and Canberra sabotaged Japan's economic life. The sudden ban on petroleum and other vital supplies undermined Japan's war campaign in central China even more than if Britain, the United States, and Australia had combined to send an army of 200,000 and squadrons of military aircraft to assist the Chinese.

Japan, economically and geographically, was a replica of Britain. Possessing a cluster of industralized islands, she depended heavily on commerce with distant lands. By 1940, though not a participant in the European war, she was suffering some of the dislocations of that war. Shipments from Europe and North America became scarce, and many raw materials could no longer be bought. Accordingly the freezing of Japanese assets in July 1941 and the embargo on most items of trade threatened to strangle Japan. To strangle Japan was of course the aim, but the embargo could also provoke an aggressive response. To withhold strategic supplies is to assume that an enemy lacks the power simply to come forward and capture those supplies. The blockade would be no more effective than a line of string across a map if Japan had the military strength to break that blockade.

v

In the Australian Parliament on 21 August 1941, W. M.
Hughes pleaded that British battle ships be sent to Singapore.
Prime minister in the First World War and now minister for the
navy, he believed that the simplest way to fend off an enemy
was to amass military strength. He knew that a successful
economic blockade, in the final resort, depended more on the
exercising of military than economic power.

'Less than a month has elapsed', said Hughes, 'since
Japanese forces poured into Indo-China. Tomorrow, they
may enter Thailand. A fortnight hence, where will they be?'
The prime minister, R. G. Menzies, was urged by his own war
cabinet to travel to London by flyingboat and use his eloquence
to persuade Churchill and the British cabinet that the defences
of Singapore should be strengthened. If at this late hour the
aerial defences of Singapore had been viewed seriously, Japan
could conceivably have been deterred from invading Malaya
and the other European colonies in south-east Asia.
Alternatively, Japan's attack on those colonies would have
been less successful; and that alone could have profoundly
affected the course of the war. For without a firm command of
the oilfields of Borneo and Sumatra, Japan could not have
carried on a long war.

Menzies did not fly to London to argue urgently his case. In
the face of a political crisis he resigned as prime minister, and in
October a Labor government under John Curtin took office.
But even if Menzies had pressed his case in London he might
not have succeeded, for the British Empire was over-extended
and could only strengthen Singapore by weakening another
strategic place close to home. Moreover the new Australian
government was not so perturbed by the vulnerability of
Singapore and was inclined to think that Japan had only
moderate strength and that warnings could still deter her from
war. The Labor ministers, much more than their predecessors,
saw the Soviet Union as a powerful ally against Japan; though
they carried their faith in Russian strength and morale too far.

They hoped that before long Russia might be successfully fighting Hitler in the west and fighting the Japanese in Siberia. The coming to power of the Labor Party in Canberra coincided with a revival of Allied confidence that Japan was not necessarily a danger. Sir Earle Page was Australia's envoy to the British war cabinet; and passing through Singapore at the end of September, he was shown a secret assessment prepared by the British General Headquarters in the Far East. The document encouraged Page to think that Japan was eager to avoid war in the next few months: 'She is consequently now susceptible to diplomatic pressure'. In Manila a week later Page met General Douglas MacArthur, the new commander of the United States Army Forces in the Far East, and heard the confidential view that Japan was already over-extended and that any Japanese attempt to capture the Dutch East Indies or Malaya could be thwarted. Page then flew to Washington where he heard that American forces were so strengthening the Philippines that those islands would soon be safe from attack. After five weeks of travelling Page reached London, where he prepared a strong submission to the British war cabinet. He argued that if Singapore's air and naval forces were strengthened, war against Japan could be avoided. The Japanese might even be forced by threats to withdraw from their new airfields and bases in French Indo-China.

The likelihood of a Japanese war came closer but in the eyes of many decision-makers the war was receding. The economic blockade against Japan gave the Allies a soothing but false feeling of security. As early as 17 September 1941 the Australian Parliament was told by the minister for external affairs that the danger of war in south-east Asia had ebbed because of 'the firmness displayed by the Governments of the British Empire countries and the United States since the Japanese incursion into French Indo-China'. In Singapore, in officers' messes, it was also observed that Japan had been quietened. So the clink of officers' glasses applauded that policy which, through misdirection, would actually force the Japanese to press south towards Singapore and Manila, Bali and Rabaul.

VI

We imagine that Japan was unalterably committed to
mounting a surprise attack in the Pacific. In fact Japan had
long wavered. Two months after Germany's invasion of the
Soviet Union the Japanese leaders still pondered what to do.
The Emperor Hirohito thought a war involving the United
States as an enemy would be too risky. Prince Konoye, the
prime minister, agreed; he sought a personal discussion with
President Roosevelt but his request was courteously pushed
aside.

Meanwhile the economic blockade weakened Japan. Her
military campaign against China was impaired; her plans for
a war against Russia were also impaired. In essence, the
economic blockade — designed in the hope that it would halt
a Japanese advance — made that advance an urgent priority.
In Tokyo on 6 September 1941, in the presence of the
Emperor, the military and political chiefs discussed the need
to capture those nearby colonial lands which were rich in war
materials. With carefully-prepared statistics, they stressed how
much Japan, before the blockade, depended on imports of
raw materials. Three quarters of Japan's iron ore came from
overseas. Rubber and nickel and nearly all the petroleum
came from overseas. More than 80 per cent of Japan's lead
and tin and bauxite and 60 per cent of the copper came from
overseas. And now these imports — except cargoes from South
America — had virtually ceased.

Petroleum dominated the discussions in Tokyo. As the
United States and the Dutch East Indies had just cut off
supplies of petroleum, Japan's military future was bleak
unless she went to war. 'Our empire's national power is
declining day by day,' confided the director of the planning
board. He predicted that even with the strict rationing of
petroleum to fishing boats and civilian industries, Japan's
stockpile of liquid fuel would be exhausted by the middle of
1942. On the other hand Borneo and Sumatra, if they were
captured from the Dutch and their oil installations were
enlarged, would make Japan self-sufficient. Here was a vital

reservoir of oil which the Dutch seemed unable to defend.

Japanese diplomats tried to persuade the United States to withdraw the embargo on the export of petroleum and other war materials. The United States was the most persistent advocate of the message that the world's disagreements should be solved by negotiation, not by force. She was willing to negotiate with Japan but unwilling to make concessions. Nor did Japan make concessions.

The western pressure on Japan came not only from the embargo but from the Burma Road. The road was opened again to the convoys of trucks which carried war materials all the way from the railhead at Lashio in British Burma to Kunming in China, 600 miles away. As the Burma Road supplied the Chinese armed forces with materials which otherwise would have been unprocurable, the Japanese leaders were inclined to blame the road for the effectiveness of the Chinese resistance. The Burma Road, however, did not carry a large traffic each month, and many of the American supplies which reached Burma in 1941 had to wait at Rangoon and Lashio for six months before they could be trucked to China. At Rangoon a mountain of American blankets, slowly eaten by white ants, symbolized the in-efficiency of much of the western support for China.

We still tend to think that warfare between nations is like a duel or a fist fight. This medieval concept lingers even though each fighter today is supported by a supply line of miners, manufacturers, scientists and other armourers and providers. In the last months of 1941 the western allies were so impeding Japan's fighting strength and so aiding China's fighting strength that they were virtually engaged in a limited war with Japan. And Japan could not retaliate unless she made unlimited war. Thus Pearl Harbor was to be just another step, though a frightening step, up the ladder of war.

Japan still held the alternative of attacking the Soviet Union. Germany urged the Japanese to make that attack, and the scope for an attack improved when the Russians were forced to neglect their defences in the far east. On 5 November 1941 the chief of staff of the Japanese army, Sugiyama, reported confidentially that the Red Army had sent 1300 tanks westwards on the Trans-Siberian railway in order to reinforce the home defences. Moreover at least 1300 Soviet aircraft had been transferred from east Siberia to the European front.

Japan's ambitions had been turned firmly south by the embargo imposed by the American, British, Australian and Dutch governments. Here perhaps was one of the great turning points in international history in this century, though we can only guess at many of its effects. Certainly if Japan, late in 1941 or in the first thawing of 1942, had attacked the Soviet Union in the far east, she would probably have captured Vladivostock and the Pacific coast, and forced the Russian defenders to retreat west into Siberia. Hitler's war against the Russians in the west would have been correspondingly aided; but whether, as a result of the military squeeze by Japan and Germany, the Soviet Union would have been ultimately defeated is extremely doubtful. Indisputably, if the Japanese had attacked Vladivostock instead of Pearl Harbor, the war would have run a very different course, might have ended in a different way and in a different year, might not have touched the south Pacific and south-east Asia, and might have resulted – when the war finally ended – in a ladder of international power which differed sharply from the ladder of 1945.

VII

By November 1941 the Japanese leaders had definitely decided on tropical conquest, unless by chance the Americans made concessions. The decision to fight was influenced partly by the weather. In the far northern winter the iced ports, fogs and short days made Soviet intervention less likely at the back door of Japan. 'It is difficult for the Soviet Union to conduct a major operation in winter', noted the chief of staff of the Japanese army on 5 November 1941. Ironically, in Singapore, the local reading of the weather persuaded the British headquarters that a Japanese attack was unlikely in the next six months. They decided that the stormy weather in the South China Sea would not favour an invader during the monsoon months from December to February. So

Singapore's life went on cheerfully: a garrison town, bazaar, naval base, at peace with the world.

Would the Japanese succeed if they invaded Hong Kong, Thailand, French Indo-China, Malaya, Burma, the Philippines, the Dutch East Indies, and a chain of United States bases in the central Pacific? The balance of opinion amongst the military and naval chiefs in Tokyo was that they would not only win but win quickly. This assessment underlay the decision of the Japanese to attack the tropical colonies rather than the Soviet Union.

Indisputably one key reason for that decision and therefore a powerful cause of the Pacific war was the Japanese estimate that the defences of the tropical colonies were feeble. The colonies seemed to lie like jelly in the sun. The Japanese high officers believed that Singapore, the great British arsenal, had paper walls. They believed that Britain's navy was weak in those waters. They believed that in the air Britain and her allies in south-east Asia were vulnerable. Most Japanese leaders believed, above all, that once their invasion was under way, Britain's hopes of sending reinforcements from Suez to Singapore would be like sending a snail to attack a mosquito.

A prerequisite for the outbreak of war — in other words a vital cause of war — is the belief of a nation that if it goes to war it will either win or, at worst, avoid defeat. Japan would have been extremely reluctant to make her attack on southeast Asia in 1941 or 1942, or 1943 or 1944, if she had not foreseen a strong possibility of victory. At a secret conference in Tokyo on 5 November — just over a month before Pearl Harbor — the army chief of staff, Sugiyama, confided that the Philippines would be captured in fifty days, after which the Dutch East Indies would be invaded. Malaya and Singapore would be conquered in 100 days. There would be assaults on military and air bases from Rangoon to the island of Guam and from Hong Kong to the Australian-held Bismarck Archipelago. Sugiyama predicted, with wonderful confidence, 'that the entire operation will be completed within five months after the opening of the war.' He did not mention, perhaps did not know, that Pearl Harbor would also be raided. Even in the circles where high policy was made, that plan was virtually a navy secret.

At that time there was no intention of invading Australia and New Zealand. The plan was to defend Japan and her new conquests by a defensive eastern perimeter of outer islands and bases stretching from New Guinea to the islands of the far north Pacific. Australia, it was hoped, would soon be isolated from Britain and the United States and be forced to withdraw from the war. On 15 November 1941 the high officials in Tokyo approved a master plan entitled 'Proposal for Hastening the End of the War'. Clause two briefly dealt with Australia:

> the connection between Australia and India and the British mother country will be broken by means of political pressure and the destruction of commerce, and the separation will be achieved . . .

If, after the war actually commenced, Japan had succeeded in severing the sea lanes approaching Australia from both Europe and the Americas, there would presumably have been demands for Australia to supply minerals and food to Japan. And the Australian government, fearing an invasion, would have been forced to trade with Japan. In that sequence of events Australia would have quickly become a satrap of Tokyo.

While Japan's leaders were confident that they could quickly capture the rich tropical lands and so acquire a strategic stockpile, they expected a long and difficult war. The evidence is clear that they had a nervous respect for the industrial might and the military potential of the United States, but they hoped that the vast distances of the eastern Pacific would help to shield them from the full weight of the United States' forces. Their plan of quick conquest envisaged a defensive perimeter — a Line of the Rising Sun — stretching from the Solomons to Wake Island and the Kuril Islands. As the distances covered by all military aircraft, and especially fighters, were relatively short, the vastness of the eastern Pacific represented Japan's main defence. The weakness of that defensive barrier was the southern end, where Australia, New Caledonia and the New Hebrides were perilously close to the Line of the Rising Sun. Early in 1942 the Japanese, in the wake of their conquests, were to attempt to enlarge their defensive Line of the Rising Sun and to include New Hebrides, New Caledonia, Fiji, Samoa and the larger islands to the north-east of Australia. That ambitious attempt failed. Thus the Line of the Rising Sun and the vast Pacific ditch had one defect. The ditch could be jumped not far from Australia.

In expecting a long war, the Japanese high command were also heartened by the belief that the European and Russian war zones would indirectly help them. They thought Germany would still defeat Britain, even invade Britain. They hoped that Germany and Italy might soon capture Suez. They expected the Soviet Union either to shrink in size or be overthrown by Germany. They also had high hopes of soon ending that war in China which absorbed over one million Japanese soldiers and mountains of military equipment and fuel. If the war in China were to end, Japanese defences in the Pacific war would be much stronger. All these hopes proved to be too optimistic; but in November 1941, when Germany was triumphant, these hopes were realistic. On such hopes rested the Japanese decision to fight.

At no time, apparently, did Japanese military chiefs believe that the United States would be conquered. It would be held at bay but would not be invaded or militarily enfeebled. War would end, the Japanese hoped, by a negotiated peace, in which the United States, shorn of allies and weary of war, would concede to Japan a large sphere of influence in East Asia, China and the Indonesia Archipelago. Surely, we say with the certainty of hindsight, Japan did not predict that she could emerge from the Pacific war with increased power and territory. In fact, erroneous predictions on the eve of a war are more common than uncommon. In human behaviour few events are more difficult to predict than the course of a war: that is one of the vital unlearned lessons of warfare.

VIII

If the Allied leaders had been able to predict the speed and success of a Japanese drive into the tropical colonies they would probably have made concessions to Japan. If they had known how strong was Japan and how weak were Singapore and General MacArthur's Philippines, there would have been serious negotiations. But nothing — no trinket, no minor concession — was offered the Japanese diplomats. The sad truth is that the Allies preferred, if crisis came, to make war rather than make concessions. They believed they would lose by making concessions. They could not, however, conceive of military defeat in those sweaty cities and tidy plantations where for generations the white pith helmet and the white face had been held high.

In Canberra and Singapore there were few fears that a war against Japan would be lost. It might be a difficult war, there might be military setbacks, but the Allies would win. Nothing aided this assurance more than western attitudes towards the Japanese. They were thought to be inferior to western soldiers in stamina, morale and leadership. Japan's victory over Russia in 1905 was forgotten, and her recent conquest of one-third of Chinese territory in the space of four years was seen more as a reflection of the weakness of the Chinese. The Japanese technology was derided, and the slogan 'Made in Japan' was viewed in Australia in the 1930s as the symbol of the shoddy: toys in Christmas stockings testified to that. It was inconceivable that Japan could make a fighter aircraft that matched aircraft made in Britain and the United States. Few western observers realised how effectively Japanese technicians had learned their craft at Douglas, Boeing and other aircraft factories in the United States.

Englishmen even more than Australians persisted in the belief that Japan was weak in the air. Two retired inspectors-general of the Royal Air Force were influential in the Pacific in 1940 and 1941, and they assumed that Japan had barely emerged from the kite-flying stage. One of these early aviators, Sir Charles Burnett, became the chief of air staff in Australia while the other, Sir Robert Brooke-Popham, became Britain's commander-in-chief in the far east. Their advice was often heard by Australia's war cabinet.

Brooke-Popham twice visited Australia in 1941 for secret discussions and confided that the Japanese were not air-minded. Menzies was not fully persuaded. In his last months as prime minister, he urged the British to send fast Hurricane aircraft to Malaya to strengthen the defences. The complacent reply he received in London stressed that the standards of Japanese aircraft were not 'even comparable with those of the Italians': in that year the word Italian – in the ears of the Allies – was a synonym for a tin soldier. Ironically, even after the Pacific war had begun and the Japanese had won mastery of the air over Malaya and Singapore, military leaders in Britain still thought the Japanese supremacy would be ended when the first British Hurricane fighters reached Singapore. Six weeks after the start of the Pacific war the Hurricanes flew over Singapore. Their inability to match the Japanese aircraft was, to many Englishmen, a shock as violent as that following the sinking of the great *Prince of Wales.*

Britain's fastest aircraft were reserved for Britain and the Middle East. In many other blunt and subtle ways the British and Australians in Singapore and Malaya tended to underestimate the Japanese nation. Japan was said to have a bath-tub navy as well as an obsolete air force; the morale of Japan's troops was said to be low after the long years in China; and the swamps, mountains and forests of Malaya were said to be obstacles too severe for an invader. The Japanese, it was said, 'dare not risk their tired army against the power of the British Empire'. Japanese pilots, it was insinuated, were unable to see at night.

A month before the outbreak of the Pacific war, the British prime minister was absorbed in the Middle East. To Mr Churchill, understandably, the Mediterranean Sea and Suez Canal and the oil of the Middle East were vital and he himself was preparing for a vigorous drive against Rommel in North Africa. As seven of every ten German divisions were now engaged in Russia, the time seemed favourable for an attack on the German forces which occupied the border of Egypt and Libya, within striking distance of the Suez Canal. To send reinforcements from Suez to Singapore would endanger the success of the drive against Rommel. Australian soldiers were wanted for that Suez campaign; British aircraft and ships were wanted. After many delays, 18 November 1941 was chosen for the beginning of the campaign in North Africa.

John Curtin, soon after becoming prime minister, had an

opportunity to recall Australian troops from the Middle East and post them to Malaya, Singapore or Australia. On 5 November 1941 he told parliament that his government had no intention of recalling them. Five days later his army chief, General Thomas Blamey, returned from the Middle East to suggest that all Australian troops – even the division which was training in Malaya – should be concentrated under one command in the Middle East. Blamey, stopping in Singapore in the course of his slow air trip, sensed no urgent danger from Japan, so imbued was he with the thinking of the high British soldiers and diplomats whom he was accustomed to meet in Cairo.

In Sydney, General Blamey was perturbed at the easy-going attitude to the European crisis. 'I am astounded at the complacency with which people in Australia view the war situation', he said. 'You are leading a carnival life, and you are enjoying it.' In Melbourne that week he observed the cheerful crowd at the horse races. Australians, he added later, were like a herd of gazelles on the grassy edge of a jungle. Even he did not realise that the jungle was so near.

Now and then Churchill, under pressure from Australia or New Zealand, promised that in the event of a Japanese advance towards the equator, he would send a fleet. On 26 October 1941, Australia received a cable from Churchill containing the good news that Britain's powerful ship, *Prince of Wales* would join the old battle cruiser *Repulse* in the Indian Ocean, 'in order further to deter Japan'. Four other British battleships were expected in the far east in the following February.

Prince of Wales and *Repulse* called at Colombo and then sailed for Singapore, arriving on 2 December 1941. Like enormous floating neon-signs, they were believed to be advertisements to the Japanese that a war would be a mistake. The Singapore naval base was a similar advertisement, designed in the early 1920s when aircraft were still flimsy and the heavy battleship was supreme. In 1941, however, the Singapore base would not be very useful unless Britain also had command of the air, the surrounding seas, and the Malayan mainland. Many Australian and British naval and air officers doubted the strength of Singapore. It is fair to say that if Singapore had stood in the North Sea, and had been designed to resist German attacks, it would not have been taken very seriously by its own supporters; but against the Japanese it was considered secure in certain conditions by Englishmen occupying high places.

The negotiations between Japan and the United States drifted on. Late in November, Washington made a cautious proposal for a continuing truce with Japan and submitted it first to relevant nations. China and Britain were wary of supporting it, and even the United States government became wary. Diplomacy could no longer avert the war.

On 7 December 1941 the Japanese aircraft-carriers launched a raid which inflicted enormous damage on the naval base at Pearl Harbor, ten miles from Honolulu. On the same day, far to the west, the American island bases of Guam and Wake were attacked. As people awakened, as sunrise succeeded sunrise between the central Pacific and the islands of the South China Sea, Japanese troops or bombs were landing at many places. In Hong Kong a Japanese division crossed into the British colony from occupied China. In the Gulf of Siam, in the dark of early morning, Japanese convoys landed troops on beaches in Malaya and Thailand. In full sunlight in the Philippines, American military aircraft which were arranged neatly on airstrips – unguarded many hours after the war had begun – were bombed by Japanese airmen. And in Singapore that afternoon the two great British warships prepared to go to sea for their last voyage, their admiral not knowing that the fighter support on which he relied had been crippled during the first day of aerial warfare in north Malaya.

In Canberra, members of the war cabinet met and resolved formally to declare war on Japan. They had no idea then of the damage which the Japanese had already caused nor the extent of her attacks across one fifth of the earth's circumference. They declared that a state of war with Japan now formally existed. The news that the United States and Japan were also formally at war was received with relief, almost jubilation, in many Australian quarters. With America in the war it might be a larger war, a more terrible war, but it would almost certainly be, they believed, a victorious war.

It is easy to be wise after the event, but it is easier to be stupid. And it would be stupid to pretend that any man holding high office could have predicted accurately on 1 December 1941 what would be the outcome of a war with Japan. And yet such predictions, necessarily hazardous and often instinctive, have a decisive influence on whether there will be peace or war. Because Japan predicted that she could easily conquer the tropical colonies and cling to them, and because the Australian and British and the American governments anticipated victory for themselves in the short term or the long term, the war was almost unavoidable. Negotiations had really broken down months before the war began. Negotiations were futile because both sides believed that their military position was superior to that of the other. Both sides wanted peace, but only on their own terms.

The way in which the Americans, in the Philippines and Pearl Harbor, were surprised by the suddenness of the Japanese raids was more a sign of over-confidence than of innocence. The way in which British, American, Australian and Free Dutch military leaders were surprised by the success of Japan's southward thrust was also a sign that during the parleying in the last year of peace they had been assuming a military strength and a power to threaten which they did not possess. Japan also overplayed her hand. An early sign of over-confidence was her occupation, by treaty, of southern Indo-China in July 1941. The sudden retaliation by the United States, Britain and Australia — the imposing of economic blockade — was in Japanese eyes a surprise and a declaration of warfare.

The moral contrast between war and peace is not simply black and white, and the distinction between warmaker and peacemaker is often a mirage.

Conclusions

17: Myths of the Nuclear Era

To reach conclusions about the causes of wars fought in the era of sailing ships and horse-drawn artillery is to provoke the question: are those conclusions relevant to the nuclear era? Are the causes of war in our era of intercontinental missiles totally different to the causes of war in the years of the first railways?

A hundred thousand articles have discussed the dangers of the nuclear era, and strategists and theologians, biologists and novelists have grappled with that vital but tantalising question of whether there will be a nuclear war in the next half century and whether such a war will be utterly devastating or somehow kept within limits. Many of the books devoted to the question see our nuclear era as unique and therefore rarely to be guided or soothed by lessons or hints from past wars and periods of peace; but our era is not so unique.

Nuclear weapons quickly haunted the imagination not only because of their power to destroy but also because of the dramatic setting in which they were first used. When the first atomic bombs were dropped on Japanese cities in 1945, warfare appeared to be transformed. The bombs gave the impression of overwhelming success because they seemed to end the war in the Pacific, crushing the spirit of a nation which hitherto had seemed defiant, and dramatically shortening a war which was not expected to end until after the American forces invaded the Japanese islands in 1946. On the other hand, if the bombs had been made and used a year or two earlier, when Japan held a position of greater military strength and was therefore less likely to surrender, they might have provoked fury more than submission. A year or two earlier, a more resilient Japan might have warned Washington that if one more nuclear bomb were dropped, Japan would kill half of the prisoners-of-war in its charge or launch an unnamed secret weapon: the exact weapon mattered little because bluff is a vital part of warfare, especially if employed by an enemy which, to western eyes, seemed as unpredictable as Japan. Even in 1945 the two atomic bombs did not inevitably have to end the war because Japan, if she so willed, could have conducted a ferocious guerrilla warfare once the American army of occupation had landed. Likewise the world in 1945 might not even have witnessed nuclear weapons if the Allied leaders, instead of pursuing their policy of unconditional surrender, had shown more mercy to the Japanese, demonstrated to them the power of the atomic bomb, and persuaded them to surrender; but there were only two atomic bombs then in America's hands, and the idea of squandering one bomb on a target of no military importance was unattractive. So the two bombs were dropped on two cities, without warning, at a delicate stage of the war, and the Japanese response happened to be tame and subdued, thus giving the outside world the impression that here was a weapon to which no answer existed.

The rush of subsequent events, even more than the flattening of two cities, proclaimed the power of the new weapon. The city of Hiroshima had been bombed on 6 August 1945, Russia declared war on Japan on 8 August, Nagasaki was bombed on 9 August, Japan first offered to surrender on 10 August, the terms of the surrender were accepted by Japan on 15 August, and by the end of the month the American troops were landing in Japan. If a less obedient series of events had followed the first atomic bomb, the new weapon would not have so dramatically shaped our imagination. Never before had a major military weapon been introduced with such success, and never before had that single success remained – for at least four decades – the sole example of a weapon's magnitude.

The new weapon's halo of invincibility also stemmed from the American credo at the end of the Second World War that technology alone could win wars. Compared to the Soviet Union the United States relied more on factories and the ingenuity of inventors and less on the sheer number and the morale of fighting men; and the nuclear weapon seemed to show the wisdom of their emphasis. Its impact was aided by the belief that it would lead to short wars. It seemed that military technology would mercifully restrict the duration of wars at last, something which field-marshalls had seen as inevitable since 1900.

The peculiar situation of the world and of Japan in 1945 gave those two bombs a spectacular and lasting influence such as no global stage-manager could possibly have achieved. The atomic bomb was superseded by the hydrogen bomb, and the methods of delivering nuclear warheads from land sites and from submarines became sophisticated and accurate, and more nations learned how to make nuclear weapons. As the thousands of missiles now had a capacity to destroy most of the large cities of the world, it became impossible to think that the world could be the same again. Any lessons learnt about war and peace during most decades of modern history now seemed to be largely irrelevant.

The belief that the world had entered an unprecedented era was shared both by the gloomy and the optimistic, though they disagreed totally about the effects of this revolutionary era. The gloomy argued that if a weapon existed it would ultimately be used and that therefore nuclear war was unavoidable. On the other hand the more hopeful leaped to the opposite extreme and argued that weapons of such destructiveness helped, more than any past weapons, to preserve peace between the super-powers. While one school of thought saw the uniquely powerful weapons as a cause for unprecedented gloom, another viewed them with optimism.

III

Many of those who saw the nuclear age as mainly a breakaway from the traditional history of war and peace still occupied some of the intellectual furniture from the pre-nuclear world. They tried to construct new versions of the balance of power theories; they detected new armaments races; and they were as engrossed in the likelihood of surprise attacks as those military observers who were shocked by Pearl Harbor in 1941. Curiously, while seeing the nuclear era as unique, they held some of the assumptions of Norman Angell, Ivan Bloch and those pre-1914 prophets who themselves had tended to believe that their own era of warfare, beginning about 1900 and culminating in the First World War, was unprecedented, and ruled by new criteria. Every era of rapid change is inclined to emphasise the new at the expense of what has not changed.

Accidental war was quickly seen as one of the special hazards of the nuclear age. For long there has been a theory that some wars were accidental, though the war in Europe in 1939 and the interlocked war that began in the Pacific in 1941 were not interpreted as accidental, nor were the Korean and Vietnam wars. It was the First World War more than any other war which gave rise to the idea that a war in its beginning could be a kind of steam-roller which, once the engine was warmed up, unintentionally slipped into gear and began to roll forward, gathering such momentum that none of its important passengers could halt it. This picture of 1914 was revived in the nuclear era when it was feared that a war between nuclear powers might follow the same steam-roller course, with appalling results. The theory, which was discussed sceptically in chapter nine of this book, gained urgency in the era of automatic weapons through the fear that mechanical errors or a mad leader might launch a nuclear missile. As that missile could lead to almost instant retaliation, it was easy to envisage one mishap triggering chaos. The possibility of human error seemed sufficiently serious to lead to the imposing of controls and checks, at least in the United States. Likewise the fear that an arms race would lead inevitably to war – a fear borrowed from the First World War – became widespread in the first nuclear era, and yet one careful study of the American and Soviet investment in offensive strategic weapons in the long period from 1952 to 1976 shows that when one side increased its investment in arms it was not usually in response to an increase by another nation. In short the idea of an arms race in which each spurt was a response to the other runner was very dubious. As the decades passed, and nuclear war was avoided, the emphasis on the uniqueness of the nuclear era acquired a new slant. The long period of peace now apparent within the western world was increasingly attributed to nuclear weapons and 'the balance of terror'. At the time of writing, the European world – and that includes the United States and the Soviet Union – has experienced four decades of international peace.

Admittedly 'peace' is a relative term, and since 1945 there have been uprisings in eastern Europe, a long civil war in Greece, upheavals in Northern Ireland and Poland, and a Cold War during which a European conflict seemed just over the horizon. Several long wars have also been fought by Europeans on the edge of this vast European expanse, with the French fighting in Algeria and the Russians in Afghanistan. Likewise European nations, trying to hold on to their overseas empires or retreat from them on favourable terms, fought wars across the seas: the Dutch fought in Indonesia, the British in Malaysia, Aden and the Falklands, the French in Vietnam and the Portuguese in Africa. Since 1945, many Europeans have been killed while fighting, but few have died on their own soil. From 1945 to the late 1980s there has been an unusual period of peace for the European peoples.

The common explanation for the peacefulness is the power of nuclear weapons and the belief that a nuclear war is probably unwinnable. That overlooks the fact that the nineteenth century also experienced long periods of relative peace, one of which ran from the end of the Napoleonic Wars in 1815 to the outbreak of the Crimean War in 1853. The fact that a later era of European peace extending from the end of the Franco-Prussian War in 1871 was exactly as long as the period of peace from 1945 to 1988 should warn us that our experience is not unique. Therefore it is unwise to jump to the conclusion that the European lands since 1945 have been relatively peaceful largely because of the role of nuclear weapons.

The long peace in the lands of European peoples since 1945 came from a mixture of causes. The Second World War, like every decisive general war, set up a hierarchy of power which made diplomacy more manageable and the resort to force less likely; the dominant nations – the United States and the Soviet Union – also knew from recent experience the terrible cost of a major war; and nuclear weapons made resorting to war less likely, for in a nuclear war both sides might suffer losses that far outweighed the gains of victory. In addition, the peace after 1945 eventually yielded a distinct contrast with the shorter period of peace which began in 1918. Whereas the two powerful losers of the First World War, Russia and Germany, had been able to regain military power with remarkable speed, the main losers of the Second World War, Germany and Japan, were not allowed to re-arm in the normal sense. Germany was divided by the victors of 1945 and remains divided, while Japan's post-war constitution curbs her military expenditure. Rarely in the history of the modern world have the losers in a major war remained under loose military control so many decades after the end of the war. As the military recovery of nations which have lost a major war tends to foster instability, the military fate of Germany and Japan has been a crucial cause of peace. Their wonderful economic performance since 1945 and indeed the absence of a major world depression have probably also promoted peace: it was the world depression of the 1930s which not only carried Hitler to power but so demoralised and diverted Britain and France that they lost their grip on an unarmed Germany and failed to prevent Hitler from re-arming at a time when such prevention was possible.

In the last two centuries it was normal, after a decisive general war or a decisive series of wars involving major nations, for a long period of peace to set in. Significantly the peace after the 1914–18 war was abnormally short, for it was weakened by the world depression and its military, economic and psychological effects on winners and losers. On the other hand our period of international peace is abnormally long, and perhaps nuclear weapons have been more important in prolonging the peace than in initiating it. The history of war and peace during the last two centuries shows that nuclear weapons are not a necessary cause of a long period of peace, but they might well be a crucial ingredient of a very long period of peace. Traditionally, after each major war, the memory of the dangers and desolation of warfare have faded, allowing war to take on a romantic appearance and thus hastening the outbreak of a new war, whereas today the nuclear weapons themselves remain a vivid reminder of the potential devastation of war. While nuclear weapons might prolong the present period of relative peace, they cannot guarantee it.

It is possible that in the peaceful years 1945–85 the advent of nuclear weapons was no more influential than another new fact, the dominance by two nations of the whole international system. This was the first time in the last two centuries that two nations had been so dominant: moreover their geographical isolation lessened the possibility of direct and dangerous entanglements along their own borders, and they lacked those turbulent border contacts which endangered England and France when they were potential enemies, or France and Germany when they were strong rivals. The physical isolation of the two superpowers has lessened the chance of any violent confrontation over a strategic point which each viewed as central to its security and therefore to be held, whatever the cost. Significantly, the most dangerous point of confrontation between the Soviet Union and the United States since 1945 has been Berlin, a meeting point of the American and Russian zones of military occupation. But if Berlin, instead of being hundreds of miles from the nearest Russian city and thousands of miles from the nearest American city, had been a fortress on the border of Russian and American soil, the Berlin crises of 1948 and 1961 would have been even more explosive. In the history of warfare, nations have tended to fight their neighbours more often than they have fought distant nations, and so the isolation of Moscow and Washington lowered the chances of intense conflict, especially in the quarter century 1945–70. But later the multiplication of submarines driven by nuclear engines and capable of shooting long-distance missiles armed with nuclear warheads virtually had the effect of turning the superpowers into close neighbours, thus making them more vulnerable to attack.

The existence of only two superpowers with their own allies and spheres of interest has also curbed the likelihood of a major war breaking out within Europe. The nations in western Europe, being mostly under the American wing, were unlikely to fight each other while the nations in eastern Europe, being under the Soviet wing, could not fight each other. A list of those European nations which conceivably might fight each other was far shorter in 1979 than in 1939.

As both the Soviet Union and the United States extended their own spheres of influence – ideological and military and commercial – they met or clashed in Africa, south-east Asia, central America and nearly every other part of the world. Those dispersed Soviet-American clashes, taking place far from home, have been fought mainly by proxy. When the United States fought in Korea and Vietnam, Russia fought on the opposing side not in person but by supplying weapons and military advice. While a Russian army fights in Afghanistan in the 1980s, the Americans fight silently by supplying the Afghan rebels with ammunition. The fact that the Soviet and American forces have fought each other indirectly and far from home is a sign that the post-1945 peace is an uneasy peace, but it is not startlingly more uneasy than the long European peace of 1871–1914 when several overseas wars were fought partly by proxy.

Certainly the evidence since 1945 gives no support to that school of opinion which believes that nuclear weapons, and the constant improving of those weapons, increases the likelihood of war. It is right to stress that a nuclear war, if it erupts, could be a terrible war, but there is no compelling evidence that, so far, nuclear weapons have endangered the peace.

IV

Since 1945 no nuclear weapons have been used in warfare, and so it could be an exaggeration to adopt the phrase 'nuclear era'. Although the major nations were possibly on the brink of nuclear war over the issue of Korea in 1953 and over Cuba in 1962, they did not launch nuclear weapons. War after war has been fought and nations possessing nuclear weapons have taken part in them, but have not used such weapons. On the other hand the label of 'nuclear era' can be justified if nations wield such great power through the mere possession of nuclear weapons that they do not have to use.

A survey conducted by the American political scientists, Organski and Kugler, tested the simple proposition that if nuclear weapons are now all-important, then in a typical diplomatic dispute the nuclear power would simply force an opponent to give in. Even if the nuclear power issued no threat, its bargaining position in theory would be so strong that its opponent would make concessions. Their survey suggests however, that usually a nuclear power did not browbeat its opponent: indeed 'nuclear missiles are not the miracle weapon they were thought to be at the beginning of the nuclear era'.

Even more curious was the evidence culled from the seven crises in which a non-nuclear power faced a nuclear power.

Clearly the non-nuclear power could have been expected to step down, but it did not step down and in six of seven episodes it actually won the dispute. The exception was the Russian blockade of Berlin in 1948 when the United States, then the only effective nuclear power, effectively used its threat to win. In the other six conflicts* in this category, the nation possessing no nuclear weapons defied or ignored the nuclear powers 'and got away with it'. In disputes involving a nuclear power the winners were usually the nations possessing 'conventional military superiority on the site of the dispute.' Their study suggests that the influence of nuclear weapons on specific international disputes was probably small, for nations were reluctant or afraid to use their nuclear weapons, while a nation which did not possess such weapons was inclined to ignore them when they appeared in the hands of the enemy. If this is true it is strange that the most powerful weapons in the world's history have achieved so little.

The study by Organski and Kugler, however, is not conclusive. The two main nuclear powers, the United States and the Soviet Union, were often over-extended because they were protecting many interests and allies in lands far from home. Remote interests are harder to protect, irrespective of the mighty armour held at home. Britain in her long naval supremacy did not always exert effective pressure on the borders of remote colonies or against remote tribes, and yet it would be as unwise to conclude that she lacked effective naval power as it would be to say that Russia and America lack great military power today. Sometimes a superpower is less effective when operating in those remote lands where her own interests are less important, but this does not mean that closer to home,

---

* The six wars in which non-nuclear forces were said to be not deterred by a nuclear power were: the Chinese civil war of 1945–49 when the winning Chinese communists were not deterred by the fact that Chiang Kai-shek's ally, the USA, possessed the atomic bomb; the Czech coup of 1948; the Korean War of 1950–53; the Hungarian revolt of 1956; the Chinese–Soviet dispute over the Usuri River in 1969; and the long Vietnam War of 1964–73. In the opinion of Organski and Kugel, these conflicts provided 'precisely the ideal conditions in which the mechanism of deterrence should operate'. It did not operate in six episodes, though it did in the seventh – the Berlin blockade. The interpretation of some of these crises, however, is open to dispute.

in more typical spheres of influence, the superpower's authority will be so open to challenge.

Organski and Kugler rightly pointed out that nuclear weapons might not remain unused in the future. They see the danger of nuclear war as highest at that time when the pecking order between big nations becomes confused. They believe that a war between the superpowers becomes likely when the world's dominant nation – dominant in the sum total of economic, social and political strength – has almost been overtaken by a challenger. In their eyes the next dangerous phase will arrive when Russia begins to overtake the United States in total capability, or when China approaches the Soviet Union and, 'decades later', the United States. At such times the two rivals, being equal in strength but so different in their mixture of economic and social and military strength, are likely to disagree on their relative might and therefore are more likely to resolve the recurring diplomatic deadlocks by fighting. A crisis provoked by the rising challenger, however, does not have to result in war. In the period 1870–1914 the United States passed Britain in overall capacity without provoking war. But if the challenger, while overtaking the leading nation, provokes acute tension, and if the leader and challenger both possess nuclear weapons, they might use them: such is the opinion of Organski and Kugler.

There is more continuity than we realise between the world of Hitler and, almost half a century later, the world of Reagan and Gorbachev. Even in the earlier time of Hitler, conventional weapons were very destructive: indeed if they, rather than the new nuclear weapons, received priority in research, they probably would be frightening today. In the absence of nuclear weapons, the conventional weapons of the Second World War would certainly have been developed more rapidly than they were in the following forty years. Today we would be more conscious of the present destructive capacity of orthodox weapons if they had not been shaded by nuclear weapons. While we have come to regard the bombing of Hiroshima as the ultimate symbol of devastation, its destructiveness was far from unique. In the same year an American air attack on Tokyo, using conventional rather than atomic bombs, killed nearly 84,000 people, and one attack with conventional bombs on the

German city of Dresden killed an estimated 135,000: Dresden in its death toll therefore almost equalled two Hiroshimas. Even if no nuclear warhead existed today, the Americans or Russians could bomb a compact European or Asian city so thoroughly with conventional explosives that the wounded and dead might exceed 500,000. By one calculation more than 10,000,000 people have been killed in wars since the end of 1945, and not one of those deaths was inflicted by nuclear weapons. In one sense the nuclear era has not arrived simply because nuclear weapons have rarely been used and because the possession of such weapons is not yet a necessary passport to military power.

v

Even if it is true that the nuclear era has not yet arrived, it will eventually descend with a mighty roar – in the opinion of many observers. They believe that since nuclear weapons exist in their tens of thousands they must ultimately be used, for in their minds it is inconceivable that major weapons will remain idle in a nuclear stockpile for an indefinite period. Unknowingly, the proponents of this view are appealing to history when they expound the principle that the major form of armament of an era will inevitably be used.

History does offer guidance though it cannot be conclusive. In certain centuries in Europe, military might was limited by strong conventions and restraints. The eighteenth century was especially noted for a limited warfare in which battles were avoided except in highly favourable conditions, an enemy in retreat was not often pursued, and military campaigns were usually suspended from the late autumn until the late spring. The fear that mercenary soldiers would desert a battlefield in large numbers shaped the mode and intensity of fighting. Ironically the soldiers themselves were the high-risk weapons of that century.

In many centuries the most dislocating tactic would have been to assassinate the enemy's monarch but it was rarely if ever attempted even during bitter wars: the possibility of retaliation was too high. Similarly, in the years 1700–1940 the killing of prisoners-of-war was rare during wars in western

Europe. As fear of retaliation has clearly been a factor
operating in every century, one should not be surprised that
nuclear weapons are treated gingerly.

At no time in the last two centuries has it been easy to predict
whether a major weapon will determine the course of a coming
war, let alone be employed. Big nations can possess a deadly
weapon but refuse to use it even though its efficiency and
deadliness have been proved. Chemical warfare is not new, and
sulphur was burned at sieges of cities in the Peloponnesian
Wars nearly five centuries before Christ, while in the Crimean
War the British proposed to burn sulphur on a large scale and
allow the wind to carry it amongst Russian soldiers at
Sebastopol. In the First World War the Germans directed
chlorine gas against the French trenches in April 1915 and
British troops used gas five months later, both armies relying
on a favourable wind to blow the gas towards the enemy.
Occasionally the wind did not obey and the attacks backfired.
Shells filled with gas could be fired accurately from artillery,
irrespective of the direction of the wind, and thousands of gas
shells were fired during the trench-fighting in France in 1917.
Both sides also used mustard gas which remained in the soil for
days and, when the air temperatures rose, escaped into the
atmosphere and wounded soldiers. In the last year of the war,
various gases were so effective in surprise attacks that one in
four of all American casualties in the war resulted from gas; by
one definition the use of gas was humane because it wounded or
disabled rather than killed soldiers. At the end of the war, gas
was clearly a major and proven weapon, and as aircraft were
becoming more effective, their ability to drop gas bombs
seemed likely to revolutionise warfare. In 1926 the Oxford
scientist, Dr C. G. Douglas, and Britain's former controller of
chemical warfare, Brigadier-General Hartley, summing up the
future of gas warfare, noted that most 'forecasts of future wars
assign to gas an important role in its use from aircraft.' The
mass-gassing of civilians in cities seemed likely in wars of the
future, and by 1939 many nations had equipped both soldiers
and civilians with gas masks. To the surprise of most observers,
gas was not used in the Second World War, though the
Germans had by then developed nerve gases which were
deadlier than any gases used in France in 1915–18.

Gas was not used directly against soldiers and civilians in the Korean and Vietnam wars, though chemicals were directed against foliage in the Vietnamese countryside in 1965. The United States used the herbicide, Agent Orange, to destroy thick jungle or crops, spraying an area equal to one tenth of South Vietnam. Initially believed to be safe both for the Americans and their enemy, Agent Orange carried tiny amounts of a toxic contaminant which the manufacturing process had failed to remove, and ultimately it was shown to be harmful to American servicemen. In 1969 the General Assembly of the United Nations passed a motion condemning the herbicide as contrary to a Geneva Protocol which in 1925 banned chemical warfare. In the following year the United States ceased to use Agent Orange. Ironically the power of retaliation lay not with the enemy but with undetected properties in the chemical itself.

The great powers of the western world have not deliberately used lethal gas in warfare since 1918. Italy, almost a great power, sprayed and bombed mustard gas on the Ethiopians, thus achieving a major victory in 1936. Five years later the Japanese artillery at Ichang on the Yangtze River fired gas-filled shells and forced the Chinese to retreat. In 1942 President Roosevelt of the United States warned that his Allies would make 'the fullest retaliation' if Japan and Germany fought with the aid of gas and his warning was effective.

There can be little doubt that the fear of retaliation was the major factor outlawing the use of gas in wars fought by superpowers, but in some wars there was little fear of retaliation. The ill-equipped Ethiopians and Chinese had no capacity to retaliate, nor could the tribesmen of the Yemen retaliate when the colourless but fatal phosgene gas and the Egyptian-made blister gas were used against them in the civil war of the 1960s. In the 1980s, Iraq used gas against Iran, perhaps in the hope of breaking the military deadlock and so achieving a breakthrough; but soon Iran retaliated. Undoubtedly the superpowers have carried out extensive research on chemical warfare, and in 1982 a scholarly book, *Surprise Attack*, argued that, of all the unconventional weapons, chemical warfare was probably more valuable than nuclear weapons for an attacker relying on surprise.

Germ warfare was also a possibility during the Second World War but was not employed. Like chemical and nuclear weapons, it is likely to lead to strong retaliation. Moreover germs can accidentally stray and so infect their original owner. The reluctance of major nations to use gas provides a message which has largely been ignored. Since, over a long period, major nations have refused to use one of their most deadly weapons, it is possible that major nations will refuse to launch nuclear missiles for fear that similar weapons will be used against them or that international opinion will turn against them. This does not mean that nuclear weapons will necessarily remain idle in the following half century. But it certainly casts doubt on the dogma, favoured by large sections of the anti-nuclear movement, that major weapons must inevitably be used and that therefore a cataclysm lies just around the corner.

As the fear of costly retaliation has always been present in the relations between nations, and is one of the determinants of whether a nation decides to fight or not to fight, the likelihood of retaliation must affect the minds of national leaders during an age of ultra-lethal weapons. In this sense the nuclear era represented continuity. Indeed the case can be argued that the proliferation of nuclear weapons or deadly gases could well be valuable because it compels nations to be even more sensitive to the probability that if they use the weapon a terrible vengeance might be inflicted on them. But it is also reasonable to suggest that the larger the number of nations which own nuclear weapons, the higher is the possibility that one nation will eventually decide, either in desperation or through one of those miscalculations so common on the eve of past wars, to employ the weapon.

The history of warfare, while offering no clear guide to future wars, should make us wary of accepting several of the key assumptions behind the anti-nuclear movement: that major weapons must ultimately be used and that a build up of nuclear weapons definitely increases the chance of disaster. The accumulation of nuclear weapons might well ensure that a major war, should it come, will be a terribly devastating war. On the other hand the fear of retaliation might mean that a major war is less likely to be a nuclear war.

The puzzle of the unused stockpile of weapons tends to colour much of the thinking about modern war, but in fact major nations have long possessed a large unused capacity to harm their enemy. Unused military capacity was visible in Europe on the large scale in 1850, 1880, 1910 and even in the wartime year of 1940. Ironically, a mountain of surplus, unused, up-to-date weapons is especially visible at the end of a war. Thus at the end of 1945 the world's combined military power dwarfed that of 1939, and most of that 1945 power was an unused stockpile, and yet it was the year 1945 – not 1939 – which ushered in a period of relative peace for the western world.

There is an understandable reluctance to accept what is true of the nuclear age as of the earlier ages: that international peace prevails when rival nations agree that they would lose rather than gain by trying to resolve their differences by war. A heavily-armed world is hardly a reassuring spectacle, but if no alliance or superpower believes it can gain victory by using its massive arms, then the peace is likely to continue. In the twenty-first century, when perhaps a formidable new weapon will have arisen to end the nuclear era, people may look back on the half century 1945–1995 and marvel that the 'balance of terror' was the label commonly assigned to such a peaceful era.

VI

In intellectual circles the idea is now widespread that a major war must be an all-out conflict and might well destroy the human species. Archbishop Hunthausen, in accepting the Thomas Merton Peace Medal on 18 November 1982, told his American audience that it was no longer possible for a political and religious leader to claim that there could be a 'limited nuclear war' instead of an all-out war. In the same year one of America's best known historians, William H. McNeill, concluded a detailed study of warfare since AD1000 with the affirmation that the only alternative to a world government 'appears to be sudden and total annihilation of the human species'. Patrick White, a winner of the Nobel Prize for Literature, expressed the parallel view held deeply in the arts that the world's people must control those national leaders 'who are prepared to destroy a world they lust to dominate'.

The concept of a nuclear winter deepened the gloom. In 1983 it was argued in the journals *Science* and *Foreign Affairs* that a nuclear war between the superpowers would create a climatic disaster and famine that would kill several billion people. In the history of the world this climatic disruption would equal or be 'more severe' than that which extinguished the dinosaurs at the end of the Cretaceous period. The prophecy influenced governments, and six nations in the Delhi Declaration of 28 January 1985 affirmed that even a limited nuclear war would turn the earth 'into a darkened frozen planet'. In the following year a critical inspection of the assumptions and statistics of the theory seemed to melt the likelihood of a nuclear winter: it was highly improbable, even on the basis of the evidence gathered by the scientists who predicted the winter. On a subject as speculative, political and emotional as the effects of a nuclear war, sensible predictions are not easy.

It is almost an axiom of our age that a nuclear war, should it occur, will be very short. The theory that nuclear wars will be waged only for a few days rather than a few years is believed so widely that its exponents usually feel no need to argue their case: they simply assert it.

The prediction of a quick, deadly nuclear war seems to rest on the dubious assumption that the prevailing machines of warfare largely determine whether a war will be long or short: accordingly the nuclear weapon, being more shattering than any previous weapon, will end a war quickly. That kind of theory is old and unreliable. Thus, from the 1860s it was believed that European wars were likely to be short because of the new railways, telegraphs and quick-firing weapons, but that prediction was nullified by the unexpectedly long First World War which gave rise to the view that in the technology of warfare the attack and defence were now in deadlock. The new prediction of long wars was superseded by a faith that the fast aircraft and the armoured divisions on land were restoring the primacy of the attack, thus making for shorter wars. Earlier chapters have shown, however, that technology has not been the sole factor, nor even necessarily the main factor, in determining the length of a war.

Another dubious assumption of those who expect a swift nuclear war is their belief that the length of a war is fairly predictable. Again and again, experienced generals and admirals have failed to predict the likely duration of a war, especially a war between major powers. It is therefore unwise to expect that an ability to predict the duration of a war will suddenly emerge in, of all times, this most uncertain and volatile military and political era.

It is possible that a war between two nuclear powers will be short, but if the war involves the superpowers and many of their allies, it might well prove to be a long war. General wars have tended to be longer than two-nation wars, mainly because they are a combination of many wars, fought on different terrains, under different conditions, with some of the warring nations very late in entering the war, and the conduct of peace negotiations becoming difficult because of the sheer number of nations involved. General wars have also tended to be long because neither side is likely to be winning on all fronts at the same time, and so the nation losing on one front might be more interested in peace than its ally winning on another front.

Those who believe that nuclear war will always be quick and decisive seem to assume that a nuclear war will be a clockwork spectacular which, once the first atomic missile is fired, triggers a series of pre-ordained attacks and counter-attacks that pulverise the weaker nations into submission. But it is still possible that after the first missiles have been fired both sides will agree to a temporary cease-fire and then resolve that it is more prudent to resume fighting by conventional weapons. It is also possible that both superpowers will be heavily damaged by the first round of nuclear missiles and call a halt: while they are battered and disorganised, some of their allies might begin fighting each other on a new front with conventional weapons. Likewise a war might begin with conventional weapons, become deadlocked, briefly launch nuclear weapons against a few military targets, and then resume as a conventional war. A major war fought by nuclear powers need not become a nuclear war until its last phase or middle phase rather than during its first phase.

Within the last hundred years a general war involving major powers usually had numerous turning points in which the war increased or decreased in intensity, a new strategy was adopted or a new front was opened, kindling or snuffing the hope of victory. It would therefore be surprising if modern nations fighting with a wider variety of weapons than ever before, and capable of waging war in so many distant regions of the globe, should be so strait-jacketed by the potential of one of their weapons that their mode of fighting, and the duration of their war, should be more restricted than ever before.

While it is easy to envisage a war suddenly ended by a crushing blow from nuclear or other modern weapons, that blow is also capable of widening a war. A knockout victory by one nation suddenly creates a vacuum in the sphere of influence of the defeated nation, and new wars often break out as a result. Thus in 1940, Hitler's conquest of Western Europe weakened France's hold on her colony in Indo-China, Holland's control of her oil-rich East Indies, and Britain's ability to defend her colonies in Hong Kong, Malaya, Singapore, Burma and India; this forced and sudden loosening of Europe's grip on south-east Asia emboldened Japan to launch her Pacific war late in 1941. Likewise, a year later, Hitler's swift march into Russia forced Stalin to divert some of his forces from Siberia and the Soviet coast opposite Japan, and that safeguarded Japan's flank, enabling her to make conquests towards the equator.

When the waterbirds fight, the fisherman increases his catch: that is one of the few accepted axioms of international relations. It would be strange if, in a nuclear war, disasters as sudden and tumultuous as those of 1940 and 1941 did not provoke similar opportunism. Thus, if one of the superpowers should be knocked out, and if the other superpower is battered and disorganised though victorious, the international system would at once become fluid and malleable.

In essence, a so-called nuclear war can involve a few nuclear and a host of conventional weapons, can involve mostly non-nuclear nations and be fought on many fronts, can provoke new and simultaneous wars by the sheer crush of military events, and in its duration and outcome can be as unpredictable as the wars of the past. It is unwise to endorse the widespread conclusion that a nuclear war, especially one between superpowers, is certain to be short.

Likewise the experience of past wars suggests that a major

weapon is not always used at the outset of the war and, if used at all, can be sparingly used. In 1914, Britain and Germany possessed the most expensive navies in history and both nations were determined to command the sea but neither could afford to fight the other on unfavourable terms. Their main clash was thus postponed for two years, until the Battle of Jutland, and even there both navies preferred an indecisive contest to the risk of a crushing defeat. Likewise in a modern war the superpowers, fearing nuclear retaliation, might continue to treat nuclear missiles as weapons of last resort, to be used only if the opponent should gain the upper hand in a conventional war fought on land, sea and air. The nuclear weapons, far from being instantly decisive, might be held in reserve and so help to prolong the war.

No category of war is at present so unpredictable as a war involving nuclear weapons. If ten American or ten Russian cities were to be hit by nuclear missiles the effect on public morale and on the will-power of the civilian and military leaders cannot easily be forecast. While some nations show a capacity to fight on in the face of overwhelming odds, some collapse or seek an early peace before the obstacles become forbidding. The wars of the past seem to offer the same gentle warning to those who expect a long war between the superpowers as to those who predict a short war: 'both are possible'. Wars, usually, have tended to be longer than expected.

VII

Never before has such a powerful peace movement preached the possibility of abolishing war or banning nuclear weapons. The peace crusade is now so confident and so large and active that it has become in its own right a factor in international relations. There have always been peace movements; Free Trade was a vigorous peace movement in the middle of the nineteenth century, and later came Esperanto and Socialism. The First World War and its horrors multiplied the numbers of those who sought a way of ending war, and the League of Nations at Geneva was seen as a special instrument of peace in the 1920s and 1930s. The Second World War and especially the dropping of the two atomic bombs in 1945 spurred a new peace movement in democratic nations but during the Cold War of the 1950s that movement was often seen as the fellow traveller, the tame friend of communism.

Meanwhile many believers in peace still held to a simple formula. Some argued that male aggression was the main cause of war and that if women ruled the world there would be international peace, but that theory wilted when women became the rulers of India, Israel and Britain and did not prevent their nations engaging in wars. Communism was for a long time claimed to be a peace movement, and that quality was widely attributed to it in the 1930s and 1940s. The only communist nation, until 1945, was the Soviet Union, and as it was an opponent of Hitler it was seen generally as peaceful, its own invasion of Poland in 1939 having been forgotten or forgiven. It was able to pose as the supporter of international peace and denounce capitalism as the persistent provoker of war until the 1950s when it was no longer possible even for an ardent apologist to argue that communist nations were averse to war if the opportunity seemed favourable.

The loss of plausibility of the old single-factor formulas for world peace was a boon to the birth of a wider peace movement which, tied to no ideology, simply stressed the peril of the world. The anti-nuclear movement, however, was not steady, rising in the 1950s, fading away swiftly after the early 1960s, lying almost asleep – curiously – when the Vietnam War was at its height, then reviving with vigour in the mid 1970s, once the war in Vietnam was over, and reaching a peak perhaps on both sides of the Atlantic in the early 1980s. Even with its tendency to blow hot and then cold, it had a strength and tenacity such as no popular movement for peace could even approach in the years before 1945. It won wide support from the young – the group traditionally expected to fight the wars but which was mainly absent from the peace movements before the Second World War. In Europe the military leaders became the special target, partly because they were American rather than European, partly because fear of Russian communism had waned, but especially because the young pacifists possessed no serious idea of the causes of war and peace. Professor Michael Howard, a fine historian of war, noted that only one generation of successful peace is necessary to lull many young idealists into believing the preposition 'that peace is a natural condition threatened only by those professionally involved in preparations for war.'

The peace movement attracted utopians who held no theory of war and peace; it attracted scientists who knew the destructive power of the latest weapons or whose field of study was nature, biology and those areas which a nuclear war might devastate; it especially attracted followers from the Left, for they did not worry if disarmament should largely affect the capitalist world but leave communist nations in full possession of their nuclear arsenal; it attracted theologians and, from 1972, many bishops of the Catholic Church in the United States where the Archbishop of Seattle was to become an advocate of the disarming of the United States 'with trust and reliance on the Lord as our security'.

Public opinion and possibly economic sanctions were the quiet weapons of the new peace movement. In 1982 a disarmament seminar at Cambridge University argued that nations could begin to discard their nuclear arms and that the world's opinion would protect them from an aggressor. To critics who saw such a viewpoint as unworldly the disarmers replied that already public opinion had prevented the use of nuclear weapons, dissuading President Nixon from using nuclear weapons against Vietnam and also from bombing the irrigation dams and canals in north Vietnam. Whether public opinion would be so vocal and persuasive if some day the firing of nuclear missiles was a way of saving Europe from invasion or protecting the national independence of the United States was open to doubt. Moreover, public opinion in favour of peace at all costs was essentially a force in the United States and among its more democratic allies: no such public opinion was visible in Russia, eastern Europe, China, Vietnam, Cuba and those communist nations whose citizens lacked the freedom to call on their own rulers to lead the way in disarming.

The peace movement could well enlist such support that it becomes a profound force in international affairs. Most followers of peace movements, however, do not appreciate that their movement could prove to be a cause of war. Few crucial conclusions about war and peace seem to be so little known as the proposition that every major factor fostering peace is also capable of fostering war; and so far no argument has been offered against that painful conclusion. A peace movement can actually promote war. It can even promote a nuclear war by giving leaders of an authoritarian nation the strong impression that the morale of their enemy has been undermined by the peace movement within its borders and that the firing of a new nuclear missile against the enemy will so shatter morale and so freeze will-power that the enemy will sue for peace. While a strong peace movement can actually prevent a war, it can also hasten the coming of a war or prolong a war that might have ended early. The peace movement in England and France in the 1930s probably was one cause of the Second World War because it strengthened Hitler's bargaining position and gave him an inflated confidence that the potential enemy had no stomach for war. A generation later in the United States the peace movement possibly prolonged the war in Vietnam.

It is natural to wish success to a mass movement which tries to prevent the spread of nuclear arms to new nations and reduce the nuclear arsenal of the superpowers. And yet success in reducing the nuclear stockpile and even in banning the bomb might not necessarily promote international safety. A few nations might then successfully devise an even more terrifying weapon, and for a time it might be the possession of a sole nation which therefore has no fear of retaliation. Meanwhile most supporters of peace movements believe that they are working for peace, and they will continue so to work, and sometimes peace will be promoted by their enthusiasm.

VIII

Normally the outbreak of a major war becomes more likely as the last devastating war fades from personal memory. As Europe has not been devastated by war for more than forty years, most Europeans have only second-hand memories of the horrors of war. Likewise most Russian and American families, not having suffered in the wars which their country has fought on foreign soil since 1945, see war as less harmful when the memory of its realities fades away. The western world looks with disdain on the fervour with which some nations in the Middle East go to war but such fervour has not necessarily vanished permanently from the lands of European peoples. The terror felt towards an approaching war can be overcome, and fear can even give way to fervour, if the goal at stake is high.

Films, plays, books and paintings can portray the terror of a nuclear war, but no horror can continue to be persuasively depicted if the horror, so often predicted, does not arrive. Even disasters in nuclear power plants seem to give only a temporary shock, the disaster slowly being forgotten. The anti-nuclear movement is sure to pass through periods of decline and revival simply because fear and horror, no matter how soundly based, cannot be kept alive year after year. A world cannot permanently live in fear, no matter how potent is the danger that nuclear nightmare might suddenly descend. The warning of danger can also be self-defeating if evidence proves that the fear was exaggerated. That seems to have been the fate of 'the nuclear winter'. As the old fable hints, the scientist who cries 'wolf' too often is no longer heeded. Equally menacing are those citizens and nations who are deaf to the cry of 'wolf'.

IX

So far the nuclear era shows considerable continuity with the preceding era. The special perils predicted in the first four decades of the nuclear era are not yet evident. So far the evidence suggests that nuclear weapons have probably been more a factor for peace than for war. The evidence also suggests that the term 'arms race' is not yet appropriate for the nuclear era, and historical evidence indicates that an arms race is not an inevitable pathway to war. While many theorists of war are certain that the great nuclear stockpile will eventually be used, with disastrous results, there are historical precedents for major weapons and tactics lying unused for long periods after their effectiveness has been proved.

Just as the despair towards the future is often exaggerated and based on a blindness to history or a misreading of history, so several of the sources of hope can also be exaggerated. Thus the peace movement in which so many trust can, in certain conditions, actually increase the likelihood of war more than

18: War, Peace and Neutrality

FLAWS IN CURRENT THEORIES OF WAR AND PEACE

1. Most of the popular theories of war – and the explanations by many historians of individual wars – blame capitalists, dictators, monarchs or other individuals or pressure groups. These theories, however, explain rivalry and tension rather than war: rivalry and tension between countries can exist for generations without producing war.

2. Governments' aims and ambitions are vital in explaining each war, but to emphasise ambitions and to ignore the *means* of implementing ambitions is to ignore the main question which has to be explained. For the outbreak of war and the outbreak of peace are essentially decisions to implement aims by new *means*. To attempt to explain war is to attempt to explain why forceful *means* were selected.

3. The evidence of past wars does not support the respectable theory that an uneven 'balance' of power tends to promote war. If the theory is turned upside down, however, it has some validity.

4. The evidence of past wars does not support the scapegoat theory and its assumption that rulers facing internal troubles often started a foreign war in the hope that a victory would promote peace at home.

5. The evidence of past wars does not support the 'one pair of hands' theory of war: the belief that a nation busily making money will have no spare energy or time for the making of war.

6. The idea that the human race has an innate love of fighting cannot be carried far as an explanation of war. On the statistical evidence of the last three or thirteen centuries it could be argued with no less validity that man has an innate love of peace. Since war and peace mark fluctuations in the relations between nations, they are more likely to be explained by factors which themselves fluctuate than by factors which are 'innate'.

7. War-weariness in a nation often promotes peace and war-fever promotes war, but there have been notable instances where war-weariness promoted war.

8. The Manchester theory argues that increasing contact between nations – through common languages, foreign travel and the exchange of commodities and ideas – dispels prejudice and strongly promotes peace. The evidence for this theory, however, is not convincing.

9. No wars are unintended or 'accidental'. What is often unintended is the length and bloodiness of the war. Defeat too is unintended.

10. Changes in society, technology and warfare in the last three centuries spurred some observers to suggest that international relations were thereby so revolutionised that past experience was largely irrelevant. There is much evidence, however, to suggest that there is considerable continuity between the era of cavalry and the era of intercontinental missiles.

A FRAMEWORK OF CAUSES

11. In their origins, war and peace are not polar opposites, and the distinction between a warmaker and a peacemaker is often a mirage.

12. The idea that one nation can be mainly blamed for causing a war is as erroneous as the idea that one nation can be mainly praised for causing the end of a war. Most current explanations of war, however, rest on these errors.

13. If it is true that the breakdown of diplomacy leads to war, it is also true that the breakdown of war leads to diplomacy.

14. While the breakdown of diplomacy reflects the belief of each nation that it will gain more by fighting than by negotiating, the breakdown of war reflects the belief of each nation that it will gain more by negotiating than by fighting.

15. Neutrality, like war and peace, depends on agreement. Sweden and Switzerland, for instance, have remained neutral for more than a century and a half not only because they chose neutrality but because warring nations permitted them to remain neutral.

16. War and peace are more than opposites. They have so much in common that neither can be understood without the other.

17. War and peace appear to share the same framework of causes. The same set of factors should appear in explanations of the outbreak of war; widening of war by the entry of new nations; outbreak of peace; surmounting crises during a period of peace; and, of course, the ending of peace.

18. When leaders of rival nations have to decide whether to begin, continue or end a war, they are, consciously or unconsciously, asking variations of the same question: they are assessing their ability or inability to impose their will on the rival nation.

19. In deciding for war or peace national leaders appear to be strongly influenced by at least seven factors:

    i. military strength and the ability to apply that strength efficiently in the likely theatre of war;
    ii. predictions of how outside nations will behave if war should occur;
    iii. perceptions of whether there is internal unity or discord in their land and in the land of the enemy;
    iv. knowledge or forgetfulness of the realities and sufferings of war;
    v. nationalism and ideology;
    vi. the state of the economy and also its ability to sustain the kind of war envisaged;
    vii. the personality and experience of those who shared in the decision.

20. Wars usually begin when two nations disagree on their relative strength, and wars usually cease when the fighting nations agree on their relative strength. Agreement or disagreement emerges from the shuffling of the same set of factors. Thus each factor is capable of promoting war or peace.

21. A change in one factor – the defection of an ally or the eruption of strife in the land of the enemy – may dramatically alter a nation's assessment of its bargaining position. In the short term that factor could wield an influence which seems irrationally large.

22. When nations prepare to fight one another, they have

contradictory expectations of the likely duration and outcome of the war. When those predictions, however, cease to be contradictory, the war is almost certain to end.

23. Any factor which increases the likelihood that nations will agree on their relative power is a potential cause of peace. One powerful cause of peace is a decisive war, for war provides the most widely-accepted measure of power.

24. Even a decisive war cannot have permanent influence, for victory is invariably a wasting asset.

25. A formula for measuring international power is essential: ironically the most useful formula is warfare. Until the function of warfare is appreciated, the search for a more humane and more efficient way of measuring power is likely to be haphazard.

PATTERNS OF FIGHTING

26. To precede war with a formal 'declaration of war' is usually regarded as normal behaviour, but the evidence since 1700 suggests that it was abnormal. The Japanese surprise attack on Pearl Harbor in 1941 belonged to a strong international tradition.

27. Wars confined to two nations were fought usually on the geographical fringes rather than near the core of world power.

28. A general war or a world war began usually as a war between two nations and then became a series of wars which were interlocked and were fought simultaneously. An explanation of a general or many-sided war should therefore be structurally similar to the explanation of several two-sided wars.

29. A civil war was most likely to develop into an international war when one side in the civil war had ideological, racial or other links with an outside nation.

30. A general war was usually, by the standards of the age, a long war. Even in the era of nuclear weapons a general war – if it occurs – will possibly be a long war.

31. It is doubtful whether any war since 1700 was begun with the belief, by *both* sides, that it would be a long war.

32. The idea that great advances in the technology of

warfare inevitably led to shorter wars was held by many generations but falsified by many wars.

33. In human behaviour few events are more difficult to predict than the course and duration of a war: that is one of the vital unlearned lessons of warfare.

MYTHS AND PERILS OF THE NUCLEAR ERA

34. The idea that a nuclear arms race will lead to war should be viewed warily.

35. The long period of peace between the superpowers is not primarily the result of the nuclear terror, but nuclear fears will be increasingly important if that peace is to be considerably prolonged. Whereas a forty-year peace is not unique, a eighty-year peace will require the presence of unusual peace-making factors.

36. The nuclear era seems to follow the same basic rule of earlier eras: that peace will prevail if nations believe they lose more than they gain by resolving their disagreements through fighting.

37. While it is widely feared that nuclear weapons will soon be used on the large scale, there are historical precedents for major military weapons and crucial military tactics lying unused for very long periods.

38. The idea that a nuclear war will be short rests on the discredited theory that the prevailing military technology largely determines whether a war will be short or long. A nuclear war could be of long or short duration.

39. The peace movement is increasingly important but it is a double-edged sword and is capable, even with the noblest intentions, of promoting war as well as peace.

Abbreviations

Works cited frequently in the Notes:

A.R.   *The Annual Register*
D.N.B.   *The Dictionary of National Biography*
E.B.   *Encyclopaedia Britannica*: the year of the edition is cited first, followed by the volume and page number. Thus *E.B., 1910–11* XXVIII 178 means the 1910–11 edition, volume 28, page 178.
E.H.D.   *English Historical Documents*
N.C.M.H.   *The New Cambridge Modern History*

Notes

CHAPTER I   THE PEACE THAT PASSETH UNDERSTANDING

page

3. Sorokin, III 351–2.
5. Richardson's negative conclusions: *Statistics of Deadly Quarrels*, ix–xiii. His technique was more capable of squashing dogmatic generalisations than of finer analysis. For instance he could show, by studying a large number of wars, that a common language was not an overwhelming deterrent to war. That did not mean however that a common language might not have been a minor influence either for war or for peace.
6. Richardson on war immunity: *Arms and Insecurity*, pp. 232–5. Sir Ian Hamilton, p. 981.
7. Toynbee, *A Study of History*, IX 322–6.
8. Toynbee on the Second World War: ibid., p. 326n.
8. Adam Smith, II 402.
10. First historian: A. J. P. Taylor, *The Struggle for Mastery in Europe*, p. 255; second historian: T. A. Palmer, p. 491; third historians: Preston, Wise and Werner, p. 199; fourth historian: Dehio, p. 188; fifth historian: Nef, pp. 353, 382.
11. David Thomson, p. 111.
12. 'Since the smoke': letter of R. S. Skirving, in P. L. Brown (ed.), *Clyde Company Papers* (London, 1959) IV 358.
12. David Thomson, pp. 541–2, 711.
12. Palmerston's influence: Southgate, xv, wrote of 'the Palmerston who was so careful to prevent a general war in 1830–1 and 1848–9'. See also xxii.
12. Bismarck's influence: Taylor, 'Otto Bismarck', p. 668 – 'he was the principal architect of the halcyon age that gave Europe 30 years of peace after the Congress of Berlin.'
13. The background to Nef's book: Nef, v–vii.
14. 'What made the peace': Nef, p. 331.
14. The expulsion of Flashman; Nef, pp. 345, 356.
14. The wars of 1848–71: Nef, pp. 354–5, made a gallant, unsuccessful attempt to explain away some of the wars that jeopardised his explanation of peace. He forgot, incidentally, to try to explain away the Crimean and several other wars.
14. The forty-six orderly years: Nef, p. 445.
15. The American historian: Gulick, *N.C.M.H.*, IX 666–7.
15. Instability of international monetary affairs: Triffin, pp. 25–7.
16. The pre-1919 cobweb: Keynes, pp. 22–3.

CHAPTER 2   PARADISE IS A BAZAAR

page

18. The Manchester creed: in selecting this name my main reasons were Manchester's reputation as a symbol of free trade and the popularity of the creed among free-trade economists.

18. 'It is something': Apjohn, p. 234.

19. The Atlantic telegraph: Cruikshank, p. 72.

19. Buckle's career: *D.N.B.*, III 208–11.

20. Praise of Adam Smith: Buckle, I, 214.

20. 'Every new railroad': ibid., p. 223.

20. 'For the peculiarity of the great contest'; ibid., p. 195.

21. 'All the leading currents': Cairnes, p. 123.

21. Volapük: Henry Sweet, *E.B.*, *1910–11*, XXVIII 178.

24. Barclay on the Americas: Barclay, p. 7.

24. 'Militarism on the Continent': ibid.

24. 'War is coming': ibid., pp. 4–5.

28. Chamberlain's faith in rational discussion: Taylor, *The Origins of the Second World War*, pp. 172, 217.

28. 'I believe it is peace': ibid., p. 231.

28. British leaflet raids: Nicolson, p. 32.

31. 'Threat systems': Boulding, *Beyond Economics*, p. 105.

CHAPTER 3   DREAMS AND DELUSIONS OF A COMING WAR

page

36. The 'iron dice': Kautsky, pp. 439–41.

36. Moltke, 12 May 1914: Fischer, p. 37.

36. Lerchenfeld: Kausky, pp. 635–41.

36. Bethmann Hollweg's four months: Fischer, p. 92.

37. Refusal to woo Italy: Fischer, p. 99.

37. Bethmann Hollweg and peace: Fischer, p. 103.

37. Bachmann: Fischer, pp. 282–3.

37. Churchill, 1911: W. S. Churchill, p. 57.

37. British oil stocks: *The Times*, 18 June 1914.

38. War as a picnic: Esher, III 180.

38. Esher's optimism: ibid., pp. 175–7.

38. Kitchener in cabinet: W. S. Churchill, p. 140.

38. Plan 17: anon., *E.B.*, *1922*, XXXII 972–3.

38. Cordonnier, 'The French Army', *E.B.*, *1922*, XXX 216.

38. Russian optimism: Paléologue, I 69, noted that the tsar was nervous and Grand Duke Nicholas, the generalissimo, was buoyant; Rosen, II 155; Cowles, pp. 285, 319.

39. Clausewitz and Angell: Tuchman, p. 142.

41. Expectations of short, victorious war: this seems to be one of the most vital areas of research into the causes of war but so far is unexplored. My inadequate survey of war-eve hopes since 1700 is a mere entrée, but it reveals widespread optimism.

42. British hopes in 1702: cited in Coombs, p. 27.

page

42. Walpole's quip: I. S. Leadam, 'Sir Robert Walpole', *D.N.B.*, xx 655. Walpole's was a minority view.
42. 1775 Congress: *A.R.*, *1775*, p. 261.
42. Major Pitcairn: Barnes and Owen, I 57–63.
43. Franco-Austrian confidence, 1792: R. R. Palmer, pp. 12, 93; Biro, II 59–68; Rose and Broadley, pp. 75 ff.
43. Dundas's optimism: *E.H.D.*, xi 886.
43. Pitt's views: W. Hunt, 'William Pitt', *D.N.B.*, xv 1260, 1269.
44. Russo-Turk 1828: Curtiss, pp. 57–8, 94.
44. The 'bear is dying': Hurewitz, I 140–1.
44. Bismarck, I 368. Bismarck might have been exaggerating.
45. French emperor and empress, 1870: Kurtz, pp. 236, 238.
45. Maps: in contrast the German army had maps of France showing roads which French War Ministry maps had not yet included: Horne, p. 40.
45. American Civil War: Sandburg, II 98; *A.R.* (1861) 231–41; *N.C.M.H.*, x 644.
46. Bloch, 'The Wars of the Future', pp. 315–16.
46. Milner: I. Hamilton, p. 128.
46. Hicks-Beach's estimates: Hirst, pp. 146–7.
47. Boers' confidence: Lockhart and Woodhouse, pp. 433, 440.
47. Burger: cited by E. A. Walker, *Cambridge History of the British Empire*, VIII 610.
48. Hitler, 14 Aug 1939: cited in Shirer, p. 625.
48. Long war unwanted: ibid., p. 643.
49. 'If Britain and France': ibid., p. 713.
49. Halifax: Liddell Hart, *Memoirs*, II 221.
49. Ironside: ibid., pp. 249, 277.
49. Stalin's hopes: R. A. Medvedev, *Let History Judge* (London, 1972) p. 445.
50. Korea: Rees, p. 36.
50. Maxwell, p. 317.
52. The French ambassador: Paléologue, I 27, 61.
54. Wilson's friends: A. L. and L. L. George, cited in Fisher, p. 244.
55. 'We have described how a man': Lester Grinspoon, in Fisher, p. 244.

CHAPTER 4 WHILE WATERBIRDS FIGHT
page

57. Secret sitting of Congress: *A.R.* (1812) 195; Maurice, p. 45.
58. Liverpool to Castlereagh, 1814: cited in Ferrell, p. 158.
58. Barbary pirates: *A.R.* (1815) 125 – 'The naval force of the United States which had been set free by the peace with Great Britain.'
58. Mexican war of 1846: Ferrell, pp. 209 ff.
59. San Domingo: Logan, pp. 41 ff.
59. Chincha Islands: *N.C.M.H.*, x 666.
59. Lord Palmerston to Clarendon, 1 Nov 1855: Temperley and Penson, p. 295.

page
59. Withdrawal of French from Mexico: Ferrell, pp. 302 ff.
60. Waterbird analogy: Tsunoda, de Bary and Keene, pp. 658-62.
60. 'America enjoys, because of the war': ibid., p. 715.
60. Serbo-Bulgarian war: Huhn, passim; *The Economist*, 21 Nov 1885; anon., 'Servo-Bulgarian War', *E.B.* (1910-11) XXIV 699-701.
61. Damaged railway: Huhn, pp. 104-5.
61. The long march; ibid., pp. 137-8, 174.
62. Austrian intervention: *A.R.* (1885) 276.
62. First Balkan War, 1912: C. F. Atkinson, 'Balkan Wars', *E.B.* (1922) XXX 373-82.
64. 'Prussians of the Balkans': ibid., p. 381; E. C. Helmreich, *The Diplomacy of the Balkan Wars, 1912-13* (Harvard, 1938) 365.
65. Haile Selassie to Assembly of League of Nations, July 1936: Keith, II 89.

CHAPTER 5   DEATH-WATCH AND SCAPEGOAT WARS
page
68. Personification of a nation or government: from time to time in the narrative I use dubious phrases such as 'Sweden hoped' or 'Prussia decided'. The advantage is a saving of words: the disadvantage is a loss of precision. In such instances I mean that the government 'hoped' or that the majority opinion in the place of power 'decided'.
68. The implications of names of the succession wars: Andrews, p. 11; J. O. Lindsay, *N.C.M.H.*, VII 5; E. Robson, ibid., p. 166.
68. Objection to interpreting the wars of succession simply as the result of dynastic rivalries or confused matrimonial arrangements is raised in chapter 10; there interpretations based on motives are analysed.
68. Most of the details on the outbreak of death-watch wars come from standard works, esp. *N.C.M.H.*, VI, VII, VIII.
69. Death of Elizabeth of Russia: cited by R. N. Bain, *E.B.* (1910-11) IX 285.
70. Revolutions as prelude to wars: a more comprehensive list of notes appeared in *Historical Studies*, Oct 1971, where the remainder of this chapter, with alterations, was published under the title 'The Scapegoat Theory of International War'.
71. Main sources for table of wars: Richardson, *Statistics of Deadly Quarrels*, passim; Wright, I 644 ff. I excluded from the table the internal troubles in France (1870), Russia (1904), many nations (1914) and Germany (1930s), though it could be argued that they merit a place.
72. Kinglake's career: *D.N.B.*, XI 171-3.
72. The 'small knot of men': Kinglake, I 470.
73. Wright, abridged edn., 169.
73. Wright, *E.B.*, *1962*, XXIII 325.
73. Woolf, p. 313.
73. Nuclear war as a scapegoat: cited by G. H. Snyder in Pruitt and Snyder, p. 124.
74. Margaret Mead, in Fried, Harris and Murphy, 221.

page

74. Other anthropologists: ibid., pp. 88–9.
74. Lack of criticism of scapegoat: Mayer, p. 298, is an exception. He argues that acute tensions could be a deterrent to war but that tensions normally encouraged a resort to war.
74. Scapegoat interpretations which were backed by no evidence included: Stomberg, pp. 581–2; Dehio, pp. 139, 195; Taylor, *The Habsburg Monarchy*, p. 251; McLaren, pp. 229–30. Absence of evidence could partly reflect the authors' shortage of space, for the above books covered a long span of time.
75. Miss Howard: Maurois, pp. 40–2; Bury, p. 72.
75. Lack of evidence to support Kinglake: Bury, pp. 72–3; Agatha Ramm and B. H. Sumner in *N.C.M.H.*, x 468–72.
75. 'A diversion in foreign politics': *Franco-German War*, I, part I, p. 5.
75. Lord Clarendon to Queen of Prussia, 28 Oct 1868: Butterfield, III 154.
76. Russia 1904: Witte, p. 250; Seton-Watson, pp. 481, 560; Pares, pp. 69, 72.
77. Fay, II 305–6.
78. Scapegoat war for Germany, 1914: Barraclough, pp. 132–3.
78. Von Moltke: Fischer, p. 33.
78. Bethmann-Hollweg: ibid., pp. 31, 50–1.
79. Harvard scholar: Deutsch, p. 152.
79. Hitler's views on Poland: Shirer, p. 570.
80. Hitler on Russia: ibid., p. 790.
80. It is sometimes argued that each of the three main Indonesian political elements – Sukarno, the army, and the communists – hoped that 'confrontation' would favour its political fortunes. See Weinstein, pp. 3–9.
83. The civil disturbances that seemed to lack links with outside nations were: France 1830, Egypt 1882, Bulgaria 1885, Libya 1911, and China 1937.
84. Greco-Turk crisis and war: *The Economist* (1897) 302, 483, 635, 742; Atkins, pp. 85–97; *A.R.* (1897) 307–13; *E.B.* (1910–11) XII 467–9.

CHAPTER 6   WAR CHESTS AND PULSE BEATS

page

87. Luigi da Porto: cited by Clark, p. 134.
88. Poor harvests of 1740: Butterfield, III 7: R. M. Hatton, *N.C.M.H.*, VII 359; Lough, p. 34.
88. 'To place the Court of Vienna': Butterfield, III 9.
88. Fleury's carriage mobbed: Gooch, *Louis XV*, p. 67.
89. 'Your Majesties are aware': Butterfield, III 9–10.
89. Kaunitz: ibid., p. 15.
89. Louis XV, 1763: M. S. Anderson, *N.C.M.H.*, VIII 259.
89. Secret despatch of 24 Aug 1786: Hailes to Carmarthen, reprinted in Browning, I 135.
89. Dorset to Carmarthen, 21 Feb 1788: ibid., II 17.
90. Hicks Beach to Salisbury, 1897: Hicks Beach, II 46–7.

90. Germany's proposed indemnity: Fischer, p. 104.
90. Toshimichi's financial arguments: Tsunoda, de Bary and Keene, pp. 658–62.
91. When 'hope is alright': Macfie, p. 95.
92. 'If these considerations are accepted': ibid., p. 96.
92. 'Grist to some historian's mill': ibid., p. 94.
92. Heckscher, *An Economic History of Sweden*, p. 211.
93. 'When the sense of well-being': Stafford-Clark, p. 99.
94. 'Final judgment': Macfie, p. 90.
94. Lack of comment on Macfie's article: In December 1970 I wrote to Professor Macfie, who lives in retirement in Scotland, to enquire whether Clark's was the only appraisal of his argument. Macfie kindly replied that he knew of no other.
94. Virtues of dissecting treaties etc: Clark, p. 147.
95. Sir George Clark's brief and courteous critique rested on four main points:

   (a) Clark criticised the belief that 'there are conditions which necessarily lead to an outbreak of war' and that wars are 'independent of our control'. In fact Macfie also opposed that belief; he was careful to use, not words such as *inevitable* or *necessarily*, but words such as *tend* or *tendency*. Macfie's last sentence strongly implied that wars could be avoided.

   (b) It was implied also that Macfie believed in 'a cycle of war and peace, and that it works through economic prosperity and impoverishment'. I can find, however, no evidence that Macfie believed in a cycle of war and peace. The only cyclical occurrence which Macfie discussed was the trade cycle. Moreover Macfie went out of his way to argue that prosperity and impoverishment were 'only one item in the basket' of the causes of wars (p. 94), and were not the most important items (p. 90).

   (c) Clark said it was difficult, but not altogether impossible, to reconcile the idea of cycles of war and peace with the principle that 'the causes of war change with the changes in the life of society'. As Macfie also appears to have believed that the causes of war change as society changes, Sir George Clark's criticism is again a misunderstanding. One should also add that the principle enunciated by Sir George Clark is an act of faith. It reflects the assumption – dubious in my opinion – that motives are the main cause of war.

   (d) Clark insisted that the dates of the outbreak of war were irrelevant to the causes of wars. Even on this point Macfie's views were not fully grasped; Macfie had argued (p. 90) – mistakenly in my opinion – that the occasion for wars was less revealing than 'the deeper causes'.

   It would be unfair to end this note without saying that Sir George Clark – rare among scholars of war – practised the belief that incompatible ideas should be compelled to fight one another rather than be permitted to co-exist peacefully. Moreover he alone thought Macfie's thesis was important enough to discuss.

95. When Macfie studied economic fluctuations of the era 1850–1914 he relied much on British data and slightly on German and Russian. Although a reading of Kindleberger, Giffen, Kuznets and a range of scholars of the business cycle generally confirms Macfie's delineation of economic peaks and troughs, more research is justified on the complicated links between wars and economic conditions both before and after 1800. That there is a case for investigating this link as far back as the seventeenth century or earlier can be seen in F. P. Braudel and F. Spooner, 'Prices in Europe from 1450 to 1750', *Cambridge Economic History of Europe*, IV 437.

96. The disobedience of Radetzky: C. Pouthas, *N.C.M.H.*, X 402.

96. Manchuria: Beasley, pp. 244–5.

CHAPTER 7 A CALENDAR OF WAR
page

97. 'The bad months for Russia': R. Churchill, pp. 11, 534.

98. List of starting dates of wars: in assembling the dates I was conscious that no such list could be definitive. Some wars began with internal fighting but I selected the dates when they became international wars. Several wars – e.g. the Austrian–Sardinian wars of 1848 and 1849 – could be counted either as one or two wars: I counted them as two. Of the forty-four wars, none began in January, three in February, three in March, nine in April, four in May, four in June, nine in July, two in August, three in September, three in October, four in November, none in December.

98. A list confined to wars starting in and fought mainly in Europe revealed that ten began in spring, eight in summer, four in autumn, and two in winter. Of the total of twenty-four, fifteen began in the period April to July. Another list – confined to Europe and excluding wars that started with civil fighting and excluding wars that could be classed as escalations of existing wars or waterbird effects of existing wars – revealed six spring wars, five summer, three autumn and one winter. Both of the above lists therefore reveal a stronger seasonal pattern than the list of forty-four wars which I discussed in the narrative.

It is curious to observe that the four North American wars – 1846, 1861, 1862 and 1898 – all began in April.

98. Trans-Siberian railway: Tupper, p. 342.

99. Danish defences: *A.R.* (1864) 220–2.

99. Icebound fleets: Temperley and Penson, pp. 267, 269, 274.

99. Montenegro *v.* Turkey (1853) was the third winter war. So far I have found no details about the origins of that war.

101. The 'most radical revolution': Taylor, *The Habsburg Monarchy*, p. 83.

102. Autumn financial pressures: Jevons, p. 163–71.

102. Stewart, p. 57.

page
103. Autumn panics: the greatest financial panic in the southern hemisphere – in Australia in April and May 1893 – fell in the southern autumn.
104. Great Exhibition's mood: Froude, II 480.
104. France 1870: Bury, pp. 180–1.
104. Olympic Games: Mező, p. 20.
106. Mijatovich, *E.B.* (1910–11) XXIV 692.
106. Germany in 1913: Fischer, p. 33.
106. U.S. 'Manifest Destiny': Ferrell, p. 218.
107. W. S. Churchill, p. 51.
107. A tabulation of the months when wars ended could also provide useful insights.

CHAPTER 8   THE ABACUS OF POWER
page
108. A siege likened to diplomacy: Clausewitz, III 97.
108. 'Diplomacy without armaments': Gooch, *Studies in Diplomacy*, p. 226.
108. 'Waged with the whole might': Leonard, p. 25.
109. 'A conqueror': Clausewitz, II 155.
109. Clausewitz on peace: On first reading Clausewitz I noticed no comment on peace. Later, realising that he must have commented by implication, I skimmed through his work again. As his references to peace seem sparse, I cannot be sure that I have interpreted his views correctly.
110. Bull: cited in Buchan, p. 34.
110. Buchan, p. 177.
110. Wright, abridged edn., p. 122.
110. Toynbee, *A Study of History*, IX 244.
111. Scholars' preference for a multi-polar system before 1945 and bi-polar system thereafter: G. H. Snyder in Pruitt and Snyder, p. 124.
111. Gulick, p. 36.
114. 'The objective comparison of military capabilities': G. H. Snyder in Pruitt and Snyder, p. 117. According to Wright, p. 116, the term 'balance of power' implies that fluctuations in power 'can be observed and measured'.
118. Simmel on exact knowledge: cited by R. C. Angell in McNeil, p. 100.
119. Castlereagh: State Paper, 5 May 1820, *E.H.D.*, XI 965.
121. On the relevance of the pre-1945 world to the nuclear world there are divergent views. Judging by the articles gathered in Pruitt and Snyder, the majority opinion is that the international system has changed drastically. The opinion however appears to rest on inadequate knowledge of the pre-1945 world.

CHAPTER 9   WAR AS AN ACCIDENT
page
127. War of Jenkins' Ear: J. O. Lindsay, *N.C.M.H.*, VII 206.
127. Bavarian Succession: M. S. Anderson, *N.C.M.H.*, VIII 270.
127. First World War: Fay, II 547; Albrecht-Carrié, p. 294.

page

127. Röling, p. 495.
128. The idea of accidental war is favoured more by political scientists than historians. See Pruitt and Snyder, *passim*, and Buchan, p. 149.
128. Farrer: cited in Maurice, v.
129. Wolseley: Clarke, p. 112.
129. Schelling and Halperin, 'Pre-emptive, Premeditated, and Accidental War', Pruitt and Snyder, p. 44.
129. Wavell, 'The Seven Weeks' War', *E.B.* (1962) xx 385.
129. Reid, *United Empire: the Royal Colonial Institute Journal* (1914) v 557; Reid was Australia's High Commissioner in London.
130. The 5000 'perceptions': Holsti and North, pp. 159–61.
131. 'More significant': ibid., p. 167.
131. 'Historical evidence revealed': ibid., p. 160.
132. A 'conflict which none had desired': ibid., p. 170.
133. 'No one wanted to fight': Higonnet, p. 57.
133. Newcastle's advice: ibid., p. 79.
135. The dangers of arms races are stressed by many political scientists. See R. Naroll, in Pruitt and Snyder, p. 151, for list of recent advocates of the argument.
136. *The Economist*, 6 Sept 1879, p. 1018.
136. Carnegie report: ibid., 18 July 1914, p. 106.
136. M. Howard, *N.C.M.H.*, xi 204.
136. Thayer, p. 301.
138. Proportion of British budget spent on defence: computed from Ashworth, p. 491.
139. German influence in China: *A.R.* (1897) pp. 280–1.
140. Clowes: cited by Ashworth, 495.
141. Hypothesis that Japan mistakenly believed she was about to be attacked in 1904 by Russia: this is only a hypothesis but since writing it I read a similar rumour in McCormick, 1 78. McCormick, a pressman at Port Arthur, spoke of a 'press telegram from London containing false information regarding the military plans of Russia'.
142. I. A. Richards, *Practical Criticism: a study of literary judgment* (Harvest paperback, New York, n.d.) p. 229 (the italics are Richards' emphasis).
143. New Orleans: *A.R.* (1815) p. 122.
143. Chinsura: *A.R.* (1760) p. 235; *D.N.B.*, vii 427.
144. Manchuria: Beasley, pp. 244–5.

CHAPTER 10   AIMS AND ARMS

page

146. In doubting the validity of attempts to simplify war aims, it should also be said that over-simplification is often necessary. Those who write political histories covering a long span of time have to simplify war aims. If space is cramped, and few sentences can be spared for a discussion of the aims of each warring nation, only one or two aims can be singled out. This is unavoidable, not intentional.

page

149. The main causes of war: e.g. Nef, p. 266, 'the causes of war became mainly economic' from 1640 to 1740.
151. 'Our people': Fischer, p. 637.
153. Lenin's explanation: Lenin, XXI 27, 301.
153. 'Tsarism regards the war': ibid., p. 306.
153. Lenin on Clausewitz: ibid., p. 304.
153. German confidence in victory: ibid., p. 28.
154. Lenin leaves Germany: Fischer, p. 366–7.
155. The frail Russian army: Lenin, XXVI 447.
155. 'They do not grasp': ibid., p. 451.
155. Delaying the peace talks: ibid., pp. 572–3.
156. The reliance on motives as an explanation of war is even more conspicuous in newspapers, political speeches, political tracts and everyday conversation than in histories of wars. It dominates secondary-school textbooks, though the dominance may derive partly from the need to simplify events. It seems normal among economic and social historians or those historians for whom war is only a marginal interest. It has fewer adherents among political historians and is perhaps the least common among military historians who tend however to be more interested in the course than the causes of a war. While there have been hundreds of debates about the causes of a particular war, the debates centre on aims and rarely, to my knowledge, on whether aims were an adequate explanation of a particular war.

   The New Cambridge Modern History is one mirror of historians' assumptions about war. While some of its contributors explained the outbreak of particular wars (e.g. the Crimean in 1853 and the War of the Pacific in 1879) overwhelmingly in terms of ambitions, many other contributors did not. For instance two excellent articles, by Michael Foot on the Franco-Prussian War and by T. Harry Williams on the American Civil War, adopted a different framework of causation.

CHAPTER 11 A DAY THAT LIVES IN INFAMY

page

159. Naroll, in Pruitt and Snyder, p. 152.
159. Nef, p. 354.
160. Horne, pp. 81–2.
162. Congress of Vienna: Wright, abridged edn., p. 198.
162. Indictment of Kaiser: Keith, 1 49.
163. Withdrawal from Rhineland: ibid., p. 61.
163. Keith, xviii.
164. *E.B.* (1962) XXIII 792T.
164–5. *N.C.M.H.*, XII 294, 314.
165. American trio: Preston, Wise and Werner, p. 305.
165. Japanese national character: Mazlish, p. 170.
165. Detention of Russian ships: Takahashi, pp. 24, 582–91.
166. Right to 'such independent action': Hershey, p. 69.
166. Evening at Port Arthur: McCormick, 1 65–7.

page
166. Formal declarations: Takahashi, pp. 6–8.
167. Grew's warning: Ferrell, p. 626.
168. Daws, p. 341.
169. J. F. Maurice's career: *D.N.B.* (1912–21) 374–5.
170. Wolseley's instructions: Maurice, p. 3.
170. French declaration of 1870: ibid., p. 76.
171. Russo-French advocacy at The Hague: *American Journal of International Law* (Jan 1908) pp. 64–5.
171. 'Convention Relative to the Opening of Hostilities': printed in full ibid., supplement (1908) pp. 85–7.
171. Chinese delegate: Stowell, p. 55.
171. Declarations in 1914–18 war: *E.B.* (1962) XIII 808.
172. Article 12: Keith, I 14.
172. Hitler's opinion: Bullock, p. 662.
173. Stowell, p. 54.

CHAPTER 12   VENDETTA OF THE BLACK SEA
page
178. Treaty of 1739: Hurewitz, I 50.
178. 'Our religion': ibid., p. 136.
178. Siege of Anapa: *A.R.* (1836) 'Chronicle', p. 370.
179. Blessing at Kishinev: *A.R.* (1877) p. 253.
179. Lithuanian masts: M. S. Anderson, *The Eastern Question*, p. 12n.
180. The Emir's destroyer: Pierce, p. 72.
181. Turk superstitions: M. S. Anderson, *The Eastern Question*, xviii p. 22n.
181. Bryan and the Balkans: Ferrell, p. 12.
181. *A.R.* (1770) p. 7.
181. English engineer: Pasley, I 435. He was a captain in the royal engineers.
183. Russian logistics: Curtiss, pp. 59–61.
184. Importance of control of Black Sea: Allen and Muratoff, p. 105.
184. Fall of Sevastopol: Bentley, ch. XXI.

CHAPTER 13   LONG WARS
page
187. Dutch fleet captured: C. Lloyd, *N.C.M.H.*, VIII 190.
187. Austrians in fields and ferries: Maude, 'Strategy', pp. 988–9.
187. Tallard's deserters: C. F. Atkinson, *E.B.* (1910–11) p. 601.
188. 200,000 deserters: M. S. Anderson, *Europe in the Eighteenth Century*, p. 138.
188. Burgoyne: cited by Temperley, p. 225. It is not clear from Burgoyne's figures whether the 1 in 5 turnover was annual or over a longer period.
188. An army like a diver: Temperley, p. 243.
188. Marlborough's long march: Atkinson, op. cit., p. 602.
189. Hesse's mercenaries on both sides: Lodge, p. 12.
189. £3 million contract: *E.B.* (1910–11) XIII 411.
189. 'Two finest cavalry officers': Chesney and Reeve, p. 65.
190. Sayings of the strategists: M. Howard, in Howard (ed.) p. 8; de Rougemont, p. 257.

page
190. Henry Lloyd: *D.N.B.*, XI 1301-2.
191. Boscawen: *D.N.B.*, II 877-81.
192. de Morogues: cited by C. D. Lloyd, *N.C.M.H.*, VIII 175.
192. Clerk: *E.H.D.*, X 605.
192. C. Lloyd, op. cit., p. 175.
193. British subsidies: Sherwig, p. 345.
194. The 'enormous debts': Smith, II 393.
194. Clausewitz: Leonard, pp. 54-5.
195. Esher, III 248-50.
198. Algerian pirates: *A.R.* (1816), 'Chronicle', pp. 230 ff.; *D.N.B.*, XV 714-15.
198. French invasion of Algeria: *A.R.* (1830) pp. 234-8.
199. Attack on Mascara: *A.R.* (1835) pp. 423-4.
199. Attack on Constantine: *A.R.* (1836) pp. 347-9.
200. Bugeaud's tactics: Liddell Hart, *N.C.M.H.*, X 320.
202. French manifesto of toleration: *A.R.* (1830) p. 237.

CHAPTER 14 AND SHORTER WARS
page
206. Thirty Days' War: Atkins, p. 97.
207. Chesney, pp. 17-18.
208. Prussia's quick transport: Portway, pp. 25.
209. 'You all know': *A.R.* (1866) p. 249.
209. War of entrenchments: Bloch, *Is War Now Impossible?*, xxvii.
209. French captain: ibid., p. 49.
210. Two years as a 'long war': ibid., p. 141.
210. 'The war of the future': ibid., p. 59.
211. Small-bore rifle: Bloch, *Contemporary Review* (1901) p. 325.
211. Success favoured defence: ibid., p. 329.
212. Role of economic strength in war: ibid., p. 306.
212. Von der Goltz: ibid., p. 321.
213. Danger zone of cavalry: Brian Bond in M. Howard (ed.), pp. 97-8.
213. *Training Manual*: ibid., p. 89.
213. Cavalry's 'speed and endurance': Maude, 'Cavalry', p. 569.
214. 'Will hang the fate': ibid.
214. 'Battle of Dorking': Clarke, pp. 1-2.
214. *The Invasion of 1910*: ibid., pp. 144-7.
214. Clarke, p. 144.
214. E. Crammond, 'Gold Reserves in Time of War', *National Review*, London, LVII 701-2.
214. *United Empire*, 1914, V 692.
215. *The Times*, 7 Aug 1914.
215. *The Economist* (1914) pp. 442, 482, 782-3.
215. Hirst, p. 311.
216. J. M. Keynes, *General Theory of Employment, Interest and Money*, passim.
216. Russia in 1914: Leites, p. 25.
217. Sir Almroth Wright: cited in Cope, p. 63.
218. Visitors to the Marne: Esher, III 188.

page

219. Shipments of horsefeed: J. F. C. Fuller in Réquin, p. 60.
220. Sir Douglas Haig: R. G. Howard-Vyse, 'Mounted Troops', *E.B.* (1922) XXXI 1008.
220. W. S. Churchill, p. 296.
221. 'Contrary to common belief': Fuller, *The Conduct of War*, p. 174.
222. Influence of Fuller and Liddell Hart on German army: Robert O'Neill in Howard (ed.) p. 164; Wavell, *N.C.M.H.*, XII 267.
222. Sir Ian Hamilton, p. 982 (Hamilton wrote of himself in the third person).
222. 'Never, in the history of the art of war': ibid.
223. Failure to study earlier wars: Wavell, *N.C.M.H.*, XII, 256; Fuller, p. 160; Lord Montgomery of Alamein, *A History of Warfare* (London, 1968) p. 459.
223. Liddell Hart on U.S. Civil War: *N.C.M.H.*, X 330. See also Liddell Hart, 'Tactics', p. 715.
223. Bloch's five fighting nations: Bloch, *Is War Now Impossible?*, xi.
224. The 'day of the bayonet is over': ibid., xiii.
225. The principle that general wars tend to be long wars: it is probable that Bloch grasped this principle, though in an intuitive rather than articulate way.
225. Honduras *v.* Nicaragua: Wood, p. 14.

CHAPTER 15 THE MYSTERY OF WIDE WARS

page

228. The main aim of this chapter is to attempt to fit familiar facts into new patterns.
228. World Wars: There is merit in the suggestion that the First World War 'is a misnomer'. See J. M. K. Vyvyan, *N.C.M.H.*, XII 329. And A. J. P. Taylor argues in *The Origins of the Second World War*, p. 41, that the war was not a world war until 1941.
234. Malmesbury's 'dreaded class', *A.R.* (1859) p. 205.
238. Churchill on Finnish war: cited by Liddell Hart in *E.B.* (1962) XXIII 791E.
239. Hitler's secret document, 1940: Shirer, p. 969.

CHAPTER 16 AUSTRALIA'S PACIFIC WAR

page

247. P. Hasluck, *The Government and the People, 1939–41* (Canberra, 1952) p. 228.
249. Tokyo secret conferences: N. Ike, *Japan's Decision for War* (Stanford, 1967) p. 60 ff.
253. Page's visit: Hasluck, pp. 543–6; A. Stirling, *Lord Bruce: the London Years* (Melbourne, 1974) pp. 209–16.
259. Japanese plan for Australia: Ike, p. 248.
260. Complacency of Allies to defences of Manila, Singapore, etc: L. Wigmore, *The Japanese Thrust* (Canberra, 1968) chs. 5, 6; H. Michel, *The Second World War* (London, 1975) pp. 321–344; S. W. Kirby, *The War Against Japan: the Loss of Singapore* (London, 1957) esp. pp. 147, 240, 287, 323–4, 506–11; Douglas Gillison, *Royal Australian Air Force, 1939–42*, (Canberra, 1962) esp. pp. 136, 138, 149–58; *Commonwealth Parliamentary Debates*, 1940–41, esp. 21/8/41 and 17/9/41.
262. Blamey: J. Hetherington, *Blamey: Controversial Soldier* (Canberra, 1973) p. 179.

CHAPTER 17 MYTHS OF THE NUCLEAR ERA
page
267. Atomic bombs on Japan: H. Michel, *The Second World War* (London, 1975) pp. 768–70; Lisle A. Rose, *After Yalta* (New York, 1973) pp. 76–82.
270. Study of Soviet and American spending on arms, 1952–76: A. F. K. Organski and Jacek Kugler, *The War Ledger* (Chicago, 1980) pp. 187–8.
275. Organski and Kugler on the seven nuclear threats: *The War Ledger*, pp. 164–76.
275. Superpowers overextended: Charles B. Marshall, *The Limits of Foreign Policy* (Baltimore, 1968) p. 162.
276. When a challenger nation overtakes a leader: *The War Ledger*, p. 226.
277. Deaths in Dresden: David Irving, *The Destruction of Dresden* (London, 1985 edn) p. 237.
277. Limited war in 18th century: R. A. Preston, S. F. Wise and H. O. Werner, *Men in Arms*, pp. 136–7.
278. 'Most forecasts of future wars': H. B. Hartley and C. G. Douglas, 'Chemical Warfare' in *E. B.*, 1926, I, p. 577.
279. Defoliants in Vietnam: Peter H. Schuck, *Agent Orange on Trial* (Harvard, 1986) pp. 17–19.
279. Gas as a modern surprise weapon: Richard K. Betts, *Surprise Attack: Lessons for Defense Planning* (Washington, 1982) pp. 245–6.
281. Raymond Hunthausen, 'Peace: A Witness of Faith' in *Peace Dossier 6*, (Melbourne, June 1983) p. 5.
281. William H. McNeill, *The Pursuit of Power* (Oxford, 1983) p. 384.
281. Patrick White, *Peace Dossier 6*, p. 1.
282. Nuclear winter: Russell Seitz, 'In from the Cold', *The National Interest* (Washington, Fall 1986) pp. 3–17.
286. Michael Howard: 'Reassurance and Deterrence: Western Defense in the 1980s', *Foreign Affairs*, 1983, vol. 61, p. 316.
286. The early peace movement: Bernard Brodie, *War and Politics* (London, 1973) pp. 258–65.
287. Post-1945 peace movements: Nigel J. Henham, 'The European Peace Movement: Its Effect on United States Arms Control Policy, 1981–82', B. A. Hons thesis, Pol. Sci. Dept., University of Melbourne. See also Donald Neuchterlein in *The World Today*, August–September 1984, pp. 322 ff.

Select Bibliography

The following books and articles are those which I found most useful as sources of evidence or most stimulating in their ideas. To make the list less unwieldy I excluded, with rare exceptions, individual articles and chapters in such standard works as *The New Cambridge Modern History*, *Annual Register*, the various editions of the *Encyclopaedia Britannica* and the British *Dictionary of National Biography*. Some of these individual articles and chapters however were cited in the Notes. Likewise the Notes cited other books which were only marginally on my particular theme.

The bibliography is arranged alphabetically rather than thematically so that a work cited frugally in the Notes can be identified more easily. Where the title of the book does not necessarily indicate its relevance I have added an explanatory comment.

Acton, Harold, *The Bourbons of Naples (1734–1825)* (London, 1956).

Albrecht-Carrié, René, *A Diplomatic History of Europe since the Congress of Vienna* (New York, 1958).

Allen, W. E. D., and Muratoff, Paul, *Caucasian Battlefields: a history of the wars on the Turco-Caucasian border 1828–1921* (Cambridge, 1953).

Anderson, M. S., *Europe in the Eighteenth Century 1713–1783* (London, 1961).

——— *The Eastern Question 1774–1923: a study in international relations* (London, 1966).

Anderson, Olive, *A Liberal State at War: English politics and economics during the Crimean war* (London, 1967).

Andrews, Stuart, *Eighteenth-Century Europe: the 1680s to 1815* (London, 1965).

The Annual Register, annually (London, 1758–1899).

Apjohn, Lewis, *Richard Cobden and the Free Traders* (London, c. 1880)

Ardrey, Robert, *African Genesis* (London, 1961).

Aron, Raymond, *Peace and War: A theory of international relations*, tr. from French (New York, 1966).

Ashton, T. S., *Economic Fluctuations in England 1700–1800* (Oxford, 1959).

Ashworth, William, 'Economic Aspects of Late Victorian Naval Administration', *Economic History Review* (December, 1969).

Aspinall, A. ed., *The Later Correspondence of George III*, 5 vols. (Cambridge, 1962–70).

Atkins, J. B., *Incidents and Reflections* (London, 1947). Atkins was a correspondent at the Spanish-American and Greco-Turk Wars of the 1890s.

Barclay, Sir Thomas, 'Peace', *Encyclopaedia Britannica*, 11th ed. (London, 1910–11), XXI, 4–16.

Barnes, G. R. and Owen, J. H., ed., *The Private Papers of John, Earl of Sandwich, First Lord of the Admiralty 1771–1782*, 4 vols. (London, 1932–38).

Barnett, Correlli, The Swordbearers: studies in supreme command in the First World War (London, 1963).

Barraclough, G., *Factors in German History* (Oxford, 1946).

Bartlett, C. J., *Great Britain and Sea Power 1815–1853* (Oxford, 1963).

Beasley, W. G., *The Modern History of Japan* (London, 1963).

Bentley, Nicolas, ed.. *Russell's Despatches from the Crimea 1854–1856* (London, 1966).

Biro, S. S., *The German Policy of Revolutionary France: A study in French diplomacy during the war of the First Coalition 1792–1797*, 2 vols. (Harvard. 1957).

Bismarck, Otto, *Bismarck: The man and the statesman, being the reflections and reminiscences of Otto Prince von Bismarck*, 2 vols., tr. from German (London, 1889).

Bloch, Ivan S., *Is War Now Impossible*. tr. from Russian (London, 1899). The book was republished in 1900 under the title *Modern Weapons and Modern War*.

de Bloch, Jean (Ivan Bloch), 'The Wars of the Future', *The Contemporary Review* (September 1901).

Boulding, Kenneth. *Conflict and Defense* (New York, 1962).

—— *Beyond Economics: essays on society, religion and ethics* (Ann Arbor, 1968).

Browning, Oscar, ed., *Despatches from Paris 1784–1790*, 2 vols., Camden Society, XVI, XIX (London, 1909–10).

Buchan, Alastair, *War in Modern Society: an introduction* (London, 1968).

Buchanan, Sir George, *My Mission to Russia and Other Diplomatic Memories*, 2 vols. (London, 1923).

Buckle, Henry Thomas, *History of Civilization in England*, 3 vols. (London, 1885).

Bullock, Alan, *Hitler: a study in tyranny* (London, 1962).

Burns, Arthur Lee, *Of Powers and their Politics: a critique of theoretical approaches* (Englewood Cliffs, New Jersey, 1968).

Burns, E. McN., *Western Civilizations: their history and their culture* (New York, 1969).

Bury, J. P. T., *Napoleon III and the Second Empire* (New York, 1968).

Butler, Sir Geoffrey and Maccoby, S., *The Development of International Law* (London, 1928).

Butterfield. H., ed., *Select Documents of European History*, vol. III, 1715–1920 (London, 1931).

Cairnes, J. E., 'International Law'. *Fortnightly Review* (November 1865).

Carlyle, Thomas, *History of Friedrich II of Prussia, called Frederick the Great*, 10 vols. (London, 1882 edn).
Chamberlain, Sir Austen, *Down the Years* (London 1935). A memoir touching on phases of Anglo-German relations from the 1880s.
Chance, J. F., ed., *British Diplomatic Instructions 1689–1789:* vol. III – *Denmark* (London, 1926).
—— *British Diplomatic Instructions 1689–1789:* vol. V. *Sweden 1727–1789* (London, 1928).
Chesney, C. C. and Reeve, Henry, *The Military Resources of Prussia and France and Recent Changes in the Art of War* (reprinted from *Edinburgh Review* 1866–67) (London, 1870).
Churchill, Randolph S., *Winston S. Churchill*, 2 vols. (London, 1966).
Churchill, Sir Winston, *The World Crisis 1911–1918*, abridged and revised edn. (London, 1943).
Clark, Sir George, *War and Society in the Seventeenth Century*, esp. ch. VI, 'The Cycle of War and Peace in Modern History' (Cambridge, 1958).
Clarke, I. F., *Voices Prophesying War, 1763–1984* (London, 1966).
Clausewitz, Carl von, *On War*, ed. by F. N. Maude, tr. from German, 3 vols. (London, 1940).
Coombs, Douglas, *The Conduct of the Dutch: British opinion and the Dutch Alliance during the war of the Spanish Succession* (The Hague, 1958).
Cope, Sir Zachary, *Almroth Wright: founder of modern vaccine-therapy* (London, 1966). Wright was a specialist on war wounds.
Cowles, Virginia, *The Russian Dagger: cold war in the days of the Czars* (London, 1969).
Cruikshank, R. J., *Roaring Century* (London, 1946).
Curtiss, John S., *The Russian Army under Nicholas I, 1825–1855* (Durham, North Carolina, 1965).
Curzon, Hon. George N., *Problems of the Far East: Japan–Korea–China* (London, 1894).
Daniel, Norman, *Islam, Europe and Empire* (Edinburgh, 1966).
Daws, Gavan, *Shoal of Time: a history of the Hawaiian Islands* (New York, 1968).
Dehio, Ludwig, *The Precarious Balance: the politics of power in Europe 1494–1945*, tr. from German (London, 1963).
Deutsch, Karl W., *The Analysis of International Relations* (Englewood Cliffs, New Jersey, 1968).
Dictionary of National Biography, The, 27 vols. (Oxford, 1968).
Earle, E. M., ed., *Makers of Modern Strategy: military thought from Machiavelli to Hitler* (Princeton, 1952).
Economist, The, weekly, London. I used it intermittently but especially in 1878, 1885, 1897, 1904 and 1914.
English Historical Documents (ed. D. C. Douglas), esp. vols. X, XI (London, 1957–9).
Esher, Viscount, *Journals and Letters of Reginald Viscount Esher*, esp.

vol. III (London, 1938). Esher conducted secret war missions in France in 1914.

Fay, S. B., *The Origins of the World War* (New York, 1965).

Ferrell, Robert H., *American Diplomacy: a history* (New York, 1969).

Fischer, Fritz, *Germany's Aims in the First World War*, tr. from German (London, 1967).

Fisher, Roger, ed., *International Conflict and Behavioural Science: the Craigville Papers* (New York, 1964).

Flournoy, Francis R., *Parliament and War* (London, 1927).

Foner, Philip S., 'Why the United States Went to War with Spain in 1898', *Science and Society* (Winter, 1968).

Franco-German War 1870–71, anon., tr. by F. C. H. Clarke from the German official account, 4 vols. (London, 1881).

Fried, Morton, Harris, Marvin and Murphy, Robert, eds., *War: the anthropology of armed conflict and aggression* (New York, 1968).

Froude, J. A., 'England's War', in *Short Studies on Great Subjects*, vol. 2 (London, 1891).

Fuller J. F. C., *The Conduct of War 1789–1961: a study of the impact of the French, Industrial and Russian revolutions on war and its conduct* (London, 1961).

Garvy, George, 'Kondratieff's Theory of Long Cycles', *The Review of Economic Statistics* (November 1943).

Giffen, Sir Robert, *Economic Inquiries and Studies*, 2 vols. (London, 1904). Includes a study of the economics of the Franco-Prussian war of 1870–1.

Gilbert, Martin, ed., *A Century of Conflict 1850–1950: essays for A. J. P. Taylor* (London, 1966).

Gooch, G. P., *Studies in Diplomacy and Statecraft* (London, 1942).

—— *Louis XV: the monarchy in decline* (London, 1956).

Gulick, E. V., *Europe's Classical Balance of Power* (New York, 1967).

Hamilton, Sir Ian, 'War' in *Encyclopaedia Britannica*, 13th edn. (London, 1926), III 981–6.

Hamilton, Ian B. M., *The Happy Warrior: a life of General Sir Ian Hamilton* (London, 1966).

Harrod, Sir Roy, *The Life of John Maynard Keynes* (London, 1951).

Hartmann, Frederick H., *The Relations of Nations* (New York, 1957).

Hatzfeldt, Count Paul, *The Hatzfeldt Letters: letters of Count Paul Hatzfeldt to his wife, written from the headquarters of the King of Prussia 1870–71*, tr. from French (London, 1905).

Hayes, C. J. H., *A Generation of Materialism 1871–1900* (New York, 1941).

Heckscher, Eli F., *The Continental System: an economic interpretation* (Oxford, 1922).

—— *An Economic History of Sweden* (Harvard, 1954).

Henderson, W. O., *Studies in the Economic Policy of Frederick the Great* (London, 1963).

Hershey, A. S., *The International Law and Diplomacy of the Russo-Japanese War* (New York, 1906).

Hicks Beach, Lady Victoria, *The Life of Sir Michael Hicks Beach (Earl St Aldwyn)*, 2 vols. (London, 1932).

Higonnet, Patrice Louis-Rene, 'The Origins of the Seven Years' War', *Journal of Modern History* (March 1968).

Hill, David J., *A History of Diplomacy in the International Development of Europe*, 3 vols. (London, 1914).

Hirst, F. W., *The Political Economy of War* (London, 1915).

Hobson, J. A., *Imperialism: a study* (London, 1902).

Hoetzsch, Otto, *The Evolution of Russia*, tr. from German (London, 1966).

Holland, T. E., *Letters on War and Neutrality* (London, 1914).

Holsti, Ole R. and North, Robert C., 'The History of Human Conflict', ch. viii, in E. B. McNeil, ed., *The Nature of Human Conflict* (Englewood Cliffs, New Jersey, 1965).

Holsti, O. R., Brody, R. A. and North R. C., 'International Relations as a Social Science: a research approach', *International Social Science Journal* (No. 3, 1965).

Horne, Alistair, *The Fall of Paris: the siege and the commune 1870–1* (London, 1965).

Howard, Michael, ed., *The Theory and Practice of War: essays presented to Captain B. H. Liddell Hart* (London, 1965).

—— *The Mediterranean Strategy in the Second World War* (London, 1968).

Huck, Arthur, *The Security of China: Chinese approaches to problems of war and strategy* (London, 1970).

Hughes, Jonathan, *Industrialization and Economic History: theses and conjectures* (New York, 1970).

Huhn, A. von, *The Struggle of the Bulgarians for National Independence under Prince Alexander: a military and political history of the war between Bulgaria and Servia in 1885*, tr. from German (London, 1886).

Hurewitz, J. C., *Diplomacy in the Near and Middle East: a documentary record, 1535–1914*, 2 vols. (Princeton, 1956).

Ireland, Gordon, *Boundaries, Possessions, and Conflicts in Central and North America and the Caribbean* (Harvard, 1941).

Jevons, W. S., *Investigations in Currency and Finance* (London, 1884).

Joll, James, 'The 1914 Debate Continues: Fritz Fischer and his Critics', *Past and Present* (July 1966).

Kautsky, Karl, ed., *Outbreak of the World War: German documents collected by Karl Kautsky* (New York, 1924).

Keith, A. B., ed., *Speeches and Documents on International Affairs 1918–1937*, 2 vols. (Oxford, 1938).

Keynes, J. M., *The Economic Consequences of the Peace* (London, 1919).

Kindleberger, Charles P., *Economic Growth in France and Britain 1851–1950* (Harvard, 1964).

Kinglake, A. W., *The Invasion of the Crimea: its origin, and an account* of its progress down to the death of Lord Raglan (London, 1863), esp. vol. I.

Kissinger, Henry A., *A World Restored* (New York, 1964).

Kondratieff, N. D., 'The Long Waves in Economic Life', in American Economic Association, *Readings in Business Cycle Theory* (New York, 1950), pp. 20–42.

Kurtz, Harold, *The Empress Eugénie 1826–1920* (London, 1964).

Landmann, George, *A Universal Gazetteer, or Geographical Dictionary* (London, 1840).

Latey, Maurice, *Tyranny: a study in the abuse of power* (London, 1969).

Lefebvre, Georges, *The French Revolution: from its origins to 1793*, tr. from French (London, 1962).

Leites, K., *Recent Economic Developments in Russia* (Oxford, 1922).

Lenin, V. I., *Collected Works* (Moscow, 1964) esp. vols. XXI, XXVI.

Leonard, Roger A., ed., *A Short Guide to Clausewitz on War* (London, 1967).

Levontin, A. V., *The Myth of International Security: a juridical and critical analysis* (Jerusalem, 1957).

Liddell Hart, Sir Basil, 'Tactics', *Encyclopaedia Britannica*, 13th ed. (London, 1926), III 714–19.

—— *The Memoirs of Captain Liddell Hart*, 2 vols. (London, 1965).

Lockhart, J. G., and Woodhouse, C. M., *Rhodes* (London, 1963).

Lodge, Sir Richard, *Studies in Eighteenth-Century Diplomacy 1740–1748* (London, 1930).

Logan, Rayford. W., *Haiti and the Dominican Republic* (New York, 1968).

Lough, John, *An Introduction to Eighteenth Century France* (London, 1960).

McBriar, A. M., *Fabian Socialism and English Politics 1884–1918* (Cambridge, 1966).

Macfie, A. L., 'The Outbreak of War and the Trade Cycle', *Economic History*, (A Supplement to *The Economic Journal*), February 1938.

McCormick, Frederick, *The Tragedy of Russia in Pacific Asia*, 2 vols (New York, 1907).

McLaren, Walter W., *A Political History of Japan During the Meiji Era 1869–1912* (London, 1965).

McNeil, E. B., ed., *The Nature of Human Conflict* (Englewood Cliffs, New Jersey, 1965).

Maguire, T. M., *Outlines of Military Geography* (Cambridge, 1899).

Maude, F. N., 'Cavalry', *Encyclopaedia Britannica*, 11th ed. (London, 1910–11) v 563–72.

—— 'Strategy', ibid. XXV 986–97.

Maurice, J. F., *Hostilities Without Declaration of War* (London, 1883).

Maurois, Simone, *Miss Howard and the Emperor*, tr. from French (London, 1957).

Maxwell, Neville, *India's China War* (London, 1970).

Mayer, Arno J., 'Internal Causes and Purposes of War in Europe, 1870–

1956: a research assignment', *Journal of Modern History* (September 1969).

Mazlish, Bruce, 'Psychology and Problems of Contemporary History', *Journal of Contemporary History* (April 1968).

Mehta, Ved, *Fly and the Fly Bottle: encounters with British Intellectuals* (London, 1965).

Mezö, Ferenc, *The Modern Olympic Games* (Budapest, 1956).

Monteith, William, *Kars and Erzeroum: with the campaigns of Prince Paskiewitch in 1828 and 1829* (London, 1856).

Morgenthau, Hans J., and Thompson K. W., eds., *Principles & Problems of International Politics: selected readings* (New York, 1950).

Moses, John A., 'The War Aims of Imperial Germany: Professor Fritz Fischer and his Critics', *University of Queensland Papers*, vol. 1, No. 4, 1968.

Nef, John Ulric, *War and Human Progress: an essay on the rise of industrial civilization* (New York, 1963).

New Cambridge Modern History, vols. VI–XII (Cambridge, 1960–70).

Nicolson, Harold, *Diaries and Letters 1939–1945*, ed. by Nigel Nicolson (London, 1967).

Oakes, Sir Augustus and Mowat, R. B., eds., *The Great European Treaties of the Nineteenth Century* (Oxford, 1921).

Oman, C. W. C., 'Column and Line in the Peninsular War', *Proceedings of British Academy* (London, 1909–10).

Ono, G., *Expenditures of the Sino-Japanese War* (New York, 1922).

Paléologue, Maurice, *An Ambassador's Memoirs*, 2 vols. (London, 1923). Paléologue was the French ambassador to Russia in 1914.

Palmer, R. R., *The Age of the Democratic Revolution: a political history of Europe and America, 1760–1800*, 2 vols. (Princeton, 1959, 1964).

Palmer, T. A., 'Military Technology', ch. 29, in Kranzberg, M., and Pursell, C. W., Jr., *Technology in Western Civilization*, I (New York, 1967).

Pares, Sir Bernard, *The Fall of the Russian Monarchy: a study of the evidence* (New York, 1961).

Pasley, Sir Charles, *Essay on the Military Policy and Institutions of the British Empire*, 2 vols. (London, 1810).

Phelps Brown, E. H. and Browne, Margaret H., *A Century of Pay* (London, 1968).

Phillips, Peter, *The Tragedy of Nazi Germany* (London, 1969).

Pierce, R. A., ed., *Mission to Turkestan: being the memoirs of Count K. K. Pahlen 1908–1909*, tr. from Russian (London, 1964).

Platt, D. C. M., *Finance, Trade and Politics in British Foreign Policy* (Oxford, 1968).

Portway, Donald, *Science and Mechanisation in Land Warfare* (Cambridge, 1938).

Preston, R. A., Wise, S. F. and Werner, H. O., *Men in Arms: a history of warfare and its interrelationships with western society* (New York, 1964).

Pruitt, Dean G. and Snyder, R. C., eds., *Theory and Research on the Causes of War* (Englewood Cliffs, New Jersey, 1969).

Rees, David, *Korea: the limited war* (London, 1964).

Rèquin, E., and others, *What Would be the Character of a New War?* (London, 1931). An enquiry organised by The Inter-Parliamentary Union, it includes essays by J. F. C. Fuller and E. F. Heckscher.

Rich, Norman R., *Friedrich von Holstein: politics and diplomacy in the era of Bismarck and Wilhelm II*, 2 vols. (Cambridge, 1965).

Richardson, Lewis F. (ed. by Quincy Wright and C. C. Lienau), *Statistics of Deadly Quarrels* (London, 1960).

Richardson, Lewis F., *Arms and Insecurity* (London, 1960).

Richmond, H. W., 'National Policy and Naval Strength, XVIth to XXth Century', *Proceedings of the British Academy* (1923) pp. 339–54.

Rodger, A. B., *The War of the Second Coalition 1798 to 1801: a strategic commentary* (Oxford, 1964).

Röling, Bert V. A., 'National and International Peace Research', *International Social Science Journal* (1965), No. 3.

Rose, J. Holland. *The Indecisiveness of Modern War and Other Essays* (London, 1927).

Rose, J. Holland and Broadley, A. M., *Dumouriez and the Defence of England against Napoleon* (London, 1909).

Rosen, Baron, *Forty Years of Diplomacy*, 2 vols. (London, 1922).

Rougemont, Denis de, *Passion and Society*, tr. from French (London, 1956).

Sandburg, Carl, *Abraham Lincoln*, 3 vols. (New York, 1959).

Sazonov, Serge, *Fateful Years 1909–1916: the reminiscences of Serge Sazonov* (London, 1928).

Seton-Watson, Hugh, *The Russian Empire 1801–1917* (Oxford, 1967).

Sherwig, John M., *Guineas and Gunpowder: British foreign aid in the wars with France 1793–1815* (Harvard, 1969).

Shirer, W. L., *The Rise and Fall of the Third Reich: a history of Nazi Germany* (London, 1964).

Smith, Adam, *An Inquiry into the Nature and Causes of the Wealth of Nations* (London: Everyman edn., 1954). Smith made valuable observations on eighteenth-century wars.

Sorokin, Pitirim A., *Social and Cultural Dynamics*, 3 vols. (New York, 1937).

Southgate, Donald. '*The Most English Minister ...*': the policies and politics of Palmerston (London, 1966).

Stafford-Clark, David, *Psychiatry To-day* (London, 1952).

Steinberg, Jonathan, 'The Copenhagen Complex', *Journal of Contemporary History* (1966) No. 3. A study of German naval fears from 1890s to 1914.

Steinberg, S. H., *The Thirty Years War and the Conflict for European Hegemony 1600–1660* (New York, 1966).

Stern, Fritz, *The Politics of Cultural Despair: a study in the rise of Germanic ideology* (New York, 1965).

Stewart, Michael, *Keynes and After* (London, 1967).

Stomberg, A. A., *A History of Sweden* (London, 1931).

Stone, Norman, 'Army and Society in the Habsburg Monarchy, 1900–1914', *Past and Present* (April 1966).

Stowell, E. C., 'Convention Relative to the Opening of Hostilities', *American Journal of International Law* (January 1908).

Stretton, Hugh, *The Political Sciences: general principles of selection in social sciences and history* (London, 1969).

Swettenham, John, *Allied Intervention in Russia 1918–1919: and the part played by Canada* (London, 1967).

Takahashi, Sakuye, *International Law Applied to the Russo-Japanese War* (New York, 1908).

Taylor, A. J. P., 'Otto Bismarck', *Encyclopaedia Britannica*, 1962, III 659–68.

—— *The Struggle for Mastery in Europe 1848–1918* (Oxford, 1954).

—— *The Origins of the Second World War* (London, 1964).

—— *English History 1914–1945* (Oxford, 1965).

—— *The Hapsburg Monarchy 1809–1918: a history of the Austrian empire and Austria–Hungary* (London, 1964).

Temperley, Harold, *Frederic the Great and Kaiser Joseph: an episode of war and diplomacy in the eighteenth century* (London, 1915).

Temperley, Harold and Penson, Lilian, eds., *Foundations of British Foreign Policy from Pitt (1792) to Salisbury (1902), or Documents Old and New* (Cambridge, 1938).

Thayer, George, *The War Business: the international trade in armaments* (London, 1969).

Thompson, J. M., *The French Revolution* (Oxford, 1959).

Thomson, David, *Europe Since Napoleon* (London, 1966).

Thomson, Mark A., 'Louis XIV and the Origins of the war of the Spanish Succession', Ch. 9, in *William III and Louis XIV: essays 1680–1720 by and for Mark A. Thomson*, ed. Hatton, R. and Bromley, J. S. (Liverpool, 1968).

Thorne, Christopher, *The Approach of War, 1938–1939* (London, 1967).

Toynbee, Arnold, *Experiences* (London, 1969).

—— *A Study of History*, 12 vols. (London, 1934–61).

Trevelyan, Humphrey, *The Middle East in Revolution* (London, 1970). Lord Trevelyan was British ambassador to Egypt during the Suez Crisis.

Triffin, Robert, *Our International Monetary System: yesterday, today, and tomorrow* (New York, 1968).

Trotter, Wilfred, *Instincts of the Herd in Peace and War 1916–1919* (London, 1953).

Tsunoda, R., de Bary, W. T. and Keene, D., eds., *Sources of Japanese Tradition* (New York, 1958).

Tuchman, Barbara W. *The Guns of August: August 1914* (London, 1964).

Tupper, Harmon, *To the Great Ocean: Siberia and the Trans-Siberian Railway* (London, 1965).

Turner, L. C. F., 'The Russian Mobilization in 1914', *Journal of Contemporary History* (January 1968).

United Empire: *The Royal Colonial Institute Journal*, London (esp. 1914).

Vernon, H. M., *Italy from 1494 to 1790* (Cambridge, 1909).

Vital, David, 'Czechoslovakia and the Powers, September 1938', *Journal of Contemporary History* (October 1966).

Wangermann, Ernst, *From Joseph II to the Jacobin Trials* (London, 1959).

Weinstein, Franklin B., *Indonesia Abandons Confrontation: an inquiry into the functions of Indonesia's foreign policy*, 'Cornell Modern Indonesia Project' (Ithaca, N.Y., 1969).

Williams, Neville, *Chronology of the Modern World: 1763 to the present time* (London, 1966).

Witte, Sergei, *The Memoirs of Count Witte*, tr. from Russian, ed. by A. Yarmolinsky (London, 1921).

Wood, David, *Conflict in the Twentieth Century*, Adelphi Papers no. 48, Institute for Strategic Studies (London, June 1968).

Woodward, E. L., *War and Peace in Europe 1815–1870 and Other Essays* (London, 1931).

Woolf, Leonard, *Principia Politica: a study of communal psychology* (London, 1953).

Wright, Quincy, *A Study of War*, 2 vols. (Chicago, 1942).

—— *A Study of War*, abridged by Louis L. Wright (Chicago, 1965).

Index